D0929790

TECHNIQUES
OF TAPE READING

Other Books in the Irwin Trader's Edge Series

TECHNIQUES OF TAPE READING

VADYM GRAIFER
CHRISTOPHER SCHUMACHER

McGraw-Hill
New York   Chicago   San Francisco
Lisbon   London   Madrid   Mexico City
Milan   New Delhi   San Juan   Seoul
Singapore   Sydney   Toronto

The *McGraw·Hill* Companies

1 2 3 4 5 6 7 8 9 0 DOC/DOC 0 9 8 7 6 5 4 3

ISBN 0-07-141490-8

This publication is designed to provide accurate and authoritative information in regard to the subject matter covered. It is sold with the understanding that neither the author nor the publisher is engaged in rendering legal, accounting, futures/securities trading, or other professional service. If legal advice or other expert assistance is required, the services of a competent professional person should be sought.
> *—From a Declaration of Principles jointly adopted by a Committee*
> *of the American Bar Association and a Committee of Publishers*

McGraw-Hill books are available at special quantity discounts to use as premiums and sales promotions, or for use in corporate training programs. For more information, please write to the Director of Special Sales, Professional Publishing, McGraw-Hill, Two Penn Plaza, New York, NY 10121-2298. Or contact your local bookstore.

 This book is printed on recycled, acid-free paper containing a minimum of 50% recycled, de-inked fiber.

Library of Congress Cataloging-in-Publication Data

Graifer, Vadym.
    Techniques of tape reading / by Vadym Graifer and Christopher Schumacher.
        p. cm.
    ISBN 0–07–141490–8 (hardcover : alk. paper)
    1. Stocks.   I. Schumacher, Christopher.   II. Title.
    HG4661 .G67   2003
    332.63′2042—dc21

                                        2002154984

CONTENTS

PART THREE

ACKNOWLEDGMENTS

First and foremost we would like to thank the past and present members of RealityTrader.com. Without their sincere interest and desire to take the journey through myth and disinformation to trading the reality of the market, this book would not have been possible.

To Steve Demarest, Ross Ditlove, and the entire team of professionals at MBTrading.com, thank-you for providing the best trading services that the industry has to offer. The Navigator is one of the best execution tools available today.

We would also like to thank those at TheStreet.com who have provided us with a forum to interact with not only other professionals in our field but also with those subscribers who offer their personal insight and views on a daily basis. Specifically, we would like to thank James Cramer for his ambition to start such a venture and Dr. Richard McCall for his constant encouragement and uncanny insight into today's changing market.

We also owe the greatest debt of gratitude to the many professionals in the trading industry:

Alan Farley, who has the amazing ability to see through the curtains of the market's uncertainty. Discussion with you is always a challenge. We continue to appreciate your friendship and conversation.

Tony Oz, it's a real pleasure to continue to see your successes as a true leader in this industry.

Chris Wheeler for your continued friendship and faith in our objectives and goals for the education of traders.

Jim Sugarman and Tim Bourquin from the Online TradingExpo.com for having the drive and initiative to create a dynamic forum for traders to learn and exchange educational ideas.

Mike Diplock for spending tremendous hours developing and fine-tuning our principles and setups into the RealityTrader Intelliscan Market Scanner.

Kenneth Reid for working with us to define the problems and the solutions that plague traders and in the creation of our interactive Trading Psychology CD Series.

  And finally to the entire staff at RealityTrader.com who burned the midnight oil to make RealityTrader.com what it is today. Thanks to Bo Yoder and Allen Zuckerman for becoming part of our trading services and helping us to grow not only as a company but as traders as well; Russ Van Der Biessen for his continued efforts; and Nestor Suarez for his endless and tireless work ethic. To Jeff Tappan, whose unique marketing insight enabled us to grow our company to what it is today. And to Vic Jung, who is simply the best IT professional and Webmaster on the planet—without you, we would still be dreaming this on paper. Last but not least, a special thanks to Larisa Bondarenko for everything you have done for RealityTrader to make it a better service. Your wisdom and guidance made this all possible. You are a true friend.

Vadym Graifer
Christopher Schumacher

INTRODUCTION

This book describes the story of Vadym Graifer, a former Soviet citizen who was forced to flee developments in Ukraine which jeopardized his company, his life, and his family's life. The story is a so-called American success story that has been told time and again about immigrants fleeing religious, economic, and racial strife in search of a better life for themselves and those around them. Although Vadym is currently a Canadian resident, it's a story that most everyone can relate to. The personal struggles, journey of self-discovery, and eventual success he attained will reveal many lessons you may have already learned, and, more important, lessons you have yet to realize.

Part One of this story deals with these events and the principles that Vadym has come to use every day in his trading. This part also delves into one of the most important aspects of a trader's development—the mindset of a successful trader. The principles discussed in these pages will show you how a totally inexperienced trader went from market illusions to market reality, from the point of near financial destruction to the freedom of everyday trading life. These principles are ultimately linked to the understanding of tape reading described in Part Two of the book. In this sense, tape reading will *not* be described to you in a manner that the majority of people think this lost art is. It will not be described to you as a verb, in the sense that you are "tape reading." Rather, after reading Part Two, you will understand the deeper concepts of how tape reading allows you to see and distinguish between the actions of smart money and the public mentality. Realizing how accumulation and distribution actions taken by market participants through movements of price and volume will give you a strong understanding of an entry and exit strategy for any system or methodology that you currently use. It's this reality at the root of price action that will ultimately lead you to knowing why and how Vadym and those who trade with him use the motto "Trade what you see, not what you think."

Part Three presents trading setups and examples taken from trading experiences over the past 2 years. Some are presented in fraction form, while others are in decimal form. These setups and examples will ultimately lead you to understand that, while methodologies and systems may come and go, tape-reading principles will stand the test of time. They have been around since the beginning of speculation some 400 years ago and have been improved over the past 100 years. The principles, therefore, can be applied to any system currently being used and to any system that may be invented in the next millennium of speculation.

Upon completion of this story, you will fully appreciate the journey of Vadym Graifer as a trader who was participating in a market about which he initially knew nothing, in an economy that was different from that of his native country, and in an environment that was difficult to function in. It wasn't his great understanding of company reports, of valuating news events, or of how GDP figures govern market movement that made him successful. It was his rediscovery of the true meaning of tape-reading principles that go far beyond what most current presentations offer. It was his movement to an unemotional state of reality and the ultimate truth of stock movement, the language of price and volume, that turned his trading, his account, and eventually his life into something to be proud of. This is the story of a true *reality trader*.

PART ONE

A Trader's Journey

CHAPTER 1

The Beginner

Everyone Starts at the Beginning

In the late 1980s—early 1990s in the Soviet Union—the birth of a new, rapidly changing economy emerged, a free economy. It started with simple co-ops but quickly expanded to encompass more complex ventures such as private banks, financial companies, and merchandise exchanges. Although welcomed with open arms by the active part of a society that had spent 70 years under oppressive rule, it also opened the door to the rise of the Russian Mafia. I was a well-educated engineer, and I started my own business in 1987 and developed it into a successful enterprise with over 100 employees.

Slowly the dark side of the transition to a free market economy soaked into every facet of business life. As time progressed, the situation became less and less stable. Economic links were disappearing, and inflation was climbing at a gallop. Citizens became the target of criminal attacks on a scale that citizens of a civilized country could not imagine. Kidnapping and assassination became the methods of choice to handle everyday business disputes. The economy and society as a whole began to unravel at an alarming rate.

Fearing for the safety of my family, I emigrated to Canada in 1996. This new life had its own set of challenges. Imagine moving to a new country and learning a new profession without speaking the language of the country. I learned English by watching popular television sitcoms like *Married with Children*. Al Bundy became my excuse for awkward, language-related situations for years to come. At the same time, I set my sights on finding and mastering a new profession, day trading. Trading over the Internet was a logical choice for me, as it allowed me to move at my own pace unlike other professions that would require well-developed language and communication skills.

Although day trading was not yet a buzzword in 1996, it was the major direction of my quest. The reason I focused on such a short time frame as intraday trading was because I realized that I lacked knowledge about the U.S. economy and couldn't make much out of company reports. Therefore, I instinctively wanted to exploit the movements that were less affected by those factors.

As I searched the Internet, I tried to uncover everything that could help me find direction. There weren't as many Web sites devoted to trading then as we have now, so my education was incredibly superficial. Here's why.

LEARNING TO WALK ALL OVER AGAIN

After a couple of months, I had an online broker and was armed with quotes and with the *Wall Street Journal* as my news source. It looked pretty simple to me. I would find positive information on a stock, buy it, watch it go up, and sell it when it stopped rising. I couldn't see why it wouldn't work.

Do stocks go up on good news? The answer seemed obvious. Yes. It was supported by comments I read like, "ABCD gained 2¼ points today on news that the company was granted big new order," or "XYZ soared 4 points after the company announced positive study results in mice."

Did I ask myself some obvious questions like, "If it's that simple, then what are all those trading books about," or "Why isn't everybody doing it?" Yes, I did. But I also managed to come up with some answers that supported my confidence. Maybe those books are for professionals who need to manage millions of dollars and not for small-time traders like me with a desire to make just a few hundred dollars a day. After much research and preparation, everything was in place, and finally I started trading.

It was a typical start for someone who commenced trading in a bull market. I made money. I always found this to be a fascinating and interesting phenomenon—a novice making money right from the start is a common occurrence. Maybe, to a degree, it was just beginner's luck. But there are two important factors to consider. First, people are more likely to start trading during the bull phase of the market's cycle. Media excitement and the obvious rising of prices attract new traders. This kind of market is very forgiving. Selecting a stock is fairly easy, as many stocks go up with the tide, and, therefore, mistakes might go unpunished. Also, in a bull market, bad timing and missed stops don't kill as surely as they do in a bear or a flat market. So it's just a matter of statistics.

The second important factor is that the novice often has no fear. In some paradoxical way, the state of the mind of the beginner may be very close to that of a great professional trader. Of course there is a huge difference in that beginners have no fear because they are unaware of how harsh the outcome of their recklessness can be. The professionals' lack of fear is based on their experience and self-control. New traders have their hard hits ahead of them, while professionals have left them behind. Later we will see how this difference is reflected in different motives for initiating a trade: Professionals take the trade when they are comfortable with the risk, while amateurs do it when they like the potential profit. Regardless of motives, the state of the mind of amateurs and professionals may be fairly similar. This results in correct action despite the amateurs' lack of experience and knowledge. However, as we will discover later, success without the knowledge of why or how it is achieved only delays learning some hard realities and making mistakes, and perhaps experiencing even total failure.

A POSITIVE OUTCOME CAN REINFORCE A BAD HABIT

I was not making a killing. But my first experiments confirmed my initial assumption that it was possible to make a living exploiting intraday movements. It was not too hard to get an order filled at that time, even with an online broker. Competition was not nearly as tough as it was later when traders discovered more online tools or when crowds started chasing and running stocks.

During that first period of my trading, I learned one extremely important thing: I saw people arguing about the value of news and about the impact the news had on a stock price. I realized that news has no absolute value. It became clear to me that people's perception of the news is what affects the stock price. This made me uncomfortable, since I had no tool for reading perception. For a while I was able to calm myself down by thinking that I could foresee how the majority of people would perceive the news. But I soon learned that this was not the case. Stocks were reacting negatively on good earnings because street expectations were higher. Stocks were reacting negatively even after beating street expectations because whisper numbers were even higher. And stocks would just drop on good news without the slightest reason that I could see.

I saw no consistency to my train of thought, and it shouldn't have been a surprise. At that time my thoughts revolved around the news—getting the best news source, evaluating the news, predicting the news impact, and—the killer of killers for a trader—forming opinions based on the news. Despite my newfound understanding of the relative value of news, I continued to make the same assumptions: "Up on good news, down on bad news." It was a dead end, but I didn't realize it at the time. I needed a push from the outside to make me overcome this barrier, and, of course, I got one.

The market sends us plenty of hints. It's always talking to us in its specific language, sending us messages about what we do right or wrong. We don't always hear these messages or understand them. And, if we don't, the market sends more. Eventually, they become louder. If we still don't hear the message, we don't change our ways of acting, thereby exposing ourselves to the same danger again and again. Then some of the messages finally come in as thunder, changing our entire lives as traders.

For me such a message came in March 1997. The stock was ESOL, Employee Solution. It came down hard from above $30 to under $15. Following the standard beginner's idea, "If you loved it at $30, then $15 must be real value," I bought 2000 shares overnight. I was totally confident that nothing awful could happen to me based on the "value" of the stock and the fact that the market was definitely bullish at that time.

The next morning I saw ESOL open at around $8. What a shock! When I was losing $100 or $200 here and there, I was okay with it. Losing is a necessary part of the game; I already knew that. However, I could not have imagined taking such a hit on a single trade.

My reactions were typical for this situation. The first thing I did was to ask the opinion of other traders about the stock. This was the wrong thing to do. Sure enough, everyone who got caught in this mess with me said something like, "It's going to be back in no time," "This is a bear raid," "Shorts are having their hoopla day, but they will get burned," and other "useful" things. It all sounded comforting, but the stock was not rebounding as sellers were pounding it even further, both from the distribution side and from the short side. Clearly, value by itself is not a timing mechanism for intraday trading, as value is intrinsic to individuals and is the basis for speculation, not for timing trades.

This was the time to make an important decision. I could stay in a psychologically comfortable zone of denial and do nothing, or I could admit the mistake and bite the bullet. The pain of watching each tick became unbearable in a few days. I sold the stock as it lost $5, effectively cutting my trading capital base by over 50 percent. ESOL never rebounded and only got lower. It eventually got delisted and is trading now on the Bulletin Board at $0.004. Following is an illustration of this disastrous trade. (See Figure 1.1.)

At this point I was in the first stage of a trader's development. My first steps were quite typical of a beginner who hadn't found the right teachers. First of all, it's very common for a newcomer to experience a kind of euphoria. Everything seems to be too easy, as if money is just waiting to be picked up. Every new trader who starts by winning experiences this feeling. Eventually, the market punishes such careless attitudes and awakens the trader to the rude reality.

In a strange way, this euphoric state of mind is combined with nervousness. Each trade is perceived as the most important one, as a battle that a trader cannot afford to lose. Therefore, the more significance that is placed on each separate trade, the more difficult it is to admit defeat. This leads to exiting positions at worse price levels than originally intended, which is referred to as a "blown stop" (assuming we are familiar with the very concept of cutting losses). I perceive my trading today as a whole, as

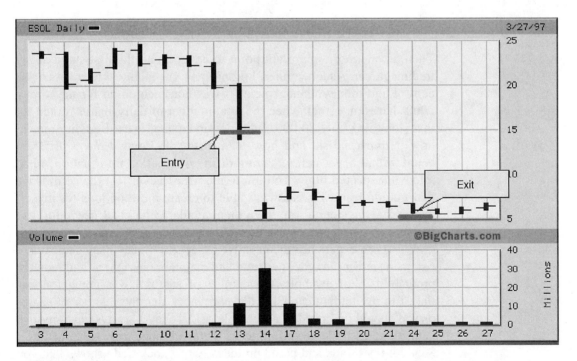

FIGURE 1.1

Graphic illustration of the disastrous ESOL trade. (*Used with permission of CBS MarketWatch.*)

a never-ending process in which each separate trade is just a separate trade, and I measure my success by the favorable ratio of wins to losses in combination with the reward-to-risk scenarios. This is the correct approach and eliminates the exaggerated significance of each separate trade, thus making it natural to take the stop if the trade goes wrong. *No single trade is so important that it would be worth tying all my thoughts, time, and money to.*

Newer traders also tend to view the trade outcome as a reflection of the people they are. A loss makes them feel foolish. They feel wrong when they take a loss. People don't like to be wrong. Our desire to be right can be stronger than our desire to make money. In trading, this feeling is evidenced by traders who hold a losing position in order to prove that they are right. Our ego takes over and keeps us from admitting that we made a mistake. I see many comments like, "Sellers are wrong. They are being fooled. They got it wrong." That is ego talking. Today, I never relate the outcome of a single trade to who I am. I do not feel foolish when I take a predetermined loss. *This trade is not who I am. What is it we really want? To be right or to be profitable?*

RISK MANAGEMENT—DON'T LEAVE HOME WITHOUT IT

There is one more important point to cover about the first stage of my trading career. As a beginner, I didn't have the slightest idea about risk control and money management. It was not uncommon for me to buy 2000 shares of a stock when the total number of daily shares traded for that stock was only 20,000. I did not understand what liquidity meant, how it impacts risk, and how to measure it. Being from a different country, and never before having dealt with market information, I had a few unexpected blows coming to me. But I never lost the confidence that I could learn. I was always able to create more options for myself and was always certain to have them available before I needed to use them.

I had to experience the negative aspects of money management and risk management in order to create and maintain the right attitude toward profitability. For example, the number of shares I was going for was linked to my trading capital. I did not realize that the number of shares played should be linked to acceptable risk. Today I always have my risk defined, and I trade according to it. If, for instance, risk is defined as a $250 loss per trade and based on the way the stock trade shows that you can keep a 50 cent stop with confidence, then my share size on this stock is 500 shares. How and where the stop loss should be placed is another matter, which I will discuss later by using a few examples I learned later in my career.

DON'T BLAME THE GUY BEHIND THE CURTAIN—YOU CHOSE THIS JOB

There is another important trait of beginner traders that they should recognize in order to get rid of it. This is that the traders feel that trading is a fight. Every day is a battle. Every trade is a battle. Every morning they go to war. If this is a war, then there should be an enemy. The next natural step is that traders define their enemies. A list of the traders' foes will most likely be familiar to the reader: market makers, specialists, analysts, short sellers, CNBC commentators, and so on. I often see something like: "Market makers run the stock down to shake the traders out and to buy stock cheap," "Darn short sellers killed the move," and so on.

This mindset creates a powerful and extremely harmful concept of the so-called *them*—some unreachable, mighty force that manages all the market movements and ruins the traders' brilliant plays. This concept satisfies the traders' ego while excusing them of responsibility for their own actions. Unfortunately many self-proclaimed gurus support this approach. It allows them to place the responsibility for their recommendations that go badly on some of those traditional enemies. They reinforce this wrong way of thinking in their followers, thus significantly lessening their chances to learn the game. *When your teacher, or the one you trust, says something like, "Their manipulation ruined our play," it's time to look for another teacher.*

Let's Compare Two Approaches

The first approach is that my trading decision was great. I figured it all out. I was right all the way. My trade outcome was a loss because *they* ruined it. *They* knew traders bought the stock, and *they* brought it down (or kept it from running). When frustrated traders sold, *they* bought from them cheap and ran the stock back up. There was nothing I could do. *They* had deeper pockets, and it was impossible to fight *them*. *They* robbed me on this trade.

The second approach is rather than blaming the ubiquitous *them*, I can assume that if the trade went against me, then the trade wasn't right. With this mindset I could assume that I timed my entry incorrectly, or I had a wrong trading idea. I had to cut off my loss to prevent it from getting bigger. The market proved me wrong on this trade. It's over. I was then able to move on with my search for the next trading opportunity. My trading system assumes losses. Each trade can turn out to be a loser. It's normal because of the uncertain nature of the market—it works on probabilities, not on certainties. My trading system provides a high enough percentage of wins, and no single loss can shake my confidence in the system.

We can see how mature and effective the second approach is compared to the first one. However, notice that the first way of thinking is psychologically comfortable. It places us in a comfort zone where there is no personal responsibility. It makes us feel warm and fuzzy. Of course there is frustration caused by monetary loss, but we feel comforted by being with the majority and by losses not being our fault.

Remember what my first impulse was when I found myself in the losing ESOL trade. I looked for comrades in disaster to ask their opinion. Was it their opinion that I was looking for? Was it a desire to make sure that I was not alone in this? And what was it that I felt after talking to them? Relief (there are plenty of traders that got caught with me); anger (darn bears that arranged this trap); secret hope (it's going to be back; if *they* orchestrated this drop then *they* should have some purpose; in this case, *they* apparently want to buy cheap shares and run the stock back).

Yes, this approach has always been a killer for a trader's account, but does this always outweigh our desire for psychological comfort? Apparently it does not. The second approach is the one that mature successful traders have adopted. However, we can feel how less comfortable it is. Undivided personal responsibility with no one to rely on but ourselves does not make us feel good. We try to avoid this cold unpleasant spot. And, if we avoid it, we effectively stop learning.

If some unmanageable higher power controls the trade we take, why learn? It's easier (and makes more sense since you can't control anything) to put on the trade and wait for *them* to decide what to do with it, hoping we get lucky this time. That's where gambling entirely replaces trading. Control is lost (or was never there in the first place). And what is it a trader needs to control? We know we cannot control the market. All we need to control is ourselves, our own behavior. And this self-control is what enables us to win in the market. It's just uncomfortable. It requires discipline; unclouded, unbiased thinking; and the willingness to admit mistakes without ego intervention. *Discomfort and profit go hand in hand.*

Does all that mean that a trader is always uncomfortable and that monetary winnings come at the price of constant stress or depression? No, it does not. The joy of self-control, of getting the best out of oneself, of being able to pull through is a huge reward. With time, this approach stops being uncomfortable and becomes the only approach that feels right.

THE FAMOUS BRE-X SCANDAL

After a few weeks an interesting thing happened in the stock market from which I learned a lot. I am talking about the Bre-X story. Bre-X was a small Canadian mining company. A huge gold mine was "discovered" in Indonesia. Soon thereafter the chief geologist committed suicide by jumping out of a helicopter. Then an independent analysis of samples was conducted and revealed them to be fakes. The incident was dubbed the "fraud of the century." Figure 1.2 shows the huge drop in price followed by the stock being delisted.

I got interested in the developing story because of its huge exposure. It was hard to believe that stockholders could be misled on such a huge

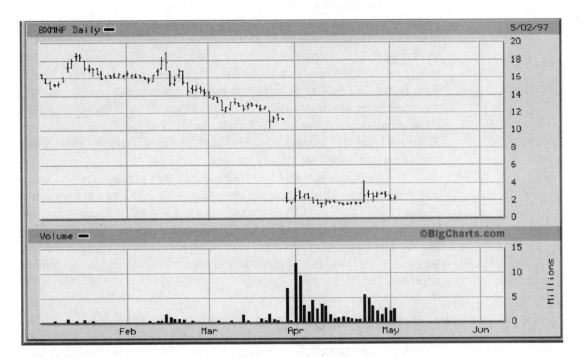

FIGURE 1.2

The story of the Bre-X stock once the fraud was revealed. (*Used with permission of CBS MarketWatch.*)

scale. When the ultimate results of an analysis were pronounced, I learned another big lesson (at no cost this time). Anything can happen in the markets. No matter how reliable and truthful information appears, we can never know all the details surrounding the story, and we cannot figure out the outcome. I read with great interest of all those investors who were full of hope only to become desperate as they realized that they had lost a vast amount of money by investing in what they believed was the truth.

A thought struck me as I followed that story. Investors started discussing Indonesian maps, comparing them to other known gold mine maps. They talked about methods of taking and analyzing samples, read geological reports, and tried to find some hidden clues in company statements, CEO correspondence, and the like. They suddenly became specialists in geology and mining. Some of the investors appeared to be well informed and knowledgeable. Yet, the outcome was the opposite of what they expected. I recently saw a story that was very similar. When some small company announced the results of a medical study, many people invested their money in the stock because of the news about the study. I checked out the stock and spent a couple of hours reading about it with those who were interested in it. Conversation ran along these lines: "I talked to a friend who is an M.D. He said it's huge." "This technology is the future." And so on. The stock price declined, but people continued to talk, convincing others and themselves that there were some evil intentions behind the decline or differents kind of manipulations, like "holding the price from running in order to buy cheaper" or just "shorting to hurt those who bought the stock." After all, the days of Jay Gould and James Fisk (gold and railroad stock manipulators of the nineteenth century) and other "manipulators" are widely known.

The irony was that all those discussions about product, technologies, and research had little to do with the stock price. Traders were trying to discuss things they didn't know much about. Even more important, those things had little (if any) impact on the price movement. That was probably the first realization of what I coined as my motto—"Trade what you see, not what you think"—the motto that governs my entire trading approach.

LISTEN TO THE TAPE; IT IS NEVER WRONG

The stock price was telling traders "Get out. You are wrong." Yet they held their position and rationalized their decision. There was something clearly wrong with this approach. It led to tied up money and to indefinitely long holding periods of a position that was supposed to be a short-term trade. This extended time frame was another indication that something was wrong.

I can't say these lessons led me to the right approach right away. In fact, the opposite is true. I repeated my mistakes several times during the next year of my trading career. Nonetheless, that was the first time that I felt I had touched a very powerful truth. I believe that the first seeds of my current approach were planted at that time.

CHAPTER 2

Turnaround

Small and Safe

The next several months of my trading were devoted to pure scalping. After the ESOL fiasco, I was afraid to stay in a trade for too long. I was taking my profits quickly. Considering that with a reduced account size I had to trade small, cheap stocks with unsustainable price movements, it was not too bad a thing. Besides, I was just as fast when I had to cut the loss, which forced me to be more disciplined. This was the case when the fear of new losses worked for me; it made me cut my losses really quickly. Yet, it was not a profitable period overall. I was making insignificant amounts of money and then giving them back. In October 1997, I decided that I couldn't continue to do this kind of trading with an online broker. It was taking too long to fill out the form, send in the order, and then get the confirmation of the fill. I already had some idea of direct access and Level 2, and I was using the combination of a quote feed with Level 2 and an online broker for order execution.

In a short while I found decent brokerage. Its routing software made a big difference to me. My scalping became better, and for a while I thought I finally had gotten a handle on this game. My discipline became much stricter. It became obvious to me that I was taking too big a risk playing the bigger lots, so I stopped playing 2000 to 3000 shares. I was trading mostly 1000 shares. And, again, in a few months I had to admit that I did not have real consistency in my trading.

I was able to get in and out very fast; in many instances I could feel the direction of a stock's movement for the next few ticks by just watching it on Level 2. And yet it was not enough for consistency. The major reason for this was (as I realize now) that I had no system. I was still trading small stocks that were getting activity on fresh news; I was effectively trying to beat other traders by getting in and out faster than the majority did. If I was right about stock direction, this game worked for me. At those times not as many traders used direct-access brokers as do now.

And most of those who did use them didn't have great routing skills. This allowed me to win "fast-trigger contests," but there was much more to trading than that. Scalping is a style of trading that requires traders to be right on a very high percentage of their entries. That's where I failed. The lack of a solid approach and impulsive trading of everything that moved were what undermined my trading at that stage. I tried applying different technical indicators but without encouraging results. I had no real understanding of their mechanics, and I attempted to use them superficially. Trading with no solid system was like trying to build a house without a foundation.

This was a challenging moment. The problem was that I did not feel comfortable with any of the traditional technical indicators or combinations of them. When I tried to apply them, I felt that I lost direct connection with the essence of what was happening; my reading was getting too formal. It was like having a conversation via an interpreter. You understand what is said, but you have trouble feeling the mood of your speaker, understanding the details of the meaning he or she puts in words. At the same time the only approach that allowed me to get this immediate feel was pure scalping. I felt trapped in a cycle I needed to break out of. I needed a system that would put a solid foundation under my entries and exits, and I didn't want this system to be as formal as most of the technical studies were. I realized that there was nothing wrong with technical analysis; it just wasn't my way of visualizing things.

As usually happens, the right door opened when it was needed. Even more than that, this door had always been there. But I saw it only when the right moment came. I read my favorite trading book, *Reminiscences of a Stock Operator* by Edwin Lefèvre, for a third or fourth time. Unlike the previous readings, this time I saw much more in it about the actual method of reading market movement. The words *tape reading* appealed to me—something in me resonated. Still, the method itself was not described in detail in the book. I could just sense the general principles of it. I needed a more detailed description of this approach.

OPENING A THIRD EYE

I searched the Internet for the words *tape reading,* and I soon stumbled across a book published in 1931. It was *Tape Reading & Market Tactics* by Humphrey B Neill. I read it twice and reread some pages of

Reminiscences of a Stock Operator. Once again, I got this amazing feeling that I was facing a very powerful truth. The major idea that I got from this research was that *smart money* acts differently from the public and that there are footprints of smart money's action. It is possible to read those footprints and take the right side, positioning oneself on the winning side. This realization was mostly theoretical then. I had no real rules or formulas as a basis for this idea. But I did feel that I was getting somewhere.

Meanwhile scalping was actually all I did in my everyday trading. For years to come I became known as a pure scalper, an image that haunted me long after my trading became much deeper than that. There is much more to my trading now than just scalping, but while we are on the subject, let's take a look at scalping as a trading style, with all its advantages and shortcomings.

Scalping

Scalping is often defined as trading for fairly small gains, like 5–10 cents. I don't agree with this definition. For me a scalp is a trade in which I do not allow the stock to go against me, no matter at what point of the trade the stock weakens. For example, suppose I bought stock at $20.05 and it went to $21 with no downtick, then paused at $21 where the ask got stronger and the bid weakened because sellers started to nail the bid. At this point I am out, and this is a scalp. If the same happened at $20.50 or $20.25, I am out and this is a scalp. I gave no regard for what profit I made—$0.95 in the first case, $0.45 in the second, and $0.20 in the third. If I bought at $20.05 and the stock never went higher and I bid $20 and got a hit, I am out with –$0.05. In order to get out and not allow the stock to move against my confidence level, I often had to sell into strength (selling when you can, not when you have to). If the stock broke my confidence level, I was less inclined to believe in its ability to give me a more profitable position.

Impact of Decimalization.   This kind of scalping, selling at the first sign of waning momentum, was possible in its pure form while the markets traded in fractions—$1/16$, $1/8$, etc. When Nasdaq trading was decimalized, it became much harder to count on an uninterrupted move big enough for substantial profit. Instead of moving in $1/8$–$1/4$s which equaled 12–25 cents, stocks started moving in cents with greatly reduced volatility. Still, I consider a trade a scalp if setbacks remain small, within 5–10 cents, which roughly match $1/16$–$1/8$ in fractions.

What Are Scalp Setups?   For me, scalp setups are any of the pivotal points or usual entries on a valid setup for intraday trading, for example, the intraday low on stock that dumps on bad news and pauses and the intraday high on an uptrending stock that shows signs of a breakout or a bottom of a pullback on an uptrending stock (for shorters, all of this can be applied in reverse). To initiate a long scalp trade, I want to see signs of momentum such as a strong *bid,* thinning *ask,* and prints at and/or above the *ask.* Of course, this is not a hard-and-fast rule. Sometimes scalpers will bid the stock while the buying side is still very weak, but their experience tells them that selling is exhausted so they will try to get their shares from last-minute panicking sellers.

Tools and Method of Reading.   Level 2 is a must. So is Times & Sales (T&S). I seldom use charts to define the exit point on a scalp. Most often it's Level 2 and Times & Sales. I also don't normally use any technical indicators for this style (again, it's just my personal preference—there are traders who use stochastic or other indicators when looking for reversal). I've found that a chart can be useful for getting an idea about a type of play or a certain setup. Then Level 2 and T&S should time the exact entry and exit.

Some Psychological Implications.   In trading, the reasons for movement are usually irrelevant ("the chart knows better"). In scalping, the reasons are as irrelevant as it gets. News, hype, short covering, bottom hunting, value buying, technical analysis (TA) setup; any of these reasons are valid for initiating a scalp trade. One day in 1998, I bought a stock on very good news. The catch was that while the headline sounded really great, reading further would reveal that it was news about a company with the same name but that was not publicly traded. I believed that traders were likely to identify the company by name and not read the whole article right away. The stock went up about 50 cents, and I hit the sell button as soon as someone shouted, "It's not the right company!"

I'm not justifying this method of trading. I use it to illustrate the irrelevance of knowing the reason for stock movement. Scalping is a game of blinking numbers. A scalper knows the pattern of the blinking and goes with this pattern, ignoring such things as company reputation, value, and so on. They just don't figure in this ultrashort time frame. People's behavior at pivotal points is all that matters. A scalper should be extremely cold-blooded, pretty fast on the trigger, have lightning-fast responses, and have good execution techniques.

The stock does what we bought it for, or we are out with no second-guessing, rationalizing for staying in it, or changing our plan as the situation changes. Each trade is "self-contained." It doesn't matter where the price of a new entry is in comparison to the previous one. We buy where the setup has occurred. A scalper has to be prepared to see a stock going much higher from our sell point, not giving us a setup for new entry. That's one of the biggest downsides of this style of trading.

How Risky Is This Style?   There is no simple answer to this question. Scalping is one of the toughest styles to learn, and the risk is fairly big if you try to start with it. At the same time, if you have mastered it, scalping is one of the safest ways to trade since your control over the trade is as close to absolute as possible.

Some Miscellaneous Points about Scalping.   A scalper usually buys with buyers and sells with buyers. If we buy with sellers, our timing has to be impeccable. If we have to sell with sellers, our timing on the sell side is most likely off. We need to be extremely precise in our trade picking and entry timing. Our average reward-to-risk ratio is not as favorable as it is for a good trader operating in a longer time frame, so our percentage of winning trades should be higher. It's one more downside to scalping.

It's important for a scalper to recognize a familiar situation in the blink of an eye. Intuition plays a big role in successful scalping. By no means should a beginner try to follow this style. Scalping is something we should come to only if our personal temperament leads us there. To make scalping worthwhile, one has to play on average 1000 shares at a minimum. So it's essential to make sure that liquidity is there. Thin issues can be scalped successfully on small lots like 200 shares, but be aware of execution capabilities. Even a stock with thick levels can be dangerous if it trades at a very fast pace and with huge volume.

A scalper usually generates more in commissions compared to other styles of traders. If this is of concern for you, do not scalp. If you do, forget commissions. *Scalping is about consistent gains, not about big gains.* A scalper has no chance to get rich overnight.

Most of the other traders jeer at me about these downsides. While some of them are great friends and traders, the others, who don't agree with scalping, consider me some sort of sour taste in their mouth, only to be scoffed at. This is fine. I don't trade to prove anything to anyone. But when you come right down to it, my portfolio speaks to my knowledge and my experience.

Of course, there are upsides as well. Good scalpers are very consistent, and their exposure to the market (and that means risk) is very small.

They are in control all the time. Consistent gains are great for confidence, for support, and for a constant good feeling about oneself. One more important thing to remember is that no matter what the market does (unless it's just dead), scalps are almost always there. It's a universal style of trading, from a market conditions standpoint. It's also a defensive style of trading suited well to choppy and uncertain markets.

CONFIDENCE GROWS FROM EXPERIENCE

Despite all the confidence I gained from experience, I was still not immune to the downfalls that the market can create. Two big lessons were waiting for me down the road. In trading, lessons are usually losses. The correct perception of the losses is extremely important for a trader. If we view a loss as a valuable lesson, then we get some value for our money. This value is knowledge, new experience, and new skill. If we don't learn from our loss, it's money wasted, and we are doomed to repeat the same mistakes.

Both lessons I refer to were of the same kind. Those were my last big losses. I never repeated that kind of mistake and never let any loss get out of hand since then. Let's look at what I did. This kind of mistake is fairly typical.

Trans Texas Gas (TTG)

The first trade involved Trans Texas Gas (TTG). This company announced that it had discovered the biggest gas well of the twentieth century. The stock went up 6 points in a matter of minutes. I bought my shares within 1 point of the top, at around $19. The stock went up a bit, topped out, and started downticking. I didn't take my profit.

Why should I? It was a huge gas well! Why shouldn't I sit out the pullback and wait for the stock to skyrocket? I was expecting further move because the news sounded so encouraging. Is this just a stupid kind of mistake that not many traders make? By no means. Time and time again, I see traders basing their trading decisions on their evaluation of the news. A small company announces that its drug got approval to be sold in China, and traders pile up on the stock because "China is such a huge market."

While this might be a reason to *play* the stock, is it the only reason to *hold* the stock? Absolutely not, but that was exactly what I did, and it still is what many people do. Let's assume that we buy the stock because we like the product announced in the news release. The stock goes up 50 cents, and we celebrate the profit we made because of our "careful research." But what if the stock goes against us? We hold our shares because it's such a great product! It very well could be, but does this really have much to do with short-term price movement? Do we know how many shares are waiting to be distributed to buyers and for what reason? Can we evaluate the potential ratio of supply and demand? And if it's possible to a certain degree, does news itself answer these questions? Of course it does not.

Needless to say, TTG never reached its former high again. The stock price slid down slowly. I kept my shares for several days, waiting for the great news to be "recognized by the market." When the stock reached important support, which was indicated by the chart, and broke it, I sold my shares. The stock proceeded lower, and eventually the company announced bankruptcy. It was not easy to take this hit, but the concept of stop loss was already ingrained in me.

It was a big lesson. Nonetheless, it took one more of this kind for me to realize what I was doing wrong. In the spring of 1998, the first sign of what was later called the "Internet craze" surfaced. Although in hindsight, it really had started with the 1995 Netscape IPO (initial public offering).

K-Tel (KTEL)

K-Tel (KTEL) shares went from $4–$5 to over $20 on news that the company had started selling its product on the Internet. This run caused hot debate. The reason for such movement looked weak, and the company's fundamentals were a subject of mockery by many. I shorted 1000 shares at $21 before the market opened. In a few hours the stock reached $24 and paused for a long time. I added 1000 shares short above $23. It *had* to go down. Weak news, weak fundamentals. Why would the stock go up?

Sure enough, KTEL went even higher, and I covered both lots at $29 and over $31. The stock closed at around $32. My broker phoned me that day and said that I had to cover my shares immediately because they had been called in. When I told him I already did, he said I was lucky. He was right. A gigantic short squeeze took KTEL shares as high as $80. (See Figure 2.1.)

I lost over 50 percent on this single trade. It was very painful, of course. But, at the same time, I felt that I finally understood something vital for my trading. I had the very strong feeling that it would be my last big loss. This feeling was correct. Never again did I take such a hit on a single trade, and the understanding I bought with my loss on the TTG and KTEL trades has served me well ever since.

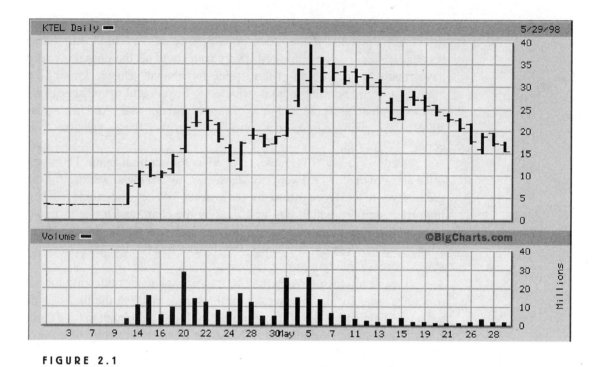

FIGURE 2.1

KTEL stock adjusted for a 2:1 split. (*Used with permission of CBS MarketWatch.*)

Learning from Experience

I realized that all those things I was looking at and using as reasons for my trading decisions were completely irrelevant. News didn't govern price movement; fundamentals did not either. KTEL was going up and up because the majority of people trading did not believe it would. The majority were taking short positions, and the market acted in a way that would hurt the majority. The public was thinking, rationalizing, and analyzing, and the public was wrong. But wait. Was it really wrong?

The KTEL price depreciated greatly after the short squeeze was over, and eventually KTEL shares were delisted from the Nasdaq. (See Figure 2.2.) So, was the public right? Actually, yes, it was. Did being right help the public make money? No, it lost!

Here is the answer. People were looking at something irrelevant to stock-price movement in this particular time frame. It did not matter whether or not they were right because it was about something other than price direction. Even if they were right, it was not what impacted

FIGURE 2.2

What ultimately happened to KTEL stock. (*Used with permission of CBS MarketWatch.*)

the stock price. Supply and demand did. People were trying to judge supply and demand from their evaluation of news and fundamentals. But the real ratio of buyers to sellers was governed by different factors, and those factors had to do with the smart money playing against the crowd. The stock market apparently worked in a way that would allow the minority to take the money from the majority. It's not a conspiracy; it's not manipulation—it's just the way the stock market works. I need to do things differently from what the crowd does because crowds are not successful in any kind of business. Those who reach the top are those who have unique vision and the ability to realize that vision. So when you see the crowd going for something, you want to view the situation from a contrarian's perspective.

After this realization, the pieces of the puzzle were coming together for me, and my motto "Trade what you see, not what you think" was again validated. We can think anything we choose of the news, of a company, of fundamentals, or of financials. But the price action is the ultimate truth. For traders to make money, they have to read price action, not all those things that surround market movements. By being around other traders of various experience levels, you can see endless variations of those things. Traders all of a sudden become experts in drilling results, medical research, software details, surgical tools, drugs, electronic devices, and business models. You name it, and they discuss it and argue points. They try to take something from the information that will help them predict price movement. But look at stocks, going from $10 to over $100 and back down, during 1999–2000. Did the fundamentals of the companies, business models, or their shares in the market change that drastically in both directions during 1 year? In some cases, maybe. But I doubt it was the real reason for all those movements of such magnitude.

Here is another example how our thoughts can take us to a dead end: If the Food & Drug Administration (FDA) approves some new drug presented by a company, stock price rises by let's say 2 points. Then the price retreats 1 point. Did the FDA withdraw its decision thereby making the stock drop? Of course not. It was the balance of supply and demand that impacted the movement and changed the price levels, while the initial press release served only as the trigger for traders' interest. Hence, in order to trade these movements correctly, you need to read this balance of supply and demand.

Remember the Bre-X story. Traders were mistaken in their evaluation, and they lost. In the case of KTEL, traders were right, and yet they lost again. Isn't this proof that traders were basing their decisions on totally irrelevant things? They were creating some other reality than the reality of stock movement.

THE TERRITORY AND THE MAP

John Magee made the following analogy in *Technical Analysis of Stock Trends*. There is a territory, and there is a map. Are they ever exactly the same? Not really. They might be close if the map is good. But they are never identical.

Think of territory as stock movement. The map is what we think of the stock movement and what we make of it. If all the reasons that traders discuss have nothing to do with stock movement, then what does? The answer is the stock movement itself! This is the only reality of the market. That's why the market is never wrong. The market just is what it is. It does what it does. As a Zen philosopher would put it, the market *is*.

Let's return to my trading situation after the two big losses. There I was, armed with good discipline, with a new understanding of how the market worked, with great execution technique, and with leftovers of my trading account—just over $10,000.

I was now under huge psychological pressure. I could not afford any more losses. This situation is known as "scared money." It's commonly acknowledged that scared money can't win. Traders refuse to take stops because they can't afford losses. Not being able to win all the time, traders let the next loss get out of hand. This is a vicious cycle. I already understood all this. I realized that I had already survived long enough to work out a solid methodology and correct mindset. Now I had to make it all work with a ridiculously small line. I knew I had to have extremely strict discipline and keep my stops religiously. I decided to work out a whole philosophy about stops, and I wrote a letter to myself about stops and their meaning for me. It was a letter written by a teacher I created in my imagination to me, the student. Here it is, with minor edits.

What Is Stop Loss and How Does One Keep It?

Let's start with the very definition of loss. When we pay tuition for college, is it a loss? It isn't if we get a good job based on the education we paid for. It is a loss if we never apply the knowledge we paid for. What if we pay much more for education than a new job can compensate us for? It's still not a loss, but we paid too much for our education. This is exactly what happens in trading. If we bought a stock based on certain criteria, the trade went against us, and we took our stop, is it a loss? It isn't a loss if we revise the criteria and avoid the same mistake the next time. It is a loss if we repeat the mistake over and over again. If we fail to keep a proper stop and wind up with a much bigger stop than we should, then we paid too much for the lesson.

However, unlike the example with college, we are given the opportunity to assign the price to the education, and we have deliberately chosen to pay the higher price! Was it a smart decision?

This is the first element of our self-tuning:

Do not pay more than we can afford!

The market is an eternal educator, but it's kind enough to let us pay as much as we choose to. Education is on sale when the stock hits our predetermined stop level. It won't be on sale in a minute, so why should we wait?

The second element of our self-tuning is not thinking of money when we're in a trade. We shouldn't count what we lose or gain with each tick. The market doesn't care if we lose or how much we lose. Focusing on money just takes us farther from emotional balance while clouding our judgment. Monitor what the market does, not how our account is affected.

The subject of our job is market movement.

We have to respond to market movement. The third element of our self-tuning is our perception of ourself when we take the loss. If we come to the market with the notion that, in order to win, we have to know what the market does every minute or hour, then how will we perceive ourself when the market does the opposite of what we expect? As a fool? As a loser?

Nobody wants to be a fool or a loser. That's where our ego takes over immediately. It tries to save us from this unpleasant feeling. The next step naturally will be to think, "I am not a loser. Those sellers are the losers. The stock will reverse in a minute, and they will be crying. I will be celebrating."

See how the ego takes us farther from the territory, making us believe our map is correct? There is a way to avoid this. We need to change the original belief with which we approach the market. Let's look at our thinking process if we come to the market with the idea that, "I don't have to know what the market does next." What I *do* have to know is "What will I do in any scenario that the market offers?"

By thinking like this:

1. We have already accepted and assumed the stop-loss possibility. It no longer comes as an unpleasant surprise for us.

2. We have admitted from the very beginning that the market is bigger than we are and cannot be controlled or predicted by us. With this understanding, our ego will be quiet because nothing triggers it.

3. We don't feel like a fool when the market goes against us. Why would we feel like that if we never thought we were able to outsmart the market in the first place?

4. We don't feel like a loser when the market goes against us. Why should we feel like that if we never thought that a winner has to be right every time?

We can see how changing our original belief reverses the way we feel and act. Realize and accept the fact that the market is an ocean. Swim with it; use its current, its ebb, and its flow. But don't think that we can change the direction of the current or that we can know all the currents that exist. When we find that the current is taking us in an undesirable direction, we swim out of it and look for another current, instead of waiting for it to reverse.

The next very important element in our self-tuning is our perception of our trading as a whole. At the end of the day many great active traders can't list the stocks they played, whereas newbies remember each detail of each trade for weeks and months to come. Newer traders perceive each trade as unique and outstanding. If the trade fails, it feels like a disaster. If the trade works out, it feels like a huge victory.

A stop loss limits the pullbacks!

When such significance is assigned to each trade, it becomes hard for the trader to accept the stop. Accept that our account cannot go up with each trade taken, just as no stock goes straight up. All have their retreats. The trend is what matters. If our account is on an uptrend, what else do we need? We need one more thing. We need our pullbacks, or drawdowns, to be as shallow as possible. But that's exactly what a stop loss does.

If we can look at our trading as a whole instead of looking at each trade separately, then we will feel compelled to apply a stop loss in order to limit the retreat.

Compare the following two patterns:

+0.50, +0.65, −0.25, +0.35, −0.10, +1.25, −0.15. This is an uptrend with three shallow pullbacks stopped early.

+0.50, +0.60, −1, +0.30, −1.50, +1.10, −1. This is not an uptrend. It's an erratic, supervolatile, jumping-around centerline. We don't want to play any stock that moves this way, and we don't want our account to look like this.

We need deep, tight self-control that will allow us to apply stop losses with no hesitation. There are certain tricks we can use in order to correct our behavior. In an interview with a great trader, I read a confession of a woman who had incredible discipline in applying the stop. When asked how she managed to achieve it, she said, "I am a very religious person. I believe God doesn't want me to lose money. I might upset Him if I do. I apply a tight stop loss and I am in accordance with what I believe in."

Define the major asset to protect by stop loss and protect
this asset religiously.

Find the motivation, the trigger, the valuable asset that can't be jeopardized. It might be something different for each of us. For example, some may find it helpful to think of our family for whom we want to prosper. A stop loss is our way to protect the prosperity of our family. It could be the car of our dreams. A stop loss takes us closer to the amount of money we need in order to buy it. It could be our mortgage, or any number of things.

Be creative with this mindset and find all the tricks that are possible to make it a loss-cutting machine. The market will reward us immensely.

COMING AROUND THE MOUNTAIN

This was a turning point for me. I learned plenty of lessons the hard way, and I had the distinct feeling that I was turning the corner in my trading.

During the summer of 1998, my account made two trips from $10,000 to $17,000 and right back down. It looked like I almost had it right. Then something important got away from me again.

Both times, the movements up and down were slow, with no big wins or losses. I knew I could make it. I just needed to stop those drawbacks.

When my account reached $17,000 for the third time, a point that was a ceiling for me twice, I stopped trading for a week. I needed to break the pattern, to get rid of the feeling that I faced some monetary barrier. All I did during that week was observe and rest. It was an attempt to forget that amount that I couldn't get past. I needed to stop thinking of money and just concentrate on trading itself. It worked. The next week I broke this barrier and made another thousand.

This was an exciting and encouraging moment. I began to feel that all my hard work and all the realizations about both the market and myself finally started paying off. I did everything I could to not let the excitement take over and make my trading careless. In a few weeks of careful trading, small stops and slow advancing, I finally saw my trading account reaching over $20,000. At the moment when it broke over $21,000, I did what I dreamed of doing for months. I withdrew some money from the trading account, leaving $20,000 in it. From then on, I allowed my trading account to grow slowly while rewarding myself with some money on a regular basis.

CHAPTER 3

The First Profitable Year

Charting Success

I decided to draw a chart of my trading account movement. The purpose was to create a certain psychological environment for myself. I realized that when I failed to break $17,000 twice, I perceived this number as a barrier. I have no idea why $17,000 was this barrier. I realized that on a chart of my account movement it looked like a resistance that needed to be broken. I wanted this chart to look like uptrending stock in which for any setback the price bounces to the upside off a lower support. In order to create this feeling of the upside from where I was and to limit the draw-backs, I started to withdraw the money from my trading account as soon as it would hit the upper envelope of the ascending channel. This trick allowed me to maintain the feeling of an uptrend. It might seem esoteric and artificial, but it worked, and I was happy with anything that did. Since trading is a mental game to a great degree, it becomes necessary to use mental tricks. It has been said often that in trading we are our own worst enemies. So it seems only logical to me that, in order to win, we need to find the way to defeat this internal foe. I don't believe it could be done by simply commanding oneself to do the right thing and to stop doing the wrong thing. If it was that simple, nobody would have any troubles winning in the markets.

If I hit the lower support and went lower by just $100, I would immediately take a day off and regroup. If, on the opposite side, I was breaking a higher envelope, then I was pressing harder and trading more aggressively. That was the right way to manage the risk: slowing down and decreasing activity when I was experiencing a setback and pushing harder when I was hot. This helped me to keep setbacks very shallow. I kept share size to 1000 or less, and stops mostly around $0.25 during this phase of my trading.

USING A TRADING JOURNAL

Charting my account movement was not the only tool I used to monitor my trading. I also started tracking my trading results in a journal, which helped me spot and prevent problems in the early stages. This journal served me as a kind of mirror in which I could see where my trading mindset deviated from the right direction. I often hear people advising others to keep a trading journal. Over the years, I have seen many versions of them. One aspect of many of them, which I've found quite questionable, is recommendations to write down the trader's feelings and thoughts at the moment of trade initiation and during its development. I don't think this is a good idea. Here is why. A trading journal fills two major purposes. The first is to help the trader develop a collection of statistics. This is the obvious purpose of a journal since these statistics help traders see which setups work consistently and where the system fails.

The other purpose is to determine by analyzing these trading statistics what is happening in a trader's mind. However, most mental changes and developments occur subconsciously. It's hardly something we realize and recognize while we're trading. Any attempt to write this kind of thing down will most likely lock us into the mindset of "what we think we think." For example, if problems with our mindset lie below the conscious level, then how would writing down these things help us determine where we go wrong? We would most likely write down not what really happened in our mind but merely repeat that same erroneous thinking process that took us nowhere during the trade. Instead, my approach led to an objective take on my reactions and allowed me to analyze my weaknesses. This journal served as a window into the inner world of a trader's mind.

I tracked:

- Number of trades per day
- Number of winners
- Number of losers
- Winners/losers ratio
- Average winning trade size in terms of points
- Average losing trade size in terms of points
- Number of points per day

Number of Trades per Day

Keeping track of the number of trades per day may seem simple and not too informative. But look at it from this point of view. How many trades do you do in a winning day? In a losing day? The rule says to act more aggressively when you're on a winning streak and to decrease activity when you're on a losing streak. Many traders do exactly the opposite. When losing, they try to get it back, to take revenge. And the result is usually not good. In this situation our trades may depend on our wishes rather than on real opportunities.

Winners/Losers Ratio

If a trader sees the winners/losers ratio below 50 percent, something is wrong, assuming that the reward-to-risk scenario doesn't allow for trading under 50 percent. My system won't allow the ratio to be under 50 percent. It tells me that I am probably overtrading, trying to squeeze something out of a juiceless trade. Also, my understanding of market dynamics and patterns is not quite right, and it's time to go back to paper trading. A ratio of 50 percent or higher seems fine, as long as winners are bigger than losers.

Average Winner and Average Loser

The average winner and the average loser show us whether we have followed the basic rule of cut our losers quickly and let our profits run. Each trader has a level of comfort, with respect to stops, depending on his or her risk tolerance, the kind of stocks played, expectations, and so on. When we look at our average loser for a month, we can see whether we managed to keep our stops as small as we wanted. If an average winner is too small, it tells us that we do many scalps or have problems staying in a winning trade. Different combinations of these statistics give us different angles. For example, a big *number of trades* combined with a low *winners/losers ratio* means that many low-percentage trades were picked.

Table 3.1 illustrates an example of such a journal with analysis. It is taken from a real week of trading. I selected a volatile, losing week (before commissions), to show how I acted to spot the problem using the numbers shown.

"Trades" in this table refers to round-trips (trades bought and sold). Flat trades are excluded. I purposely ignored the impact of commissions; I wanted to see what was going on in my mind, not just calculate my monetary achievements.

YABLE 3.1

Traing Statistic

	No. of trades	No. of winners	No. of losers	W/L ratio	Average winners*	Average losers*	Total*
Mon.	12	8	(3)	2.7	.35	(.173)	2.28
Tues.	15	8	(6)	1.3	.25	(.237)	0.58
Wed.	11	2	(6)	0.3	.23	(.273)	(2.10)
Thurs.	18	8	(8)	1	.156	(.22)	(0.512)
Fri.	10	6	(2)	3	.23	(.156)	1.068
Total	66	32	(25)	1.3			1.316

* At the time the trades occurred, the numbers were in fractions. I converted them to cents so that readers who are accustomed to decimals could understand the numbers easily.

Monday: As you can see Monday was a very nice day. There was a good percentage of winners (67 percent), and a not bad winner/loser ratio (2.7/1, which is fairly decent for a scalper).

Tuesday: Tuesday was not that great. The percentage of winners dropped to 53 percent, and the ratio went almost flat. Taking commissions into account, Tuesday was a slightly losing day, most likely resulting from overconfidence after a very nice start to the week. The number of trades went up too—a possible sign of reckless picking.

Wednesday: Wednesday was a total disaster. Over 50 percent of my trades were losers, and the losing trades averaged more than the winning ones. Apparently I was trying to press hard to resume my winning streak that was interrupted by a sluggish Tuesday. Losses were not cut effectively. Did I try to hold despite the market telling me to get out?

Thursday: Whoa! Look at this sucker's reaction to a losing day! The number of trades is way up—revenge trading, pushing hard instead of becoming less aggressive while on a losing streak. There are an equal number of losers and winners—churning, trying to jump on everything that moves with fairly random results. Winners are small—I got scared and started taking any profits, just to win? Losers are still bigger than winners—misplaced hope, "Maybe it's going back to my entry."

Friday: Friday is somewhat better. I evidently attempted to pull myself together. I didn't trade aggressively—lowest number of trades for the week. I was more selective with my plays, which could constitute a not-bad day but could not save the week. I made 66 trades, 132 tickets plus some unavoidable partial fills, $20 per ticket (usual commissions at that time), down almost $1500 for the week.

As this kind of analysis built up, I was able to see the problem as it just appeared. Familiar patterns of my behavior became visible to me at early stages thanks to the tables I created. For instance, I already knew that I tended to overtrade after a losing day. I had to keep myself from doing that by effectively improving my reactions. I could track my reactions when I was on a winning streak and spot the moment when I was getting too reckless. All this monitoring gave me a good look within myself. As a result, I became constantly aware of my inner state and could diagnose a problem just in time to prevent it from getting worse.

USING YOUR CHART OF YOUR ACCOUNT

Let's take a deeper look at how to use the chart of your account. I use mine in many different ways. First I match the chart of my portfolio equity to the Nasdaq chart. If I see them going together, it may possibly mean that the bull market works for me, and that my thoughts are not relevant to my success. There is a good chance that a bear market will take my portfolio down. You can see such a situation in Figure 3.1.

As I viewed this situation, I decided to stay put and sharply decrease my activity during a down market to reduce my drawbacks. I would also analyze to determine whether I was fighting the market. For example, am

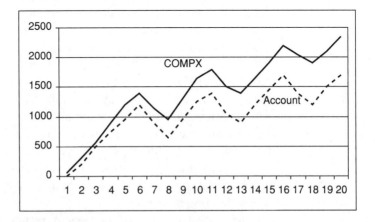

FIGURE 3.1

The comparison of market and account movements.

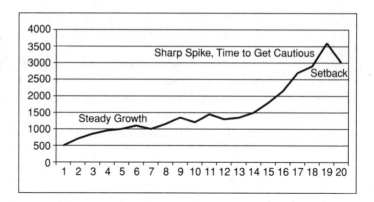

FIGURE 3.2

A sharp spike usually precedes a setback.

I trying to go long no matter what, buying false breakouts while the trend is down? This could be the case if my account was drifting down at the same time as the market drifted down. Therefore, I would need to adjust my strategy and listen to the market more carefully.

If I saw my account steadily moving up, I would become more aggressive since I would realize that I was in tune with the market. But if I saw sharp upward movement, an almost vertical line, I would start backing away to avoid or smooth out a setback that usually follows a sharp spike. My experience shows that this kind of spike rarely continues for more than 3 days in a row. (See Figure 3.2.)

Another situation I faced frequently was that my portfolio equity would reach a certain number and then inevitably drop, like a stock that cannot penetrate the resistance level. This situation is illustrated in Figure 3.3. It's most likely some kind of psychological barrier. How do I deal with it? A variety of ways are described in some of the books devoted to traders' psychology. A solution might turn out to be simple (for instance, taking some amount of money out of the trading account when it reaches that upper level again). This would allow me to trick my mind into thinking that my account was at a low envelope (800–850 in Figure 3.3) instead of an upper line (1200 in Figure 3.3), which presented resistance.

This kind of analysis can give great insight into what's happening within us and serve as a troubleshooting of sorts. We will get back to the troubleshooting theme later.

My quest for a trading system resulted in a much more solid approach than simply pure scalping. Even my scalps were not based on only Level 2 strength, as in strong bids and thin offers. I started to get a

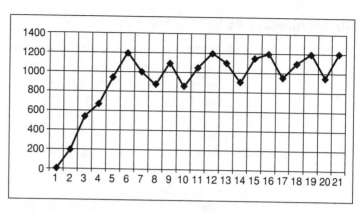

FIGURE 3.3

Account resistance caused by a psychological barrier.

good feel for what Jesse Livermore meant when he talked about smart money playing against the public and how to differentiate their footprints. Rereading old books devoted to this topic and careful market observations led to a trading system that was becoming more and more clear for me. I was adding new principles to it, learning to read the volume hints. The way prices changed and the pace of those changes were no longer a great mystery. There were apparent clues on the tape.

In many instances I was able to see stages of stock movement, such as slow accumulation followed by an increased volume and a faster price advance. Then I saw when the public discovered the stock, and the movement was becoming almost hysterical. That was the moment when all the shares that had been accumulated during the first stages were dumped into a volume and price explosion. I learned to take the position during the first stages when I could spot it and wait for the crowd to come in and take the shares off my hands. That was incredibly exciting. Instead of blind wandering, I was now trading on the right side. I was not part of the crowd anymore, but I was using the crowd's emotions.

At the same time, scars from my big losses constantly reminded me about the risk involved. I was avoiding overnight positions, and my risk was strictly limited. I realized that such strict limitations were holding me back, but I could not afford any losses. Slow, steady growth was what I wanted.

In a few months, my trading account reached $25,000, and I was taking money out of it on a regular basis. By adding the amount I took out to the amount I kept in, I was able to see that I had recouped my losses.

IMAGINARY FRIENDS ARE IMPORTANT PEOPLE TOO

In early 1999, I incorporated one more trick into my mental tune-up. In Chapter 2, I talked about how I taught myself to keep stops. I wrote the letter to myself as a teacher to student. I went farther now. I created a model trader in my mind. I thought through all his traits as a trader. He was the master that I wanted to become. I was not the one who was trading; he was doing the trading. I was merely an observer, an admirer. I can't tell you what a huge help this trick was. It allowed me to stay detached emotionally because I was just an observer. In some cases I would give him final approval for a trade, after making sure that his trade matched my system criteria and wasn't prompted by emotions.

My model trader was cold-blooded, calm, and humorous in a cool, dry way. He was absolutely disciplined, and totally focused and relaxed at the same time. So was I; it's easy to relax when you are watching someone else trade. My tension went away completely once I started doing this. Trading became fun! There was no ego involved anymore. If the model made some stupid mistake, I just laughed at him. He knew he was being watched, and this made him cut his losses very quickly. I cannot tell you how much this trick has helped me. It resolved plenty of problems I had previously experienced with emotional control. Instead of attempting to get rid of my emotions (as if that were possible!), I found my way around them: I detached myself from my emotions enough to not act under their influence.

Does this all sound crazy? Sure it does, but trading is a crazy business! It requires an unusual state of mind, so that unusual tricks are justified.

In October 1999 I finished the third year of my trading. My results were spectacular. I took $10,000 up to $70,000, keeping just $25,000 in my account and withdrawing everything above that. That was a 700 percent annual return. At that time my immigration case was finalized, and I became a Canadian resident. I felt more confident than ever. I knew that my success was not just luck. It was a careful approach and a valid trading system. And, most important of all, it was the correct trading mindset. The next year confirmed that as I took my account to over $200,000, still keeping the same amount of money for trading. Trading what I saw, not what I thought, was what I managed to do in my actual trading.

CHAPTER 4

Learning to Trade for a Living

Let's take an in-depth look at learning to trade. This topic is the subject of a completely separate chapter for two reasons. First, somehow many beginners feel that they can just jump in and start making money. Some think they can learn trading in 2–3 months. Can you imagine any serious profession that could be learned in such amount of time? Trading is certainly not the easiest of professions. In fact, it is the opposite: I have heard many people say that this is the toughest endeavor they have ever undertaken.

The second reason is that before you start learning, you must know what you must learn. Far too many traders think that in order to trade successfully, they need to learn about indicators. They believe that they only have to find the "one that works" or some magic combination of them. Then they think they have the key to the bank. This is a big mistake. This approach leads beginning traders to believe that there are secrets known to the top traders, and, if they only could get ahold of those secrets, they could make money easily. I am confident there are no magic bullets, no great secrets hidden from the trading masses. So in this chapter I discuss different aspects of the process of learning.

I always find it interesting when some traders talk about their huge gains or profits, but never much about their losses. On the other hand, some traders like to tell horror stories. After all, what doesn't kill you makes you stronger! This is an interesting dichotomy, as trading is about profits and losses, not just profits. It is easy to spot the worst traders in any crowd; they are the ones who talk only about their profits. Successful traders don't have to prove anything to anyone and they are 100 percent responsible for their own trading. They know that the successful trade is the one that worked as planned, which means the knowledge needed for the trade was actually acquired already. It is the losing trade that carries the lesson to be learned. No matter which method you follow for learning, the market will always be your main teacher—and its lessons are served in the form of losses.

LEARN OR YOU ARE BANKRUPT

I have met quite a few traders who have never even tried to learn. They thought they could use stock-picking services or newsletters, and trade their picks without deep understanding. I don't know any of them who could make money consistently. Pure followers of stock pickers will never be around long. Traders have to be their own leaders in order to survive. Furthermore, stock pickers rarely tell you how they pick stocks; they'd rather you just pay for their insight. Let's face it, followers don't trade for a living. Followers exist for a while as they continue in their learning phase. But they have to emerge as leaders for themselves if they are to be traders that are worth their salt. The only kind of stock-picking service I would recognize as valid would be the one where the leader explains the reasoning for the play so that the traders can follow it, check if they are comfortable with it, make sure the risk is acceptable, and so on. In this case it's not about following anymore. It's a normal process of learning in which a teacher shares knowledge and experience.

Among the traders I have communicated with are a few who went through the process of learning along with me. Problems they encountered are quite typical and instructive. For example, one particular trader, a woman from Russia, was easily one of the most intelligent people I've ever come across. As intelligent as she was, she still experienced many of the same problems as I did when I was learning to trade. She took a bit of a different route, however. She started with a trading outfit that taught traders. She spent many months with this outfit to no avail. Much of her account was depleted, the same as mine was. For all I know, the system offered could be sound, but the method of teaching was missing much of what trading is really about. No system offers profits to everyone. Some systems don't offer profits to anyone. This is another interesting aspect of selling in America: "If I can't make money using it, I can make money selling it." Fortunately, I learned to trade without having to pay for something from someone that wasn't proven reliable. I paid the market for my education instead, and what a great teacher it was! Relentless too.

After a few months and a lot of capital spent, the woman began to listen a bit more to what I was saying. After I began to take my profits to great heights, I wanted to share with her some of the principles that had brought me my success. Some traders listened; some didn't. Some even went so far as to dismiss me and my ideas. But, as a trader, I didn't care. My account profits spoke for themselves. I don't have to prove anything to anyone who doesn't care to accept what I say. I don't need to fight with people to make them see my point.

The woman's intelligence helped bring her closer to trading reality. She and I would trade together almost every day from this point on. She told me of her trades and listened to my opinions of them. I wouldn't so much offer her a trading strategy as a deeper look into why the stocks were moving the way they did. I didn't realize it at the time, but this was when I began to really refine my principles of trading. I began to apply some structure what it was that was working for me. Previously, these principles were simply ideas that were distributed in an illogical manner throughout my head. Now, they began to take shape. So while she was learning from me, I was progressing as well. It worked for both of us. Even more important, we often talked about the state of mind of a trader, and I tried to put into words everything I learned about trading psychology.

Her trading account stopped taking wild rides up and down. Instead, her account grew steadily and slowly. She put her own spin on my method, and it worked well for her. I have seen this many times: The most successful students are those who find their own slant on the approach they are being taught. They apply their personality to the system they study and produce their own version of the system. That's their edge and a comfort zone for them.

Eventually, we began talking openly about other traders. From these small trade reviews, I began to see interesting parallels between me and them. They were all going through the stages of learning curve that I had just gone through. They asked the same questions and experienced the same situations. I saw many of these traders taking the same journey I had taken.

KEYING IN ON THOSE AROUND ME

As I observed other traders, I saw that they went through different stages of trading. Their beliefs about the market all seemed to stem from a misunderstanding of it. They heard certain remarks from commercials, brokers, and the financial media. But they had a hard time adjusting their beliefs to market reality. I realized that any successful learning process must start with correcting those beliefs. Teachers who instill the right mindset in their students do more good for the students than does the teacher who only teaches a trading system.

First, let me define a belief from my perspective. A *belief* is a feeling or concept, within any individual, about some future outcome, based on past experiences or memory. We all have past experiences from early childhood all the way up to 5 minutes ago, and these experiences shape our beliefs about the future.

In general we all hold certain beliefs about life. For instance, the harder we work and the more effort we put in, the more money we will make. The less we work, the less money we will make. The person who works three jobs will make more than the couch potato. But the problem is that this belief does not hold true in trading. It takes virtually no effort to trade stocks. Anyone can buy and sell stocks and have winners and losers with no effort at all. I remember telling my daughter, who was thirteen at the time, a bit about what I was doing at the office. She noticed the green and red numbers and figured that when she saw green, she would buy. When she saw red, she would sell. It sounded so logical to me that I just had to smile. Once a simple observation is learned, with no effort, a person would buy and sell stocks with no reason or thought. Some of those trades would make money and some would not.

When new traders come to the marketplace, ready to trade stocks, they buy here and sell there based on opinions or systems they don't really understand. This is a good reason why many do not stick around for too long. They make trades, winning and losing, with no effort at all. If they win more in the beginning, they believe that trading is easy, a piece of cake. How hard could it be? You just buy here and sell there. It's not until a string of losses, or one great loss, comes along that they begin to redefine their thought process. If traders lose and lose, their belief is that trading is impossible, no one can do it. Once they encounter a string of winners, or a big win, then their belief begins to change to thinking that maybe it is possible. They had an initial belief, based on some criteria, or string of memories. Once a different criterion was placed in the experience pool, the belief became somehow distorted or was changed.

I started trading, making and losing money with no effort. I continued, lost money with no effort (it doesn't take any effort to not press the sell button). I continued, learning all I could about the market and myself (considerable effort). I am here now, trading again with basically minimal "effort."

NOT EVERYONE GETS AN A FOR EFFORT

What is the difference between my beginnings, when I traded with no effort, and where I am now, trading with minimal effort? I traded with no effort from the beginning because I did not feel fear. There was nothing to tell me that there was something to be afraid of. You learned of a few of my horror stories and they certainly instilled fear in me. I learned risk and management principles, and I geared my inner self to trading. Now I have nothing to fear again. I don't believe that the market can take more from me than I'm willing to give it. It's interesting how a beginner and an experienced trader can have the same belief yet a different understanding of the market.

The biggest difference at the beginning stage was the lack of responsibility—the beginners' belief that trading is based on "the market making and taking their money." Experienced traders know that it is they who are accountable for their trading and the money they risk and make on each individual trade. Beginners will never become professionals without being accountable for their own actions. Trading has nothing to do with what the market "does to you."

Another aspect of this belief adjustment relates to my Russian friend. She tried to learn a certain system from a trading service. Systems are not "one size fits all" entities. There are numerous systems and numerous books about systems. And I'm sure there are many more to come. "If I can just find the right system, trading will be a piece of cake." We know this to be false, since no system provides consistent winners from individual to individual. If a system existed that provided winners to all who used it, there would be far more traders making a very good living. But the fact is that 90 percent of traders lose money. Within a group of traders applying the same system, one trader makes more money than another, and some don't make money at all. The system is the same, so why are the profits different? Trading again is about us and is just a reflection of who we are at any given moment. Let me illustrate. You are in the stock, and it makes a couple ticks in your favor. Are you confident and calm? If you are, then you will let it run, allowing the profit to develop. Are you a coward, or do you feel unsure? If either is true, you will take your profits prematurely. Your position is moving against you—are you a cold-blooded trader willing to accept the risk even before you put on the trade? Or do you feel like you just can't accept monetary loss? If this is the case, then you are going to take your stop loss in the first case, and you will be subjected to a horrible emotional spiral in the second.

We see simple market movement every day. The market moves up and down, as aggregate shifts of demand and supply lean to one side or the other. This happens at all price levels. The basis for movement is what we as traders try to define and profit from. Some see it on a tape-reading platform, some by technical analysis, and some don't use anything (they make it up as they go along). The last kind are my favorite kind of traders. They try to buy and sell a stock based solely on opinion, and then try to hide behind the word *intuition*. I believe in intuition a great deal, but not when it's used to mask a lack of skill in stock trading. When I first brought up a chart of a stock, I saw a hill. I didn't see support and resistance. I didn't see capitulation events. I didn't see euphoric events. I didn't see accumulations. I saw a hill. Why? Because there was nothing from previous experience to tell me what that hill meant, what moves within that hill were made up of.

YOU DECIDE YOUR FATE; THE MARKET DOESN'T

Those who think that the market provides profit and loss are mistaken. You and the choices you make decide this. If you accept the notion that the market dictates your profit and loss to any degree outside your parameters, you lose control of your trading. The market is neutral. It will go up and down regardless of your position. It's you who engages and disengages, making a profit or loss. The market doesn't know who you are, nor does it care. It goes up, making emotional longs happy and emotional shorts unhappy. Vice versa with downward moves. Emotional trading is a killer of traders. The idea is that you, at this very moment, have some feeling within you about yourself, your trading. Either you made money this morning and are eager to trade again because you feel confident, or you didn't make money this morning and are feeling frustrated and ready to give up today. Or you might have made a profit and are willing to rest this afternoon, or you lost money and are ready for revenge this afternoon, as if the market owes you something. The markets owe us nothing.

Many people might wonder, "But if the market does what it does, then how do I still have control? The market moved to make me money or lose my money." We still have to hit the exit button, right? How many times early on in our careers do we have a great profit, only to turn it into a loss? How many times do we have a small loss turn into a larger one? The point is that we are still the ones who make the decisions for entry and exit, and that's what we are in control of—our decisions.

The market doesn't care about us. If you believe that the market is trying to hurt you, you're misguided. The market isn't something to be at war with; it's something to move with. When you do, you regain control. When you regain control, what is there to fear? If there is nothing to fear, then you can make quick decisions for both entry and exit. Even if you don't profit, if you trade unemotionally, where each uptick or downtick is neither euphoria nor pain, then you trade successfully. The idea is not to get rid of all your emotions. I don't think it's even possible. The idea is to distance your trading decisions from your emotions. Understand that most traders experience the same set of emotions, and most of them lose. Doesn't this tell you that you need to learn to stop your emotions from governing your trades? Even more than that—you can *use* your emotions as a mirror to reveal what the majority thinks and feels, thus effectively allowing you to exploit the fear and greed of others. And, again, in order to be able to do it, you have to be emotionally detached; you need to be an objective observer of everything, *including* your own emotions.

ADDITIONAL IMPORTANT BELIEFS

One of the worst problems I had in the earlier stages of my career was listening to the opinions of others about my position. For example, when I went long in a stock and then heard someone mention that the market should sell now, I became anxious and eager to get out of my position.

If the market cannot hurt us, then other traders' opinions of stock movement can't either. We enter a trade based on our own experience and perception. We don't enter a stock and then immediately exit because someone suggests it's a bad idea. This is like cheating off the paper of another student, changing your answer from the right one to the wrong one because you think the other student knows more than you. If we make a choice in entering a trade, knowing that the market cannot hurt us outside of our predefined risks, then we shouldn't let an outside opinion change our minds so fast.

The biggest problem I see with traders' application of their systems is that the systems tend to create the illusion of certainty and predictability. Systems do not tell the future. They simply provide us with signals for entry and exit. Systems offer a probability of success, not a certainty.

Once all the traders see an obvious pattern, there cannot be a profitable outcome. The majority can't win in the market over time. The market can't exist this way. When traders' beliefs aren't close to market reality, they will continue to allow us to feed off their misguided notions. Fortunately these beliefs will never change, because the market never changes.

One of the most common beliefs is that the more we learn about a particular stock or company, the better we can read the price movement. Many times throughout the early learning stage of my trading, I fell prey to the notion that I "had" to know what the market was going to do or what an individual stock was going to do. For example, the market maker, PUNK, was selling an amazing number of shares at $20. What did it mean, and what happens next? NDX is under 1900; what does it do next? Eventually my answer came to be, "I don't know. You can't possibly know. No one knows. And you know what? I can trade successfully without knowing!"

TRADING IS NOT A NEED-TO-KNOW BUSINESS

As I talk with other traders throughout their training process, I am often asked, "I *need to know*. Otherwise how can I trade?" This is the major question traders have to answer. The answer can be found in the general approach to the market and in the understanding of its mechanics.

Let's take a simple situation and determine whether it is possible to know all the factors that will impact future action. If it is, would this knowledge really help us to foresee what the market will do? Let's go back to the market maker example. PUNK is selling a healthy number of shares at $20. The buyers hit him with continuous orders, and the orders get filled, yet PUNK is still there. The trader then thinks, "OK, how do I figure out how much is for sale because I can't trade not knowing it."

Is it really possible to know how many shares PUNK has to dump? It's virtually impossible. Let's assume that he has an order from a big client and sells for the client. Sometimes even the market maker does not know the size of an entire order! Many times a client will not give the whole order to the same market maker. The client will split the order up to see who can get the best price, and possibly route remaining shares to the better of the market makers. Or the client might be trying to avoid letting the word out about a huge position change. There are a whole slew of things a client can do with an order.

For argument's sake, let's assume that in some mysterious way the trader actually has information about what the client is doing. Now the trader knows for sure that PUNK has 3 million shares to dump. Does this knowledge help the trader see what happens next? No, because the trader cannot know how many shares buyers are willing to buy. If they want 10 million shares, the stock will most likely go up after PUNK is done. If they want 500,000 shares, the stock price will most likely drop when the buyers are done.

Let's make the next step in our unrealistic assumptions and pretend that our trader *knows* that buyers want 5 million shares. This still won't help the trader because the market is not static; it's changing all the time. When PUNK is done, how can we know that other market makers won't move to the same price with their liquidity, because they just got a call from their client? Or, how can we know that buyers won't change their mind after they bought 2 million shares and decide to wait out a bit to get shares at lower prices or maybe limit their exposure for now?

MAKING THE ODDS EVEN

Now let's pretend that we are conspiracy-theory idiots and that we really think everything in the market can be known or figured out. We *know* everything I've already discussed. It still won't help! As the stock prices move, the balance of power changes, and new forces become interested in taking or liquidating positions. I know that people in their right minds would never suggest that anyone could ever possibly *know* all the current intentions of all market participants, and I also know how the intentions will change as prices change.

As you can see, the very nature of the market is uncertainty. There is no such thing as "know." The market works in probabilities, not certainties. This is what makes trading so challenging, and it is what makes trading different from many other careers. Engineers calculate and apply learned methods and know how a construction is going to act under certain circumstances. They don't have to deal with wondering whether a bridge will hold if a certain amount of pressure is applied. They had better know it will hold. Our entire system of education is built on this approach. We gather information, analyze it, make conclusions based on facts, make a decision based on knowledge, and finally act on this decision, getting the result we determined in advance.

What happens to people who try to trade using this kind of approach? Naturally, they attempt to gather as much information about the markets as possible. Then the information is analyzed. The traders now feel armed. They act on this information according to the analysis. Then they observe that despite their preparation, results are random. Sometimes the market acts as they thought it would, and sometimes it doesn't. Naturally, traders next decide that their information is not enough or that their method of analysis is not perfect. They delve further, applying new systems and new indicators, thereby making their analysis more and more complicated. All this activity convinces the traders that they are on the verge of finally figuring it all out.

We all, I am fairly sure, went through this vicious cycle in which each new piece of information seemed to be the missing piece of the puzzle. If a trader takes this journey, frustration is unavoidable. What happens here is that traders are trying to apply a method that has nothing to do with the way the market works. This methodology of collecting, analyzing, and

concluding works in the environment of certainties, and the market is not
such an environment.

Our next question naturally is, "How am I supposed to trade with
confidence if I can't know anything about what happens next?"

MAKING THE PROBABILITIES WORK FOR YOU

We are supposed to go with the odds of probabilities. Every time we put
on a trade, we accept that this trade and any other can be a loser no matter how good it looks. That's how we get rid of frustration caused by the
fact that our brilliant analysis took us nowhere. If the loss is assumed and
accepted in advance, it comes as no surprise. It's just one of the scenarios
we can foresee. This is the key. Instead of thinking that the market is definitely going to do this or that, think in terms of *if* the market does this,
then I will do that. You need several scenarios in if-then terms. Now you
are protected from frustration because you never tried to predict anything.
No prediction—no surprise—no frustration.

It's unusual for human beings to think like this, which is exactly why
few traders succeed. The minority learns to think like this. The majority
either never does or never even realizes that a different way of thinking is
necessary. The majority seeks certainty to no avail, trying to find it in
mythical inside knowledge or in trading systems. When I make a successful trade, does it mean that I knew it going to happen? No. I did not
guess, either. I saw familiar price and volume action with a recognizable
setup. I knew all the possible outcomes of this setup. If the stock moved
through $20, then it was most likely to go higher. If $20 was never broken, then the trigger for the entry was never given, so I would do nothing.
If it moved through $20 but then lost to $19.75 on pullback, then it's
weaker than I thought, and this would be a stop loss. I have a set of scenarios based on the range, on the trend, and on the support and resistance
levels. As soon as the stock shows a break out of the range, violating the
resistance in the direction of the overall trend, a buy is triggered.

Do I know what the stock is going to do after that? Of course not.
No one does. I react to a scenario I have prepared in advance and that is
triggered by market action. The market gives me a signal, and I go with
it, letting the market do its thing and reacting on what it does. For me this
is the *only* way to approach trading. Don't ask why and don't try to predict, meaning don't try to figure out why this or that movement occurs. It
doesn't matter. You need to spot the movement, to categorize it, and to
exploit it if it fits into a set of familiar scenarios. That's all there is to trading, aside from mental preparation. If you feel the urge to know why

something happens, then you should understand that you want to be an analyst, not a trader. By the way, many brilliant analysts make very poor traders.

TAKING STOCK OF IT ALL

To sum up, the market is merely a by-product of the actions and intentions of all its participants. As prices move and events happen, those intentions change all the time. Thus, it is impossible by definition to *know* what the market will do next. Trading is not about knowing, figuring things out, and so forth. Trading is about acting in familiar situations on familiar signals.

Learning to trade requires two things. The first is that set of familiar situations and signals, which is not too hard to learn or to teach. In this regard trading is not rocket science. The second is adopting the unusual mindset that allows us to act in an uncertain and highly liquid environment. This is obviously harder since trading is a somewhat esoteric field. It's not easy to learn the mindset, the mental state, the discipline. You can explain these things, but can you teach someone how to achieve them? In my opinion, yes. For example, samurai fighting techniques and martial arts are based on a specific mindset. And there are teachers and students. Such skills require a different kind of teaching, not the one we find in school. It's not enough to just tell the student what to do. The teachers must be able to demonstrate what must be done. At the very least they have to have once been successful at what they are teaching. Without the first-hand knowledge and experience, the teachers will have nothing to tell their students about the hardest to learn and most vital element—correct mindset.

People who teach trading must demonstrate the correct approach. And at the same time, this process of learning requires strong dedication and sincere desire from the student. I don't believe the people who say, "You can't teach trading; one either learns it or not." However, as with anything, you can show and explain, but you can't make anyone do the right things. We need to accept the fact that not everyone can be taught to do this. After all, we all have different psychological profiles, and trading requires such an unusual attitude toward risk and an unconventional state of mind. There must be a certain percentage of people who are just not cut out for it.

There is one more aspect to learning this profession. No matter how intensive your educational process may be, you still need a lot of personal experience. Many good trading habits come to a trader only through the process of actual trading. You hear many times that you need to hold your stops, and you do realize the importance of this. Yet knowing this doesn't mean that you are going to take the right action when you face a losing trade. Going through certain experiences is an irreplaceable part of a trading education. The beginning stages of trading are hard because they are almost inevitably sprinkled with losses. It's imperative to keep them as small as possible, because so many traders run out of capital before they get a real chance to learn. You have to grind it out, survive this period of the learning curve. And it could be really long, often a year or two, possibly longer, and very seldom less than a year. I don't mean to suggest that after you have gone through this stage, you know everything there is to know. The market will always offer new challenges, and you will always find something new to deal with. But this provides an opportunity for you to refine your skill.

CHAPTER 5

The Trader's Circle

Bridging the Gap between Art and Science

Most people refer to the journey a trader takes as a *learning curve*. Let me step away from the "curve" portion of this phrase and focus on trading as a progression into one's self. As we discuss earlier, trading isn't a logical $1 + 1 = 2$ or a mechanical "all you have to do is see this system and you win." Traders need to think in a different paradigm, one that includes mechanical information with mental strengthening.

Mechanical information is easy. Anyone can read a few books, observe a few trading sites, and learn a trading system. Every professional trader knows what a cup-and-handle formation is, what Bollinger Bands are, what Fibonacci lines are, and so on. Professionals may not use all these things (there are only so many indicators that one can use), but they have a general understanding of their purpose and their relevancy. Furthermore, professionals do not negate mechanical ideas. Rather they accept them as complementary and assume that they are based on reality, and not illusions created by passing fads and corrections, where in a few months, the mechanics no longer work. I have seen numerous examples of where a bull market strategy no longer works in 2000–2002 and might very well not work for the next couple of years.

Mental strengthening is not easy. It's especially difficult for those who think that trading is purely mechanical and nonartistic. Traders such as these continue to try to prove that if you find the right system, you will be successful. These traders often contradict themselves as they talk of emotional control, egoless trading, trading what you see, and crowd psychology. However, if everything were purely mechanical, then there would be no need to discuss any of these issues. Furthermore, if everything were purely mechanical, then everyone using the system would perceive the market in the same way. If there are 1000 traders using a system, why can't all of them actually make money?

Clearly, trading does have artistic aspects. Well-known physicist Yakov Zeldovich said it best, "Science has one answer where art has many." To illustrate, imagine a stone, a simple stone. When an engineer or a math professor or a carpenter look at it, what is it they see? Just a shapeless stone, right? But when a sculptor looks at it, he or she sees a beautiful masterpiece. Let's have two sculptors look at the same stone. Will they see the same thing? Of course not. Each will have his or her own idea of what shape the stone will take. Similarly, two traders don't see the same trade in the same market action. It is how artists apply themselves that defines what comes out of a shapeless stone. And it's how traders apply their personality that defines what kind of trades they make. We can't shape the market in the same way a sculptor shapes the stone, but in both cases we have something that we need to apply our vision to and extract what we want from it. The subject of our artistic work is our trade—this is what we shape in a way that is governed by our skill, our perception, and our vision. Later we provide examples of how traders see different ways to play the same setup. All those ways can be valid, as are valid different works of art seen by the sculptors in the same original shapeless stone.

There is a fine line between flexibility and the tendency to change your approach as soon as your system produces a loss. After all, we are wired in a way that makes it hard to repeat doing the same thing when we know it doesn't work. But that is exactly what a good system assumes us to do. You have to endure a string of losses sometimes in order to allow probabilities to work in your favor, because you can't know which trade is going to end your losing streak. At the same time, when you see the market changing its tune in a way that requires significant adjustment, you need to make the adjustment, or you are destined to stay with a losing strategy indefinitely. This is one more side to trading where art plays a big role.

My partner and I both use tape-reading principles to define the majority of our exit and entry plans. We both are very close to market reality and have emotional control in our trading. We complement each other. Yet, we can look at the same stock and have two totally different ideas on where that stock is moving. This proves that mechanical setups by themselves offer only the raw material for something deeper and more important.

STRENGTHEN THE MIND AS WELL AS THE SYSTEM

Traders must condition their mental processes to enable them to create synergy between mechanical strategies and the mental capacity to follow through on the signals of exit and entry.

If we think of trading as a circle, then the beginning stage is one spot on the circle. The circle represents something tangible because traders can move around on the circle to different phases of trading regardless of whether they are professionals or beginners. Some new traders have characteristics that are more developed than those of professional traders. Conversely, some characteristics in professionals seem more related to beginners. This is further evidence that mechanical trading leaves out much of what is important. Ego, emotion, anger, and revenge can be found in a trader of any level if the trader allows it.

The goal of newer traders should be to get as close to reality as they can, but not too close lest they feel that they have everything all worked out. When they feel they have it all figured out, traits of new traders come back to haunt them and create drawdown periods. The goal of the trader is to develop an unemotional, egoless, and clear perception of stock market reality. Getting from the first part of the circle to the last part and staying there is an extremely difficult process, which is the reason why traders' success ratios are low. As I've noted before, only the minority is successful.

For example, in sports, we have little league baseball in which everyone can participate. High school teams have tryouts, and only the better players are selected. College takes the cream of that crop, and eventually professional sports takes the best of the best. The minority succeeds. There are numerous examples of how the minority succeeds. One of the things that contributes to the success of members of the minority is that they don't think like the majority.

This is how, in tape-reading principles and trading, what you see, not what you think, allows you to become the minority. There are four stages—newer trader, developing trader, striving trader, and reality trader—that take you from majority thought to minority success. These were the stages I went through and that I see others go through all the time.

As a newer trader, I traded on what I thought. My opinion ruled my world. I had no real understanding of how tape principles (accumulation/distribution) governed the market's behavior. I did not seek out any type of system that provides structure to the chaos of price movement. I used phrases like, "Day traders ran that stock past our stop." "When you think a stock is too high, then it's time to short." "Market makers are a conspiracy group existing to take a stand against my position." "If you want to make money, just do the opposite of what I do." (This last one is my favorite since it proves minority versus majority thinking in an indirect manner.)

I usually had mixed results, much about which you have already read. There was a string of losses or wins, but I did not make a profit consistently over time. The market was a constant struggle. Jealousy, anger, frustration, and fear of failure were what I experienced as this type of trader. Even more interesting is the fact that all these emotions were creating distortions in my perception of the market without my being aware of it. I had no idea that mental change was necessary in order to get me closer to the last phase of the trading circle.

FINDING OUT MORE ABOUT MYSELF

When I moved from a newer trader to a developing trader, I began to realize that there are ways to bring structure to chaos through systems and principles. I started to relax a bit more. Feelings of frustration and anger began to give way to little bits of hope and "trading eurekas" in my head. I started seeing market realities. My initial thoughts about how the market works began to break down as the walls of illusion crumbled. I started to question things I had often heard. For instance, market makers weren't really a conspiracy. Now trading the market became less of a struggle. I began to see how market discounting worked. And I understood why Aristotle couldn't have succeeded in the market (everything is a fuzzy probability, not a logical certainty).

At that time, I also started playing a little psychological game with myself. I would either get down on myself or be happy with myself as each trade closed. I was having trouble disassociating my trading from my self-worth. So I came up with the trick I mentioned. When I came to the computer to trade every day, I viewed myself as someone other than me at the computer trading. I would act as this other person's mentor, watching what he was doing, reviewing his trading, and helping him to be a better trader. When he was trading well, I was just his admirer. I separated myself from this trader. Therefore, any trade he made, he made. It had nothing to do with me. I was there only to watch what he was doing. Eventually, I became that detached observer, and that detachment is essential to a trader's state of mind. Since then, emotion and ego have ceased to be part of my trading plan.

However, my trading results didn't really get me to the point where I could make a living. I was still in a fear of failure, since I wasn't sure I could support my family as well as meet all of Canada's requirements for citizenship. It was a heavy burden to know that at any moment I might have to leave the country. While most people could simply quit trading and go find a job, any job, I didn't have this luxury. Therefore, when traders do finally quit and go out whining that they have to go find a job, I have sympathy for them, of course, but I can't help thinking, "Try quitting your job *and* leaving your country!"

GETTING THROUGH THE STAGES

When I finally got to the stage of striving trader, I had told myself that I had to make this work. I had no alternative. I was always used to having backup plans, and, for the first time in my life, I didn't feel as if I really had one. I had to make trading work. I started to work on my understanding of true market reality. I was no longer a slave to common thought. I was beginning to understand and work on thinking the way the minority thinks. I now understood how to use common thought for my benefit, that is, to profit off the majority and to position myself on the side of smart money.

For example, market makers were no longer a group of conspiracy players. They exist to provide liquidity to stocks and often fight each other more than they try to hurt us. We are last on their list for trading intentions. This is just one example of my adjustment in thought. I wasn't at war with the market makers. I was happy they were there to sell me shares and buy my shares when I felt it necessary for them to do so. I started to develop a stable portfolio (a plateau, if you will), which eventually took a slow uptrend. I used tape reading and other market principles such as fundamental analysis or technical analysis effectively and in a complementary way. Books, friends' ideas, research of ideas, and so on were all becoming a part of my arsenal. I was using them to get closer to the true reality of the market.

THE FINAL STAGE

When I finally got to the stage I call a reality trader, I found myself in the ultimate state of trading, which allowed me to take my $10,000 to over $200,000 in just 20 months. I accomplished this with consistency—no huge wins or major drawdowns. My unemotional and egoless self allowed me a true and clear perception of market events and created the edge needed to trade profitably.

I believe that the first two stages of the circle were the hardest. I can see this same struggle in other traders. The market is a struggle, stock action is unclear, opinions are formed, executions are impossible, and so on. If there was a problem, this was the stage in which we'd find it. I asked myself why all these traders who were posting gains were entering here and there, exiting here and there. I had no understanding of what they were doing. I remember almost being angry with financial TV personalities because all they had to do was report the news. And they got paid handsomely for it, while I was having to trade to make a living. Yet I chose to trade for a living. It was just another example of how far from reality many new traders are.

Now that I'm at the last stage, a reality trader, I realize that the hardest phase is actually the third phase, that of a striving trader. It is easy to be new traders. They allow ego and common thought to dictate their trading. They feel that it is okay to be far from market reality.

As a new trader, I was being fed information for the benefit of others, not my own. I was told that a certain stock was a strong buy; it was targeted to go another 50 points higher. I was told to hold on; it would always come back. "Don't stop out. A loss is a loss only if you take it." Look at the price of New World Restaurant Group (Nasdaq: NWCI) in Figure 5.1.

My friend bought this stock because he was told it was going to be the next Starbucks, and he believed it. He jokes to me that he still owns it as a memento of his stupidity.

I never understood how traders could lose money and not seem to be bothered by it because they were in good company. It appeared that losing money was fine as they belonged to the club. The traders' job is to read stock action correctly so that financial rewards allow them to be the persons they want to be, not because they want to feel comfortable in financial destruction. Yet, I see this all the time as newer traders struggle to get through the learning phase.

If you are trading like a newer trader and have this mindset, you might as well buy and sell stock arbitrarily. If you lose, it's the market's fault. If you win, then your confidence creates a false sense of security. Worse, you allow random successes to reinforce habits that aren't conducive to long-term success. Averaging down, justifications, and turning intraday trading strategies into long-term investing strategies are just another way to rationalize a losing position: "Oh well, it

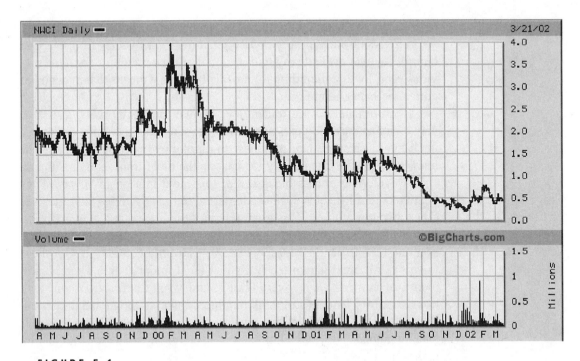

FIGURE 5.1

New World Restaurant Group (NWCI) stock. (*Used with permission of CBS MarketWatch.*)

goes into my retirement account." I want my retirement account to be filled with more winners rather than a bunch of losers. I've never been a big fan of mixing trading strategies from intraday to long-term investments.

Consistency isn't found in these stages because traders are not seeing reality. There is no accountability and little pressure. They trade what they think. They focus on money. It was not until I got to be a striving trader that I realized that price and volume are what matter. Traders should read price action, not guess or predict market value. Money comes as a reward for a trade well read. Our risk is reading it wrong. We still take accountability for that trade.

COMPLETING THE CIRCLE

Traders in the newer trader phase need to build on a foundation of incorrect assumptions and false thought processes. Then later, when they see the reality, they are able to tell the difference. It is the same idea as competing against the best to make you better. Once you improve, you can see your earlier faults and therefore be less inclined to repeat your mistakes. As I progress from year to year I laugh at my inadequacies from the year before. If I ever evaluate my trading and don't see problems from the previous year, I will quit trading for a while because it means that my ego has gotten the better of me.

Unfortunately, I see traders I've known for years trading the same way today as they did years ago. Their accounts bleed, but they continue unchanged. They let their blindness to market reality feed their ego. The market eventually finds a way to separate the mule from its nourishment.

Developing traders break out of this mold in a positive way. They begin to see some tools such as charts or "trading systems" that they see others using profitably. This gives them a little hope that they can do this as well. They see the trade setups, the postings of traders, the participation, the records, and so forth. This creates a little confidence. But these factors don't break down the walls that most traders have. There is still plenty of emotion, ego, overthinking, and wrong perceptions of stock market reality. Traders still think that mechanical trading is all they need. They don't understand yet that when traders are successful, the reason is usually mental. They have limited ideas about risk evaluation and money management.

During this phase, traders usually come to the point that they either decide to give up or take the next step. If they make it past the newer stage of trading, this next stage is the one where the market does its second cut from the team. Traders understand that while some structure begins to come into trading, there is still plenty that is not working right.

My friend who bought NWCI, interestingly enough, made the transition from a developing trader to a striving trader without consciously doing so. I told him to read the trading classic, *Reminiscences of a Stock Operator,* which completely changed his perceptions of the market

He told me that as he was reading this book while flying back from California. His reading led him to understand that he had more to learn. I feel that in every successful trader's life, there is an event or a progression of key events that turns one's mind around from common thinking to minority or "out of the box" thinking. It wasn't until he read the book that he really began to make the transition into the next part of the trading circle.

He was a trader for one of the trading services I was using as a means of finding trading ideas. He was a young man, in his mid-twenties, sharp, but with a bit of an ego that always kept him at arm's length from me. However, he drew my attention by an interesting contradiction between his apparent abilities on one hand and his misguided approach to the market on the other. He was obviously very bright and capable of learning quickly. I saw him trading for this or that reason, winning and losing. When he lost, he would change his trading plans again and again with each new breakthrough of understanding. He was able to see what worked and didn't work for him. Although he learned trading basics very quickly, his coworkers and work environment were pushing him in the wrong direction.

He used the formal approach of attempting to apply simple logic to market movements—the same old "good news, bad news, too low then time to buy, too high then time to short." It was interesting to observe him outgrow this approach. At one point, to my amusement, he tried applying a system called "momentum" trading. I could never understand how trading tops and bottoms, in effect, reversals, could be construed as momentum trading. He had a breakthrough to reality when he figured out for himself that momentum should refer to trading in the direction of the trend. This realization allowed him to see a whole new world of opportunities.

I could see his thoughts and trades begin to change ever so slightly, moving away from the strategy that he was struggling to find peace with. The service he worked for wouldn't allow methodology that contradicted its foundation to be traded, much less taught. He could see he was in a dead end. He didn't want to limit his trading progress, and I could see he was conflicted when he discussed trades with others in class or after class. This is when I noticed a change. His class discussions migrated to realism. He talked about basic mindset issues that he was using as he approached the day. It was these subtle changes that drew my interest. I was not in a position to try to reorient him since he was working for a company that demanded strict adherence to guidelines.

At one point, he decided that his traditional brokerage firm wasn't appropriate for day trading. He switched to a direct-access brokerage, placing some of his trading funds with an outfit that I was using at the time to test out its reliability and usefulness.

DISCOVERING THE SATISFACTION OF TEACHING

It was at this point in his trading that our personal discussion began to expand. At first, he asked me about the functionality of the software and its features. After he became a bit more familiar with the software, he moved his attention to the execution functionality. I was a recognized expert in the field of order routing. He knew this and came to me for some advice on one function or another, such as routing rules like the ISLD crossing/locking quotes problem that seems to plague many traders and the SOES 5-minute rule. There were a ton of them, and our conversation was mainly about getting him up to speed on them. Furthermore, the functions were always changing. And because the service leader wasn't day trading, he didn't keep up with the changing execution environment enough to help. Therefore, almost by default, I was the logical choice for help on execution technique.

Our brief discussions here and there did not lead anywhere for a while because superficial exchanges were not enough to get a dialogue going. Most of his questions about functionality required a minimal response, and he did not yet want information about my specific trading style. Then, as fate would have it, he was about to hit a major blowup, as most traders do, that would push him in the direction in which he needed to go. He was playing his usual top/bottom, false momentum strategy, and, this time, it almost killed him.

He had bought a stock, one of the major players, and saw it move in his general direction for a bit off the low of what he considered to be a support area. At this point, he began to see the profit dwindle and eventually turn it into a small loss. Then the stock got away from him, the market began to tank, and he was looking at a margin call. This error didn't have so much to do with his trading methodology as it did with his trading mindset. However, if his stock was experiencing a true momentum, instead of going long off that low, then the base made near that low, when failed, would have given him a beautiful short setup that could have led to a profit. So his general approach to the market, being against trends, in his own words to me later, caused this snafu.

However, it was this snafu that led to a much better dialogue between us. His problem, at this point, was how to regain his confidence, not his money. This is where we really began to make the connection between his appetite for knowledge and my desire to offer all that I had learned from my own experiences.

He knew that he had to look for alternative strategies in order to avoid going through the same problem that he had just faced. At this point, he asked me how I kept my risk minimal and my consistency high enough to enable me to make a living doing what I was doing. This was during a period in which I was averaging 12–25 trades a day, with no losing weeks or months. My desire to explain was equal to his desire to learn.

We began to talk about trading with the trend, about effective routing avenues, and eventually about more interesting issues such as trading intuition. I could see that his interest in the "voodoo" of the market piqued his ambition to learn more. As I mentioned before, I suggested that he read a couple of books such as *Reminiscences of a Stock Operator* by Lefèvre and *The Intuitive Trader* by Koppel. He read them and couldn't believe how they brought him to the world of reality. This was the time when we started discussing my method of tape reading. It didn't take him long to see that my approach was connected to market reality, and it allowed him to break the barrier he had encountered in his trading. He studied my method with real enthusiasm, and his hard work brought results quickly. His personal trading improved greatly in just a few months. He felt much more confident now. He was able to read the reality now.

REVELING IN THE TRIUMPH OF ANOTHER TRADER

One of my proudest moments came in May 2000. The market was reeling from the March 2000 highs and was taking a huge hit. I awoke to find an e-mail from my friend. He started by expressing his appreciation for the time I spent with him. And he told me that his progression was due in large part to our numerous conversations. He told me that he and his wife had discussed all the people that had helped him throughout his life. During their conversation, he noted to his wife that he felt he owed me something for my time and my guidance.

He had put a check in the mail to me for 10 percent of his trading profits from the month of April as a sign of his appreciation. Mind you, this was a month that had wiped many out. Yet, because of the time we spent online, he had experienced one of his best months ever.

In the beginning of my friend's striving trader stage, Jesse Livermore, in a way, became his mentor through *Reminiscences of a Stock Operator,* pretty much as Livermore was for me earlier. Livermore's ideas, his understanding, didn't really teach a system. Rather, it taught reality and how to think like a real trader. This was Livermore's effort to remove all he thought he knew that came from ego, false perceptions, and the like. My friend began to read a lot about trading. He was in constant talks with those he trusted and was trading with everything he could gather. He took in all the information he could from those who were willing to give it to him. It's because of this aggressiveness that he progressed through this striving trader stage very quickly. My friend didn't realize just how quickly until I showed him these stages. There are people who have minds you can unlock and inspire. My friend was one of those people. You could see his enjoyment in his progression, and I'm sure he could see the same in me as I watched him grow.

REDISCOVERING THE CIRCLE

Let's review the stages in the circle. New and developing traders find it easy to trade with no effort, with random wins and losses. Striving traders read all they can, ask all they can, develop all they can with their system, and so on. They spend a lot of time on developing the winning and correct trading attitude. I'm not talking about work as in endless research of stock charts and trading journals, spending an inordinate amount of time on trade reviews, tracking, and so forth.

I'm talking about seeing reality and becoming a realistic trader. I'm talking about working on getting rid of ego, emotion, and thoughts based on illusion or an incorrect understanding of tape-reading principles. All the research you do by reading books, reviewing charts, and so on needs to be taken to deeper levels within you, thereby enabling you to understand why the market works the way it does. Self-control has to be learned for profit and for loss.

There is an amazing amount of progress needed in this stage, and it's up to the traders as to how fast they get through it. As we move through the stages of the newer trader to the reality trader, we can see why the third stage is really the hardest, because it takes the most effort.

As noted earlier, newer traders trade without much effort, buy and sell with basically no fear. Reality traders also trade without much effort, buy and sell with basically no fear. But the difference is that reality traders understand that trading is more than just "buy and sell." They understand that there are principles of tape reading that are complementary to technical analysis and fundamental analysis, how these principles lead us to the footprints of the minority, and how they show us the crowd psychology of the majority. They understand how to trade unemotionally, to trade what they see, not what they think. They understand that everyone has a different perception of the market and that it's this difference, when there is a shift in the aggregate of supply and demand, that dictates stock movement. They understand why the demands of trading require a greater understanding of our mental capacity. They understand that the market works randomly, that the best setup can fail, and that the worst can produce profit. They understand that a system is based on probabilities, which in turn inherits losses—nothing is right 100 percent of the time.

Reality traders understand that risk evaluations and money management enable them to trade the next trade. When their probability system produces a loss, they keep the loss small. They know not to average down, not to justify a loss, not to chase the market, not to. . . Basically, they understand what not to do, and they don't do it. Let me use once again an art analogy. There is a well-known saying by a famous sculptor that explains how he created his masterpieces. He said that he was just cutting off all that wasn't needed and that what remained was the beautiful sculpture. In exactly the same way, traders get rid of everything that gets in the way, of everything that is not needed in terms of their system. What remains is a state-of-the-art trading system, and each successful trade becomes a masterpiece.

On a deeper level, a reality trader knows his rules, and he knows when to break his rules. He knows that he doesn't answer to anyone. He doesn't have to prove anything to anyone. Trading is his. Trading is his passion, his life, and his reason for getting up in the morning. The bell rings for him. The market exists to provide him with funds to feed his family, go to soccer games, play golf, take trips, and provide freedom. He trades against the best traders in the world and beats them. No one can rattle his cage, and no one can tell him about his business. He does everything he does, in trading and in life, based on the situations before him. And no one can knock him off his pedestal. He is the king of his own castle, and it's a castle built on reality. This is the environment in which I exist.

One more thing about the trading circle. This circle should never be closed. There is a point in many traders' development when we feel we have it all figured out and that we can close the circle. If we do this, then we are right back at the new trader stage. This often leads to drawdown periods as our ego becomes more pronounced and our reality becomes distorted again. We begin to integrate thought processes with the new trader, and this leads to a string of losses or "dumb trades." This happens to me every so often as I am trading. For example, during a range market, I was trying to trade trend setups. It cost me thousands of dollars. I was fighting reality in this case and allowing something within me to want a trend rather than to play the range. This is proof that mechanical trading isn't the key. You have to be able to clearly identify what kind of day you are in, and you can do so only with clear mental strength based on true market reality.

The longer we trade, the more will happen to us. If we ever close the circle, we go right back to ego, misperceptions, and mistakes that new traders make. It is impossible to close this circle. For if we close it, ego, emotion, and trading what we think happens again.

The market is our teacher. It teaches us new lessons each day. It teaches me that I don't have things all figured out. It teaches me that I need to stay a reality trader if I'm to make it, to keep my account in a steady uptrend. It teaches me that I am an eternal student and that, if I ever close the circle, I can expect the market to separate me from my money faster than I can say "sucker."

CHAPTER 6

A Trader's Edge

I'm often asked about my risk tolerance. This became especially important during the bear market of 2000–2002. It's not an accident that trading has a fairly low rate of success, and market conditions often don't help at all. The ability to adjust to new markets is the strength in any trader. In the bear market that began in 2000, it became necessary to find a way to survive in this profession.

First, traders have to form realistic expectations about their gains. The problem is that trading offers unlimited opportunities. And when you look at market movements after the fact, it seems easy to make any amount of money. When newcomers expect to make a couple of thousand dollars a day, they take enormous risks in order to achieve that goal.

Established traders know that their primary purpose is to preserve their trading capital. In order to do so, they have to limit risk. However, limiting risk also limits profit potential. One day I was watching a few illiquid issues with a few of my friends. What I mean by illiquid is that there really aren't many participants in this stock. There were about four market makers, and a couple of ECNs (Electronic Communications Networks) would show up from time to time. The spread was wide, and the depth of the stock was very thin. One of these issues caught my attention because it moved from just under $11 to over $15 in a matter of minutes. It was Qiao Xing Universal Telephone (Nasdaq: XING) (see Figure 6.1). I watched this stock and its behavior and knew it wasn't to be touched by professionals because of slippage concerns. If I was wrong with my entry, risk was way outside of my parameters at the time.

One really anxious trader who can never stay on the sidelines asked me why I wasn't trading it. He was long 2000 shares and was happy to see that

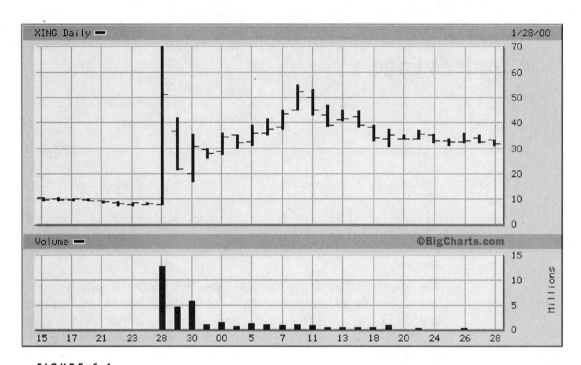

FIGURE 6.1

Example of short-term volatility. (*Used with permission of CBS MarketWatch.*)

the stock had climbed from his entry at near $12 to just over $14. He said to me, "Why didn't you take position on it? You were in front of the computer the entire day. You could see it." While he was saying this to me, the stock went from $14 back down to just under $11 again. But he refused to sell it. He ended up taking a considerable loss for the size of his portfolio. He made two mistakes. The first was not seeing the risk of this stock. The second was not' taking the profit on such an extremely risky stock while he had it.

All stocks move. But you don't have to trade them all, especially ones that trade in dollars a minute. It is hard to imagine anything more risky than this monster with a huge spread and almost no volume. Of course there was opportunity to profit, but this is what amateurs go after. As a trader, I know to manage my risk first, and there was no way to do it on that stock at that time.

PROS ASSESS RISK; AMATEURS ASSESS POTENTIAL

For professionals, risk evaluation always comes first. If you are uncomfortable with the risk on any particular stock or trade, just stay away from it. The skill of staying away is one of the most important one could learn. Unfortunately, for many traders, this never sunk in. The market might not present any opportunities on a particular day. In such a situation, any trade would be an attempt to squeeze blood from a stone. Furthermore, if the market presents movements that are not readable by the system we use, any trade would be just gambling.

The market might present readable opportunities without favorable reward/risk ratios, and any trade would be too great a risk from the perspective of risk management. In all cases such as these, the trader has to stay away. An urge to trade just for trading's sake can lead to big losses in the worst case or to slow bleeding with many stops in the best case. During 1998–2002 we went through all the markets one can imagine. A running market with incredibly strong uptrends, crashes, dull phases, slow sliding, and so on. And I went through each one unscathed, while many of my colleagues were forced to stop trading altogether.

The first market stage (a huge run-up) brought many people into the market who thought it was easy. Their goal was to buy anything in sight and hold for double, triple, or even more profits. I don't envy those who started their learning at that time. It was easy to believe that buying and holding are really all there is to it. Those were the salad days, to be sure, but not for everyone. I saw plenty of people trying to short the market all the way up. One self-proclaimed great trader who admitted to not trading any longer, kept calling the QQQ short, losing hundreds of points for the traders who followed him. We only heard of him calling a great market bottom. This is a sucker's game. This is plenty of evidence that following someone blindly will not make you a great trader.

Traders were losing on the long side as well, because no stock goes in just one direction. Upward movement was interrupted by pullbacks. When traders tried to hold through those pullbacks, they sometimes got burned badly. It happened in situations when volatility was too big for them to handle and the risk taken was too big. This leads us to the next important concept that needs to be understood for market survival.

YOU DON'T HAVE TO BE IN THE MIDDLE OF EVERY BATTLE

It's not necessary for traders to trade everything. In fact, stocks that grab the most attention are often the most dangerous. I remember in 2000 when JDS Uniphase got dumped badly. It was the most dangerous stock in the market that day, and many people lost big by trying to go with the hot action. The same happened with Emulex in 2001 when a false press release sent it down 60–80 points. Many feel that they have to take part in the action that the entire market is focused on. They go home, talk to friends, and are asked, "Hey, there were such huge swings on ABCD today! Did you take advantage of them?" Answering "no" would make one feel like a coward. But remember, as a trader, I don't have to prove anything to anyone.

Many people who look at the action after they get home from work ask, "OK, we can't get access to a computer. But you can. You see it all happening. How come you don't play?" Do not be tempted to look like part of some elite class of traders. The hottest market action is where the biggest risk is. Don't trade for action; trade for profit. But keep in mind that profit always goes with the possibility of loss. Evaluate the loss you might take if things turn nasty and decide whether you can afford the risk and whether you want this risk and/or reward.

Traders spend much more time in the ambush than they do in the battle. They limit their risk by limiting their market exposure. The biggest problem for traders is risking being thrown out of the game. I know a trader who lost his entire trading capital on a *single* trade. Whatever we do and however strongly we feel about a trade, we must *never* risk our entire capital on one trade. This doesn't mean that we should ignore any opportunity in which the risk is too big, even if the reward/risk ratio is great. We do have the ability to decrease the risk by decreasing our share size.

Imagine a stock with a great upside of $20. We see that it moves in such a way that if our entry is wrong, it would cost a $2 stop. Many cannot afford a loss of $2000. However, the 10/1 ratio is really tempting. We can still go for it if we take shares that put us in a position of affordable risk. By decreasing our share size, we limit our profit potential. That's the price of risk control. Limiting risk and capital preservation go first. I never feel that I have to trade. I don't feel bad if the market action happens without me, and I don't go for profits if the risk is greater than I can afford. By learning this kind of restraint, we preserve our capital.

During the late 1990s, it was astonishing to see how many traders mistakenly thought they were experts in the medical field, in reading geological mining maps, or in some other profession that requires more study than a simple company 10-Q quarterly report. Speculators are not about determining the future value of a company's net worth. They are detached observers of the psychology of the market. Too often we see opinions based on the illusions of people who pretend to be something they are not. As I mentioned before, early stage speculators are born of the need for some certainty. They want reliable patterns, proven and provided on a basis from which they can trade. Eventually they realize that simply following systems and patterns does not provide the desired results. Sadly, more often than not, this leads to frustration rather than to a continued quest for reality.

THE DICHOTOMY OF THE GUILTY

The belief that people fear what they are guilty of holds true for the market. An early speculator most likely is not a great trader and so believes that no one is. This early stage is part of the learning process. Furthermore, these early speculators form opinions about subjects they do not understand. Their opinions may certainly sound reasonable, but the reality is that they may well be off base. For example, I have no idea about physics, but I'm sure I could write a paper on gravity just from simple observation. I might even get a B grade on the paper, but would you trust me with the design of a plane?

Forming opinions is the greatest threat to early speculators. The market has curtains. Unless we pull back that curtain, we will never see the reality. For example, let's assume a trader is screaming about a company's new product. This is not happening because he is excited that the product will be great for humanity. He is excited because he wants to attract interest so that he can sell his shares at a better price. The trader wants to lead me down the path of excitement so that I would buy into the stock for his benefit, not mine.

Taking this in the broader sense, the market wants to show me one thing and hammer me with the opposite. The early speculators fall prey to these instances. They are not properly trading a system because they have no sense of reality and no sense of how their own personality traits are affecting their trading. Their trading is akin to gambling. Henry Emery, a late-nineteenth-century American economist, suggested that, in gambling, one must win and one must lose. In speculation however, this is not so. A gambler *creates* risks in the marketplace with wrong assumptions and by following opinions. A speculator *assumes* risks and responds accordingly. Unless they progress from the early stage of accepting ideas at face value, early speculators will cease to exist.

Bernard Baruch, a noted economic adviser to American presidents for more than 40 years, said about speculation, "It is a dangerously addictive habit which involves an appeal for fortune, and is often accompanied by delusional behavior, and is dependent for success on the control of emotions."

As early speculators begin to pull back the curtains of obviousness and take a deeper look at the market, they begin to see the world of market psychology. They realize that traders are not experts in every field, and, even if they were, it has no bearing on the stock price. They realize that a stock moves when supply outstrips demand and vice versa. Therefore, they read the psychology behind the move and not necessarily the reason for the move. To these people, the stock market is no longer a carnival of fools, with playful intentions and obvious deceptions. At least they are no longer a part of this crowd even if it still does exist.

They understand that what were once thought of as simple manipulations and cons are in fact just normal parts of the game. Experienced traders do their job, while the early speculators fall for traps. What many fail to realize is that what seems really obvious usually is a trap. If you see a road with no obstacles, it most likely doesn't lead to anywhere. It works for reading stock movement. It works for many of the general principles that market moves are based on. There are many common phrases on Wall Street, and all the pundits have heard them. But there are different views on things that seem to be absolutely nonarguable. It's often the case that one's edge is found exactly in the niches where few go. Let's go over some of those common phrases and see how true they are.

"Do Not Overtrade"

A trading leader tried to argue with me about my many trades per day, maintaining that I was doing something wrong. He argued that we only have to find that one great trade per day to make us profitable. I must have left my crystal ball back in Russia, because I can't seem to distinguish how, in a market that is based on probabilities, one will always know which trade will be the best one every time.

Many people say that we should pick the best of the best trades and not jump on every one of them, trying to go for as few trades as you can that suggest the highest potential. This is not true for all traders or for all styles. I practice my system, which puts a high probability on my side, and I would be better off trading as much as I can. A trader should enter any opportunity that his or her system has generated. After all, that's exactly what casinos do. They do as many "trades" as possible because the probabilities are in their favor and the more bets that are made, the higher their profit. This leads us to conclude that the principle "do not overtrade" is style-dependent. If your approach is trading a low percentage of winners, small losses, and big runs, then, yes, don't overtrade. It will lower your overall profits.

But if your style is trading a high percentage of winners, relatively small profits, and even tighter stops (as is the case with scalping), then it sounds strange to not overtrade. Overtrading will work in your favor. Instead of assigning the right number of trades per day, I would rather define what overtrading really is. To me, overtrading is taking the trades that don't match your setups. If you get three setups a day, then the fourth trade is overtrading. If you get 30 valid setups a day, then 30 trades do not constitute overtrading.

"Do Not Trade Illiquid Stocks"

I mentioned earlier my decision to stay away from Qiao Xing Universal Telephone because of its lack of liquidity. This doesn't mean that all illiquid issues should not be traded. I have seen many great traders trade stocks with low liquidity. It's their edge. They have to know how those stocks move—the "jumpiness" of those issues they use to their advantage. One reason for this phenomenon is that on stocks with huge liquidity and a wide following, too many conflicting interests interact, which often makes the stocks hard to read. For instance, when I watch monsters that are traded by everyone, like Microsoft, Intel, and so on, I know that they almost never go straight up or down. They're always struggling.

In addition, trading houses know very well that there are plenty of traders who try to squeeze the juice out of these stocks, and they have the best of their best traders assigned to these monsters. I see plenty of online traders and institutional traders with their cloudy intentions in these stocks. You have the best traders in the world trying to fool everyone, including their neighbors (by neighbors, I mean the Goldman Sachs trader wants his or her intentions to be hidden from the Merrill Lynch trader). I rarely want to be in the middle of such a battle. Meanwhile, on stocks with lower liquidity where there are fewer players and fewer contradicting interests, I may find a much higher level of readability. It doesn't mean of course that the stock with 10,000 shares in volume is safe to trade. There should be a balance in everything. But it shows how "obvious" things become less obvious when we think to look below the surface.

"Buy Low, Sell High"

The next so-called road to success is "buy low, sell high." This idea alone is probably responsible for more trading failures than any other. It is a dangerous idea because the trend is extremely important in trading. If you know the trend, you are trading safely and with a high probability of success. If you buy low, you are not trading with the trend. In fact, if you try to pick the bottom on a falling stock, you are going against the trend. It doesn't mean you have to avoid buying low completely. But at the very least you have to know what you're doing and understand that until the trend has reversed, you are on dangerous ground buying the bottoms. I am sure you have seen plenty of cases in which traders have been hurt badly by attempting to pick the bottom (known as "catching a falling knife"). There are other ways to play that enable you to follow the trend. For example, "buy high, sell higher" and "sell low, buy back lower" is a style that matches trading to the trend. An uptrend is a series of higher highs and higher lows. As long as the trend is intact, you are safe buying every high, and you will be wrong only once at the very top. Even when you buy the pullback bottom on an uptrending stock, it's not really buying the low—it's just a particular detail of your timing, your microstrategy of entry.

"You Can't Go Broke Taking Profits"

The next adage I want to discuss, and negate, is, "You can't go broke taking profits." We've heard it a zillion times. Well, it's wrong! Of course you can go broke if you take losses that are bigger than profits. There is no trading without losses. They are a natural part of trading. If you allow your losses to be bigger than your profits, you certainly can go broke taking your profits. Considering that this adage is usually used to justify "selling too soon," I do consider it to be wrong.

"A Loss Is Not a Loss Until You Sell"

"A loss is not a loss until you sell." This saying is very dangerous. If traders keep their losing trades, they lose more than just money on one particular trade. They lose focus and the ability to pick other trades. In such situations, traders are nervous and often angry. The losing trade sucks all the energy out of them. Not all gaps are filled (one more wrong assumption). Any particular trade is not guaranteed to be the one that will come back sooner or later. For instance, my three hardest losses (I mean, really hard) would have taken me out of the game if I had held them. I owned ESOL at $15 and sold it around $5. Try to find it on a Nasdaq map today. I owned TTG at $20 and sold at $12. Where is TTG today? It went bankrupt. I was short KTEL at $22 and covered at around $29. It went to

$80. So much for the theory that one should hold a losing trade until the gap is filled.

"Short Sales Take Stocks Lower"

One more idea that can be heard frequently among traders is that shorting makes stocks go down; it's shorters that kill our excellent picks. This is not true. If a stock is really strong and has more demand than it has supply, it will overcome the selling pressure, and shorts will only add fuel to the run-up as traders try to cover. If a stock is not strong enough and shorts are right, traders will provide support for the stock on the way down while they buy to cover in order to realize their profits. In my strong opinion, shorting is an absolutely necessary part of the game because it provides liquidity, somewhat limits volatility, and provides a cushion as stocks reverse.

"Selling Attracts Buying, Buying Attracts Selling"

The last saying I want to discuss, and probably the toughest to negate, is that selling attracts buyers by creating "value" and that buying attracts sellers by creating the incentive to take profits. It seems *so* obvious that it has always bothered me, even in the early stages of my trading when I didn't really have arguments against it. Let's think of it this way. If "selling attracts buying, buying attracts selling" were the case, would we see anything but the same trading range on all stocks? A stock drops from $20 to $15, and happy buyers nail it. It goes back to $20, and sellers hit it. We see every day that stocks continue to go up or drop, making new lows. In other words, it's just one particular case of a more general law. There are several cases, and those are: (1) Buying attracts more buyers, (2) selling attracts more sellers (or, if you wish, scares more traders into selling), and (3) the case we started with.

The first two are called the *trend*. If the third case were the only one, we would never see any trends. The third case calls the range, and it works only for stocks that trade in a range. The problem is that failing to realize this leads to all those disasters in which traders try to short every top or buy every bottom. I can tell you that during the huge market run-up in the fall of 1999, there were plenty of killed traders who could not believe that the market still had the courage to go up. They were shorting and shorting. Some got burned holding their shorts, and some were covering and shorting again, mistakenly thinking that it was a normal trading process.

Traders try every next top to short or every next bottom to buy. In doing so, they try to identify the point of a trend reversal. There is only one of these reversal points. By doing this, traders try to find that one reversal point that is going against the prevailing trend. It just doesn't make sense. It's quite clear when you think of it in these terms. You are better off going with the trend at each interim point. You find yourself wrong once at the reversal point, and then you can reverse the direction of your trades to be in accordance with the new trend.

FINDING THE ELUSIVE EDGE

As you can see, many things that seem to be obvious in reality aren't. All this leads to the topic of *edge.* When you read trading forums and message boards, you will see questions like, "What is your edge? How can I get it?" Do these questions make sense? Yes and no. Yes, traders need an edge in order to be successful. And, no, you cannot ask someone, "What is your edge? Tell me, and I will use it." You can't simply get someone else's edge.

By observing traders in action, you can see a group of traders that apparently has an edge, whatever it is. They are confident in their action although they don't necessarily sound confident in their comments. They are consistent, they are in a good mood most of the time, and they don't get frustrated or overexcited. Their plays are easy to distinguish; they have a very distinctive style. The trades they make are apparently "their" plays. They often have their own spin on traditional setups. You can see other traders asking them what they do and how do they do it. They often share their "secrets" with no hesitation. Yet, rarely can someone do the same thing. It may be easy to understand what they do, but it is not that easy to do it. How did they get where they are? And why is it so individual that their style is so difficult to copy?

That's exactly *their* edge. *Their* is the operative word here. There is *no* edge that could be found, shared, and used by others. Edge is *yours* only.

For a long time I viewed the market as a big jigsaw puzzle. I was figuring out this piece and that piece, putting them together one at a time. Things would look clear for a short while, and then I would realize that there were more pieces that I didn't even suspect existed. So, I would try to find them and fit them into the puzzle. At the same time, however frustrating and never-ending this process seemed, one other thing was happening: I was not only adding new pieces, but I was also getting rid of pieces that did not fit, that were not mine. They weren't necessarily wrong, but I wasn't comfortable with them. Step by step, only things that were "mine" remained in my arsenal. When I looked at a certain stock, at its chart or Level 2, I could tell whether it was "mine" or not. My plays became distinguishable. Traders I communicated with began marking some plays as "my style." That was a sign that my edge was emerging. I was comfortable with those plays, I had a feel for them, and I could tell what the signs were of them working or failing.

Did I try to find out what other traders' edges were? Sure I did, as any trader would. Did someone else's edge work for me? Never. Did other traders try to copy my edge? Sure. My results were posted, and traders could see my calls in real time so they tried to do what I did. Did it work for them? No, it did not work for those who tried to buy when I bought. But, yes, it did work for those who tried to learn and apply the principles I was following.

But it worked only for those who found their own spin to my edge! See the point? It's not necessarily about right or wrong. It's about what *you* and only *you* can read. It's about what *you* and only *you* can get a feel for.

Look at setups on any system. They might be clear enough and easy to understand, but can you apply them with no differentiations and expect consistent profits? No, you cannot.

By observing traders in action, you can see that each plays the same setup differently. Some use setups directly, some skip the trigger itself and wait for a setback, and some don't even look for setups that work and prefer hunting for those that fail in order to fade them. The same happens with exits. Some traders scalp and keep their sure easy money, while others scale out, letting profits run.

Which way is better? *Yours!* The way you feel best with, most comfortable with. So how do you find what is yours? There is one and only one way to find your edge: *experience.*

Trade after trade, day after day, you must apply tight risk control in order to survive while you are learning; and you must still be around when things start clicking. Accept the fact that consistency will come only after you find your edge. You may read many books, take courses, and participate in discussions. The purpose of all this is to find the edge that's *yours.*

How do you recognize it? Don't worry. You won't miss it. You will get this amazing, absolutely wonderful feeling of control, of knowing what you are doing, of feeling that there is a segment of the market action where you are on top. Your edge may be something not many other traders do, like trading at lunchtime or trading thin, illiquid stocks or trading right at the open or . . . Or you may have a different angle from what many others do, like fading a breakout that everyone else buys. When you find your edge, the rest of the market ceases to exist. You ignore everything that is not your edge. You wait for your play to come around. When someone asks you, "What? You haven't played QCOM today? It went from $400 to $600." You just shrug and respond, "Really? Never even looked." That's because you found your edge, and QCOM doesn't fit.

Do all traders see the same thing when looking at the same setup, such as, "Cup and handle ABCD, trigger $20.50, stop $20.25"? No. One of them may see, "Buy ABCD when $20.50 is getting hit." Another one may see, "Wait for ABCD to clear $20.50 and go up, pull back, and then buy it if it holds new support at $20.50." Yet another may see, "If ABCD clears $20.50, no play for me. But if it loses $20.25 first, I'll short it." Do you see the resemblance to the art analogy and Zeldovich quote we discussed in Chapter 5? This is how your personality, your vision, shapes things for you, and this is where your edge emerges. In Chapter 12 we demonstrate how traders can play the same setup in many different ways depending on their edge.

Trade and observe. Listen to yourself and wait until things become clear, easy, and *yours*.

CHAPTER 7

A Trader's Intuition

The Real Art of Trading

Throughout this book I discuss how my trading mindset gradually formed. I talk about the tricks I invented and successfully applied. All this led me to a new state of mind. It is the highest possible level a trader can reach—intuitive trading. There are many discussions among traders about intuition. Some deny its existence, and some swear by it. I was lucky enough to experience this amazing state of mind and profit from it.

In my opinion, most of the disagreement surrounding intuition's role in trading arises from misunderstanding. Many think of intuition as of some kind of sudden revelation about the future. They expect intuition to be some kind of tip-giver. This isn't true. Newer traders don't get true intuitive impulses. For them, it's going to be hope or wishful thinking that they will mistakenly take for intuition.

WHAT IS INTUITION?

As we gain experience, we reach some critical mass that results in automatic reactions. This is similar to the way we learn to drive; at first it takes conscious thought. The more we drive and the more road situations we face, the less we think and the more we respond. At some point we find ourselves driving from one place to another without noticing intersections or other cars. Does this mean that we didn't see them? Of course not. We certainly did. But we didn't have to think about them. Unless we encounter an extreme situation, we are able to drive on autopilot. Our brain establishes a series of links between the situations we face and our responses.

Similarly, a master of martial arts responds to an opponent's action without thinking. To an observer, it might seem like an experienced fighter knows in advance each move the opponent will make before he or she makes it. Such automatic and correct responses are possible through highly developed intuition, which comes with a great deal of experience.

In exactly the same way, the more we trade, the more we establish certain links in our brain. Certain situations start looking familiar enough for us to respond to them without thinking. The number of familiar situations grows. The fewer the number of situations that look totally new and unfamiliar to us, the more confident we feel. The market ceases to be a great mystery. It becomes a set of situations—most of them familiar—and we know how to respond to them. Some situations are not recognizable, so we don't trade; we observe and learn.

As you can see, on the surface intuitive impulses work like driving—getting there without knowing consciously how you got there. You go from A to E without taking notice that you went through B, C, and D. But B, C, and D are still there, and the process of going through them is still there. It's just that this process ceases to be conscious. Thanks to your experience, you know how to get to E once you recognize A. In Chapter 4 we say that, in learning to trade, you have to go through many situations and experiences yourself. This is the process that establishes those links in our brain, collecting the "bank of familiar situations."

BE CAREFUL OF INTUITIVE TRAPS

Is it possible to develop trading intuition? It is, and there are excellent books on the subject that helped me greatly. But there are also traps on the path to intuitive trading. For example, you cannot push too hard; you cannot try to make the intuitive impulse come to you. As soon as you attempt to do that, you won't be able to tell a true intuitive impulse from wishful thinking. The intuitive impulse comes to you as a reward for having the correct state of mind—clear, nonopinionated, open, calm, relaxed, and focused. This is that unclouded state of mind that comes with great confidence and a lot of experience that enables us to hear the subtle voice of intuition. When it comes, you just act, without second-guessing or hesitation. It feels as though your finger pushes the button by itself, and you observe what's happening. There appears to be a direct link between your eyes and fingers, with no brain interruption.

In Chapter 6 we discuss having an edge and that in order to obtain one, we have to trade for a long period of time and go through different market situations, sorting them out from the point of view of what we feel comfortable with. While traders develop their edge, something else is going on. By establishing the correct state of mind, intuitive trading becomes accessible. Eventually traders come to the point where both processes merge, and this point constitutes a new level of their trading career—a level where traders make consistent profits without feeling stressed. Trading becomes effortless, easy, fun. Everything becomes clear and simple. The way to this simplicity takes you through many complications, but when they are behind you, they become nothing more than things to laugh about. This stage is any trader's dream.

A close friend and coworker of mine developed great intuitive vision of price movement. He started his trading journey as a part-time trader. His regular job was as a New York cab driver. His great interest and devotion to the markets kept him near the screen during market hours every day for years. By reading the news and observing stock reaction, he learned to feel which stock was going to move and which wasn't. Eventually, he moved from news plays to tape reading. We discussed price patterns during the day and observed stocks together. Sometimes he would make a remark about where a particular stock was going, assigning it a price target that seemed to come from nowhere. The percentage of cases when he was right was amazingly high. He still amazes me with his intuitive impulses. Sometimes he gives this kind of reading for a stock that has just been sitting without any movement, then it really explodes a short time later. We named this "the feeling of hidden tension." To an outside observer it appears that he just knows in advance what is going to happen. At the same time, it is very easy for him to admit when he is wrong. This is that great stage when a trader acts effortlessly and naturally.

TRADING MANTRAS

But wait! Should we assume that, when you get to this stage, trading is no longer a problem? If only it were that simple.

Shortly after I started trading intuitively, I faced another obstacle, which I learned was not unique to me from numerous discussions with other traders. The problem was that this beautiful state of total clarity tended to disappear for a while. It came and went without warning. Some subtle changes in me were making this clarity go away. I felt that I had no control over this. My understanding of the market processes was still there, of course, and I continued to trade within my system parameters. But the disappearance of this inner clarity lowered my percentage of winning plays.

As I continued trading, I managed to make those periods of black-
outs shorter and shorter. I accepted that they would happen, without frustration or panic. When they occurred, I cut back on my activity and tried
to minimize my losses while waiting for my clear state of mind to return.
Step by step I developed some new ideas for returning to the correct mindset more quickly. I wrote several mantras that I would read and repeat, in
a sense meditating on the subject. After a while I wrote mantras for specific trading problems. Regular repetition of them helped me reduce the
number of those undesirable periods and make the ones I did experience
much shorter. I regained control over myself once again. The mantras
follow.

1. General State of Mind

Responsibility for Your Own Trading.   No one has control over me. I am
controlling myself. Any changes in my account are caused by me. I am
looking into my actions to find the reason for any changes that occur. I
have the power to make positive changes in my account. No one can hurt
me, since I am protected by my rules and discipline. The market is not a
hostile environment; it's just a sea of opportunities. I am giving myself
money or taking it from myself. I am not hiding in the comfort of blaming someone else. I want the result—profit or loss—to come from *my*
choices.

Opinionless State of Mind.   The market has no firm link between reason
and outcome. I don't have to figure out the future. I don't need the weight
of opinion on my shoulders. I am free to react to what happens by relying
on my reading of stock action. I keep a flexible state of mind. Nothing prevents me from changing my tactic if the market doesn't act as I expect it to.

Confidence.   I don't know what the market will do next. I don't have to
know. I know how I will react to anything the market does. I am confident
in my ability to react correctly. I have a strategy that works and the discipline to carry it out. I am independent-minded. I don't trade to please others. I am self-reliant. I question any trade I take, but I don't question my
ability to make the right decisions. I trade effortlessly and automatically.
I manage risk and assume losses. I trust myself.

Living in Reality.   I do not convince myself that I am right. I just watch
stock movement and make my conclusions. When market behavior

changes, so does my strategy. Market movement is the ultimate truth. I am not trying to outsmart or outguess it. I live in the here and now. My mind is open to possibilities.

Emotionlessness.   I am objective and calm. I am a detached observer. I don't get angry about stocks not doing what I expected. I know they do what they do and that the market is what it is. I don't get frustrated with stop losses; they are part of the game. I don't get overexcited with winning trades; they are just one more confirmation of my correct approach. I feel good about my trading and about myself. My performance as a trader doesn't reflect on my self-worth.

2. Morning Tune-up after a Winning Day

I am relaxed and confident. I have an optimistic, winning attitude from yesterday. I remember the feeling of doing the right things, and I am going to repeat those things today. I am focused. I can see everything that happens. I evaluate events quickly and precisely. I see myself in control.

3. Morning Tune-up after a Losing Day

Today is a separate day, which has nothing in common with yesterday. Today's performance is fresh. It is I who have the power to do the right things. The stock market has no power over me. It's not after me. It has no memory of yesterday, and neither do I. I remember how I feel when I win. I am going to remember this feeling of victory. I can identify and execute winning trades.

4. Recovery after a Losing Streak or a Heavy Loss

I am starting fresh. I know what to do to win. I am doing the right things right now, and not trying to get back my money. I am not taking revenge—there is no one to fight with. I am taking it slowly until I get a good feeling. I am not complaining about my loss. I paid money for the lesson. Now I am applying my new knowledge to my trading. I am taking only trades that match my set of rules. There is no memory of money lost—my trading account is not money. It's a tool for making money. I am rebuilding my confidence with many small wins. They let me feel the taste of winning. I don't let events control me. I am in control of myself. I am going to remember the feeling of every win.

5. Stop Loss

Stopping out prevents losses. It's not losing; it's preventing a loss. I am not trying to control the market. I admit to its independence. I am willing to act in tune with it. If I find myself in the wrong place at the wrong time, it's in my power to get out. I have the responsibility to keep my trading account in good shape, and stop loss is my way to achieve this. There is nothing wrong in being stopped out. A stop does not make me a loser. It makes me a winner, serving as the line of defense for my account. This is my way to control events. This is my salvation. I want to be in control and be happy. A stop is not a loss. A stop prevents a loss from growing. The market is in endless motion. No trade is so significant that it's worth holding onto if it doesn't work. The next opportunity comes right away. I switch easily from the trade that doesn't work to another that will. I enter any trade accepting in advance that it can stop me out. If the trade doesn't work out, it won't come as a surprise to me. My trading strategy has the inevitability of losses built into it, but no single loss can get out of hand.

6. Fear of Trading, Hesitating to Pull the Trigger

Trading is a game of probabilities. I don't have to be right every time. I just have to follow my rules. I know my system works. Every trade is either a profit or a stop. Any given trade is not of significance. The results over a certain time period are what matter. Trading within my proven system puts the odds on my side. I have to play to allow opportunities to materialize. I know I can trade by my rules. All I do is react to signals— a signal to enter and a signal to exit—that are generated by my system. They take me in and out with no hesitation. I can observe the market and emotionally detach from it. Any stock movement is simply numbers that change following certain patterns. I know how to read those patterns. I am totally focused on what the market is telling me. I can hear it and react to it.

7. Letting Winners Run

I don't have to be right all the time. I don't have to take a profit as soon as my position shows one. I have to sell when my system generates a sell- ing signal, not when I have a profit. My goal is to play within a set of rules, not to make money. Things once set in motion tend to remain in motion. I want to ride them while they move. I just trail my stop until the stock proves that it has reversed or until a sell signal is generated. My system is profit-oriented. I am going to let it generate profits.

8. Overtrading

I have only one reason to put on a trade. This reason is a valid setup in terms of my system. There are no external influences that can make me trade. Boredom is not a reason to trade. Being down for the day is not a reason to trade. The market doesn't care about my being up or down. It generates profitable opportunities regardless of what I want. I wait for the market to create a situation I can recognize. I am not eager to find the trade. I will know when it comes along. I don't have to be in the market all the time. I sit and wait for the right opportunity. My money works when it's in a trade that exploits a profitable opportunity. My money works when it's sitting on the sidelines being ready for the right moment.

You can use these mantras or design your own for your specific problems. Their repetition really helps instill good habits and tune up your mindset. In early chapters we discuss a trading journal as a way to pinpoint a specific mindset problem. A combination of such diagnoses with mantras creates a powerful way of troubleshooting your trading.

CHAPTER 8

Rules for and the Mindset of a Mature Trader

The Dos and Don'ts of Trading

There are times when I think I could write a manual on trading that would take just a few paragraphs. In fact, after I went through all the hassles of learning to arrive at such simplicity, it is difficult to remember and describe all the hassles. A very brief explanation wouldn't be too helpful to newer traders, since they need to be informed about the process of learning. I've discussed my trading history, my experiences, my trading education, my tricks of the trade, and my horror stories. Now I'd like to pull it all together.

Trading should be natural and easy. Don't force anything, and don't fight the market or yourself. Perfect trading is like breathing. You inhale and exhale, enter and exit. Be calm and relaxed. Look for recognizable opportunities. Be focused and alert. Detach yourself from the heat of action. Be an observer and wait for opportunities to find you. Don't trade what you can't read. Don't think you have to trade everything. There are just so many opportunities that fit your personality, your ability to read. Take those, and ignore the others. Don't try to be a universal trader who can trade any type of market on any given day.

Don't fight. Trading is not war. The market is not after you. It has no idea you exist. In fact, it has no ideas at all. Stock doesn't know you bought it. It does its thing—just go along with it. The market is your boss. Obey it and get paid, or rebel and get fired. You don't fight the ocean; you swim in it. If you find yourself in a current that takes you in an undesirable direction, you don't try to change its direction. Look for another current.

Don't guess. Don't personalize the market. Don't expect the market to care. It doesn't care. It's not hostile. It's not friendly. It exists. That's it. You are free to engage or not. Trading is ultimate freedom. You are free to decide when to go in and when to go out. The market is an endless flow of opportunities for profit and loss. It's for you to choose. The market presents opportunities to you. Be open to perceive them. Be open-minded as the market talks to you in its language. There is just one language of the market. It's the language of price, volume, and pace. Any tool you use to read the market is derivative of that original language. All the junk surrounding this direct conversation between you and market, like rumors, tips, analysts' opinions, other traders' opinions, can only distract you from the reality of price, volume, and pace.

Forget that your money is at stake. Money in a trading account is just a tool for making money. Preserve your tool. You need it in order to make money. By taking stops, you preserve your tool from grave damage. The market is not certain; it works in probabilities. Hence, stops are unavoidable. Take them with no hesitation when the market says you are wrong, and your tool will survive to serve you another day. Admit when you are wrong. Now and then, a stock will shake you out and reverse. Don't let it force you into ignoring stops. You can always reenter a position, but you can never get back your loss. Each loss carries a lesson, and it's up to you to assign the price to that lesson. Do not pay more than you have to. Think of your trading as a whole, as a never-ending process. Don't put too much significance on any one trade; it's just one of many. Allow yourself to lose, and move on.

Do not take a trade out of revenge or because you need money. The market has no memory or knowledge of you. It's just a giant pool of actions of other traders. It's not going to reward you just because you need to be rewarded. You are the one who is in charge. You have the power to take the money out of the market or to lose it to market participants.

When traders engage in market activity, they put their money in a big pot. From the moment they start a trade, this money is faceless and nobody's. Anyone is free to take it if his or her skill allows. By putting money in the pot, each player assumes the risk of losing it. This risk is balanced against the opportunity to take the money from the pot. You assume this risk; you put your stake on the table, like everyone else. Never feel guilty about taking money from the pot.

Understand that risk is inherent and a natural part of trading. You accept the risk when you move from a less volatile commodity (money) to a more volatile one (stocks or whatever market vehicle you choose to trade). You do that because this volatility is what you need in order to make money. With opportunity comes risk. You can't get one without the other.

Trading can and often should be boring. It's normal. You are not in it for excitement. It's okay to spend hours sitting in front of your screen doing nothing. This is not a job where you get paid by the hour. You get paid for doing the right thing. The right thing to do is often to stay away from the action. If you want excitement, look for it somewhere else. Learn to find the joy in self-control. Accept the boredom that is a part of good trading.

Never think, "I know what the market is going to do." You don't. Nobody does. Think, "I know what I am going to do in any scenario the market presents." Determine your action for any possible scenario. This is your ultimate freedom and protection. The market can do nothing to you outside of your set of if-then scenarios. In every one of those, "if" is for market action and "then" is for your response. You cannot control what the market does, but you can control and should adjust your response.

Decide what it is you are going to trade. If it's a trend, follow its direction. If it's a range, fade it. Buy high and sell higher in an uptrend. Sell low and cover lower in a downtrend. Buy low, sell high in a range. If you play a trend reversal, don't do it on price alone. You need a more solid reason to buy than, "It's cheap enough," and a more solid reason to short than, "It's too expensive."

Define your signals. A signal generated by your system is the only valid reason you have for making a trade. The rest is emotions. Don't let emotions dictate your business decisions. When your trading system generates an entry signal, take the trade with no hesitations. When your trading system generates a sell signal, close the trade. If you question your trading system, test it on paper. Don't trade if you're testing.

Establish your level of aggressiveness. Know your trade-offs. A highly aggressive approach maximizes your profit in cases when you are right but reduces the number of cases when you are right. A conservative approach allows you to be right more often but diminishes your profit potential in each case.

Stay flexible. Modify your trading system to correspond to market changes. Adjust your level of aggressiveness and the setups you choose to the kind of market you are dealing with. Constantly check whether what you are doing matches market conditions.

Define what a sucker is. Suckers think they are smarter than the market. Suckers think they can figure it out. Suckers think there are secret systems and indicators. Suckers think they can avoid losses. Suckers don't apply stops because they know they are going to be right. Write down all the traits of a sucker and read them often to see if you spot any such traits in yourself. *Don't be a sucker.*

Define how a winning trader thinks. Write down all the traits of a good trader and read it often to see if you are there yet. Use this comparison to see where your weaknesses are and what you need to work on. Be brutally honest with yourself. Everything you don't tell yourself, you will hear from the market, and it won't be pleasant talk.

Whatever happens to you in the market, it's never the market's fault. It's not the market maker or specialist's fault. It's not the mysterious manipulator or evil short seller. It's always you. You make the decision. You implement it. You engage and disengage. Accept full, undivided, absolute responsibility. Be your own person. Don't complain and don't explain. With responsibility comes control. Gain total control of yourself. Trading is the ultimate exercise in self-control. This is a cold and uncomfortable feeling at first—the feeling of being alone in your castle. The joy of having your edge and being the best at it will come and compensate you for that discomfort. The feeling of great self-control, of total power over your own actions, will be a great reward for all your efforts. Be the master of *your* universe.

Learn self-irony. Don't take yourself too seriously. You don't have to prove anything to others. Be the first to laugh about your mistakes. Unburden yourself of the pressure of trying to be perfect. Excellent is good enough.

PART TWO

Trading System

CHAPTER 9

Tape Reading

Revitalization of a Lost Art

Part One of the book describes Vadym's journey as a trader—from newer trader to reality trader. This part of the book describes our trading system. We talk about criteria we use for entries and exits, and about our method of reading price movement. We go over the major principles of tape reading and show how they help to identify the forces behind the scenes. We also show how we build the setups—the logic that lies under this process. This part will not only help you understand our setups, but it will also help you build your own. We describe our setups and explain how they should be played. We go over the concept of stop-loss placement and trailing. In this part, you will see examples and real schematic charts. When there is no symbol of the stock in a chart, it means that the chart is an example, created manually to illustrate the idea in the text.

Finally, we present numerous examples of real trades with detailed descriptions of trade development. We want this part to be somewhat of a "pulling it all together," so we describe not only particular trades but also the logic, philosophy, and psychology of every move.

ONE SIZE DOESN'T FIT ALL

You need to keep several things in mind. First of all, by no means do we consider our system to be "the one and only." There are many of them out there. Some work today and will frustrate their users tomorrow. Some suit your personality and risk tolerance; some don't. You already know from our discussion of the *edge* that eventually the only system that is going to work for you will be the one you create for yourself, either from scratch or by applying your own spin on something that already exists. What we describe is ours. We have taught many traders this system. They use our system either in its pure form or in their own variations of it. You will see our system and you will also see how it's built. As a result, even if your ultimate approach is totally different, you will still be able to use our major ideas. In addition, the principles of tape reading will be helpful for you no matter what system you use. What we describe is not a system that works for a year or two and then fades away. The major principles of this approach stem from the things that never change, since human reactions to market events have not changed in hundreds of years.

Second, what you will see is fairly simple. We are not fans of over-complicated systems that rely on dozens of indicators. When we say *uptrend,* we mean a series of higher lows and highs. When we say *downtrend,* we mean a series of lower lows and highs. You do not necessarily need a formal indicator to see whether there is a trend; a simple look at the chart is usually enough. You don't necessarily need any calculations or indicators to see the strength of a trend; the steeper an angle, the stronger the trend. A working system isn't necessarily cumbersome, oversophisticated, and incomprehensible for anyone but those with a Ph.D. in math, chemistry, philosophy, and economics. It should be transparent for you, or you will trade on "black box" tips. At the same time, don't be fooled by the system's simplicity. This is the kind of simplicity you arrive at after many complications.

You will also notice that this system is more the reading of certain visual formations than of certain numbers and their relationships. We often hear that a "real" trading system should be quantifiable. This is not necessarily the case. Attempting to tie your action to quantified indications can easily lead you to a search for the Holy Grail. As we discuss in Part One, art is as important an element in trading as is science. And there is no place for the word *always* in trading. Chart readers use visual formations to make their decisions. Everyone knows about flags, pennants, and the like; those are visible formations. Similarly, our setups are created when a certain formation takes shape on the chart, not when one number exceeds another. This can be complemented by some indicators.

Third, this is an intraday trading system. Principles of reading are pretty much the same for any time frame. You need to apply them to the one you trade in. But we are intraday traders, so each of the examples you will see is happening within a single day. Also keep in mind that it's largely a trend-following system. It performs well in a trending environment and leads to a diminished percentage of winners and lower returns in ranging markets. This doesn't mean that you need a strong trend throughout the day to use this system. The market often produces several trends within 1 day. From the point of view of a trader operating in longer time frames, each trend is just a noise, but an intraday trader switches easily from long plays to shorting or from longer holding times to 20–30 cent scalps. Don't forget also that no system works in every market environment. Narrow ranges and choppy movement are conditions a trader avoids.

Fourth, while tape-reading principles are the same for any market, there are many fine distinctions in each market's mechanics. Our personal experience is limited to the Nasdaq, and the fine details concerning time considerations, price ranges, and other pieces of mosaic could and will be different for other markets. You will see references to the NDX as a general directional indicator, but Nasdaq futures may be used as well. Also, if you trade a stock that moves in conjunction with a particular sector, you can use this sector index to gauge broad strength. All this does not mean that this system will not work with different markets. You just need to know the specifics of your trading vehicle.

Fifth, this is mainly a trend-following system. It's based on the premise that the trend continues until it reverses. Until you see clear signs of the reversal, you need to play in the trend direction. There are two reversal setups that we tend to use as reasons for an exit strategy rather than an entry strategy. In these cases, we identify that the trend has a lower probability of continuing from these points.

We will mention confidence levels. A *confidence level* is simply a level between the current price and the stop price that allows us to gauge whether the trend of the stock is still intact given our time frame. If the stock breaks this confidence level on any kind of retracement, then we normally look to exit the trade on the movement in the direction of the dominant trend to get a better exit price than what a stop price would give us. (See Chapter 11 for details.)

Finally, no matter what system you use, ours or someone else's or your own or a combination of these, always remember that no system works by itself. It's you who makes it work. It's you who follows the rules or breaks them. It's you who patiently waits for the valid signal or reacts impulsively on everything that moves. It's always the trader!

DISCOVERING WHAT TAPE READING REALLY IS

The principles of tape reading date back nearly 400 years to the beginning of commodity speculation. Whenever there is disagreement on the perceived or intrinsic value of a product, there is cause for speculation about where that price will move. Principles of tape reading take you right to the heart of this speculative arena. They match price movement to crowd behavior in the form of a *rate of volume*.

Tape readers see price movement in relation to the rate of volume and can determine when the footprints of stock action are made. Tape reading allows one to understand the actions of the minority and eventually the majority when it climbs in. These principles are applied to an individual security's behavior and to the broader market trend's behavior. Why a stock is moving is not an issue. The evaluation is concentrated on where it is moving and how far it can move in that direction. Trading tips often don't pan out, and news creates countertrends to what is deemed logical. This is where tape reading saves us from our ego and ourselves. The truth of stock movement lies in the tape, not in our ego.

Over the past years, we have watched thousands of traders bring new methodology to the marketplace. There is literally a system for every speculative tool available. A few of these systems are quite good, and others are just plain ridiculous. However, with the advent of the great bull market of the 1990s and Internet mania, even the mediocre system could produce fairly good results assuming it didn't dictate going short on any new high. This is where the beginners' understanding of market reality, which was far from true reality, lead them to great losses. This is what happened during the bear market of Nasdaq in 2000–2002. What worked even 1 year ago doesn't necessarily work today in the majority of these systems. However, it is clear that one system has stood the test of time. More interesting, no one had been teaching it.

Tape-reading principles, having been around for 400 years, have seen every possible market there is, and they continue to produce consistent results in bear and bull markets. As you can see, Jesse Livermore's principles and understanding of market behavior need to be taught to the trading community, but not in a way that we have ever seen before.

With something so universal that has stood the test of time, it's necessary to revive an in-depth understanding of how tape-reading principles can take us to the root of price and rate of volume. They show us the footprints of the minority and how to capitalize on the irrationality of the crowd when it finally figures out what the minority already knows.

The next section may be somewhat too basic for an advanced reader. However, we would like to take you through the entire logical chain to show you how tape-reading principles give us the correct approach to the market.

ARE YOU THE MAJORITY OR THE MINORITY?

Tape-reading principles suggest that the majority is usually wrong. The idea of tape reading is based on the obvious fact that, in the markets, only a handful of players take the money—from the majority. The market usually moves in a way that hurts as many players as possible. The path of least resistance is opposite to what the majority expects. To define the direction that the crowd does not want or expect means to define the way the market is going to move. The mechanics of this phenomenon are quite obvious when you think of this in the following terms.

Imagine a situation in which *everyone* has bought a certain stock. There are no more buyers. What happens when people decide to liquidate their positions? Obviously, they won't be able to find another buyer until they offer the stock at a price that is far lower than the price the last trade occurred at. This creates a snowball effect in which players decide to unload their holdings, some because their targets are reached and others because their stops are hit.

The direction changes to the opposite—opposite of what? Not only the opposite of the previous trend but also the opposite of what all the players that bought the stock expected. They were buying the stock because they expected a further advance. In this hypothetical situation where everyone has already bought this stock, you will see overwhelmingly positive and optimistic opinions about the stock. It's very important to understand since this is what makes stocks reverse to the downside when the situation looks the brightest and to the upside when everything looks totally dark.

Indeed, this example is extreme. In real life it's impossible for 100 percent of the participants to have bought a certain issue. Still, it illustrates the idea that at some point the correlation between those who want to take a position and those who have already taken it creates an imbalance to such a degree that *potential* sellers outweigh *potential* buyers at any given price. That's where expectations of the buyers are no longer valid and trend reversal occurs.

Add to this the fact that every buyer who has already taken the position becomes a potential seller. Now the picture becomes crystal clear. The chain of events is simple. There are not many players who have an established position at the first stage of the move. Thus, there are not many potential sellers who are waiting for the price to rise. The path of least resistance is up, so the minority starts accumulating shares. Then the price movement attracts attention and more players get in. The crowd discovers the gem, and aggressive buying hits the stock. As the majority hits the stock, too many players are in and too many potential sellers are lurking. Distribution by the early buyers starts, while the lack of new buyers leaves the stock with no support. Ultimately, late buyers are left holding the bag.

MARKET IRONY

What we have just described is a major law of all market-related events. The same mechanics work with setups that become too popular. They cease to work when they are followed too widely. Any inefficiency or window of opportunity created by the market exists until it's discovered by the majority. SOES (Small Order Execution System) bandits used a new direct-access SOES to exploit inefficiencies by market makers that were not used to being this open to added liability due to their requirement of having to maintain an orderly two-sided market. These SOES bandits enjoyed their window of opportunity until the crowds discovered their strategy. So-called ECN arbitrages were taken out of the game even faster. When a CNBC commentator said that it was probably time for the masses to learn how to short stocks, the market staged a staggering 500-point bounce the very next day, July 24, 2002, after months of steady decline! This example will be a classic for years to come.

Let's get back to price movement. Evidence of accumulation and distribution in the market at levels where the minority (smart money) is participating to a greater degree is often masked to the public until the time is right. Then positions are unloaded as the majority catches on. This can be seen in numerous examples in any given week or month. The market is a discounting mechanism by which the majority usually enters and exits at the wrong time. The major idea is that the public is the last to participate, so when the public comes to buy, there is no one left to buy from them. Thus, majority participation creates the final stage of the movement, which is followed by a reversal. The same happens when the majority sells in aggregate. There is no one left but buyers. Note that when we say "masked," we don't mean anything conspiratorial. It's simply recognition of the fact that smart money tries to act in a certain way and tries to control the impression its action makes. On the other hand, the public acts in an unorganized way, driven by chaotic emotions.

We see examples of this during times of capitulation, where the majority creates selling pressure that is so strong that it exhausts selling. The majority participates in this aggregate selling phase as a crowd. Meanwhile, the minority (smart money) finds the point where the majority sells. When selling becomes exhausted, the smart money reverses and goes long. The same thing can be seen on the long side, where the majority feels as if it has missed out on a major market or stock move and can't stand to see it rise more without it. This brings in majority buying and euphoria, until buying becomes exhausted. The minority then begins to distribute shares to the crowd buyers from positions it has accumulated at lower levels.

The best example of this can be seen in the 1998–2000 move from Nasdaq 1500 to 5100 and then back down to 1600 and back up to 2300. Euphoria took the market to 5100, and capitulatory events, not to the degree we saw in 1998 but still strong, took the market to 1600. Then, as the market consolidated during the accumulation phase near 1600 as the majority was still selling, the market began to move upward, discounting that the worst of the economic and business cycle was over. The minority then began to distribute shares as Nasdaq neared the 2200 level, as the majority began to feel as if it was missing out on the resurgence of the bull move.

THE ACCUMULATION/DISTRIBUTION RELATIONSHIP

This cycle of accumulation and distribution favors the minority who can read the tape of the market and participate at levels that feed off the usual ignorance of the majority. It may not be fair, but it's how the game is played. Tape-reading principles allow you to watch how the minority is participating and then how to profit from when the majority creates the herd movement, which signals a short-term stop to the current trend.

As we defined the role of the smart money and the public in the price movement, we must now learn to distinguish their action. The major difference that allows us to distinguish the action of smart money from that of the public is the character of price movement and volume changes. As a rule, smart money action can be seen as a slow, gradual price movement with steady or slowly increasing volume. The public's action is characterized by hysterical and parabolic price spikes, almost vertical movement with a sharp volume increase.

Let's pause here and define the way we progress from this point to build a sound trading system. We know how to distinguish the smart money action from that of the public, and we want to position ourselves on the smart money's side. In order to realize this in practical trading, we must establish principles that allow us to see different combinations of the price and volume changes and their meaning. The next element we need is timing so as to allow us to find particular entries. This part is solved by setups that govern our points of entry and the direction we take. Setups also provide us with the structure that shows us where the stop should be placed because this structure will show also the signs of the trade failure. And, finally, after our position is established, we read the tape to find the moment when the movement becomes exhausted, in order to liquidate the position. We will take you through the system, building in this order. Careful readers will find that, by using this methodology, they will be able to create their own setups, trading systems, or modifications of an existing system. The value of this skill is hard to overestimate as the market changes make us adjust while we are constantly tweaking different elements of our strategy.

There are six principles that will allow you progress in your tape-reading skills. They are discussed in the following pages.

Major Principle

1. Euphoria/Capitulation.   *An acceleration in the price advance, almost vertical movement accompanied by a volume surge, is usually not sustained and indicates the end of this stage of the move (euphoria stage).* (See Figure 9.1.) This is a perfect example of how the majority is usually wrong as it lets greed overtake fear. This is often the last stage of the move, as the majority finally sees what everyone was trying to hide and jumps on the bandwagon. Distribution takes place by smart money. Since our understanding of the tape principles dictates that the majority is usually wrong, it is time to unload positions or at the very least, not get caught up in the buying frenzy that usually signals the top of the move. Ask yourself how many times you bought the top. We prefer not to count them (on both hands and feet), as we move through our learning phase regarding true market reality. This is a feeling of unbearable pain from missing the train, from standing on the sidelines while "the entire world is making money" that causes those late entries on a parabolic stage of the move—and those entries are being punished severely.

An acceleration in the price drop, almost vertical movement accompanied by volume surge, is usually not sustained and indicates the end of this stage of the move (capitulation stage). (See Figure 9.2.) Once again, tape-reading principles save us from our ego and misunderstanding of market behavior. The capitulation scenario is the opposite of euphoria. The majority is selling in aggregate during the phase where fear overtakes greed. In this case it's still the same unbearable pain; this time it is the pain of holding the plummeting stock that causes this screaming reaction, "Just get me out!" Traders or investors just don't care anymore. They

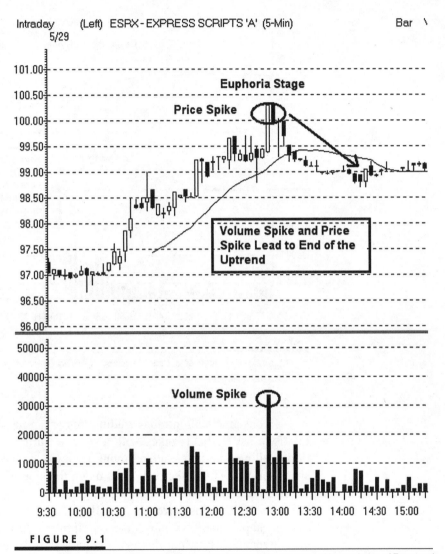

FIGURE 9.1

The euphoria stage of a trade movement. (*RealTick graphics are used with permission of Townsend Analytics, Ltd.*)

want to forget this stock. Their pain has reached the threshold where their loss has exceeded all expectations and effectively numbed all their feelings but "sell and forget!" The smart money waits for this level of selling to slow down and looks to support the stock for a trend reversal by establishing a position favoring the long side or by covering portions, if not all, of its short positions.

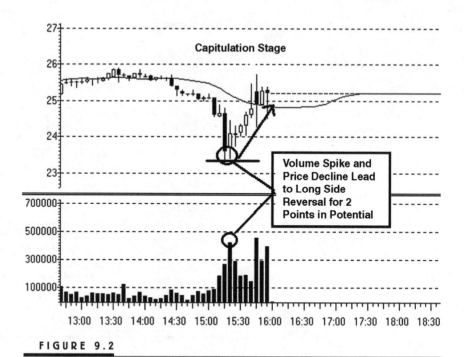

Capitulation Stage

Volume Spike and
Price Decline Lead
to Long Side
Reversal for 2
Points in Potential

FIGURE 9.2

The capitulation stage of a trade movement. (*RealTick graphics are used with permission of Townsend Analytics, Ltd.*)

In our practical, intraday trading this principle serves two purposes. First, we use vertical spikes with a volume surge to liquidate our positions, selling our shares into a buying frenzy or covering our shorts into a sharp sell-off. This effectively puts us on the side of the smart money as we ride the trend while it's slow and get out when the crowd comes in. You can see how this corresponds to the ideas we discuss at the beginning of this chapter and how those ideas tie into practical reading of the market movement. By using this price/volume correlation, you can position yourself on the right side, trading against the majority instead of being a part of the losing crowd.

Many traders we taught over years have told us that this approach of liquidating their positions into price/volume spikes entirely changed the way they traded and made their trading orderly and more profitable. It helped them cure the problem of selling too soon, since they stopped taking little profits just because they had some measly 10-cent movement in their favor. This also helped them solve the problem of holding too long, which allowed profits to evaporate. Instead they started selling or partialling out into those spikes, which brought nice structure to their trading.

Second, we start hunting for a trend reversal when we see hysterical movement. We talk more about this in Chapter 10. For now, let's say that this kind of play is based on the same idea: When the movement becomes parabolic and the volume surges, it is an indication of majority action. Since the crowd is last to act, we can assume that the trend is about to reverse.

Supporting Principles

2. Trend Beginning (Aggressive Accumulation). *Slow, steady movement upward with consistent volume indicates so-called good buying and means the start of upward momentum.* (See Figure 9.3.) Those who are accumulating need to be very careful in such situations. They are buying enough shares to support the stock's direction, but they aren't buying so

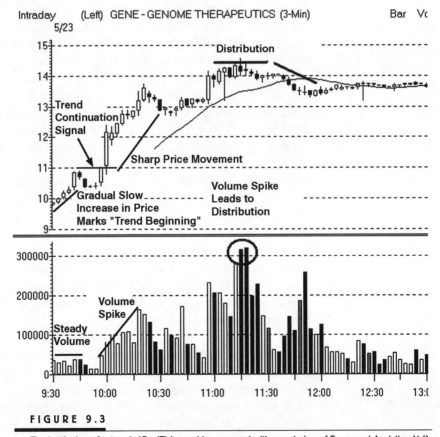

FIGURE 9.3

The beginning of a trend. (*RealTick graphics are used with permission of Townsend Analytics, Ltd.*)

much that it attracts the majority. This is often a tough game to play because any hint that the footprints are being seen by the majority will initiate a price and volume spike, thereby ruining the intention of the smart money to establish a position at better prices. This is why we often laugh about upgrades and downgrades or stock picks. If the company really wanted the best prices, it certainly wouldn't tell the world to buy it, thus making it harder to buy the stock at a low price. This leads us to the conclusion that the company has already established its position and then alerts the public to buy it, so it can begin to unload shares. Unethical or unfair doesn't matter to us as traders. Our job is to understand how the minority works in order to feed off the usual ignorance of the majority.

The movement of stock being quietly accumulated is slow and often accompanied by nasty pullbacks. Those pullbacks are caused by smart money desire to keep the upward movement in check. Buyers who try to establish a large position don't want the stock to rocket out of sight on their own buying. If they need to buy 1 million shares, they most likely are going to buy 1.5 million and sell 0.5 million, switching from the buy side to the sell side now and then, jockeying around, and keeping the lid on the movement when it becomes too fast. Level 2 players in the recent past could see this phenomenon when the market maker who sat on the bid, chasing stock up for hours, all of a sudden appeared on the offer with size, thus causing panic among those who had decided they figured the market maker out. That is a visual example of *masking* intentions. Switching the sides, using ECNs (Electronic Communications Networks) to hide the buyers' identity, showing sizes that are intended to scare traders into taking certain action rather than getting that size filled, and many other tricks were and still are being used to mask real intentions. That's why we are always skeptical of attempts to trade on a pure Level 2 reading. Attempts to beat professionals in this game are not likely to be consistently successful considering the professionals' experience, big arsenal of tricks, and access to big money. Instead, traders are better off focusing on the bigger picture, on reading the movement with methods that allow them to separate what is shown to the public from what is really happening behind the scene.

3. Trend Confirmation (Aggressive Accumulation).   *The trend confirmation principle describes a slow price advance with steady increasing volume that indicates continuing upward momentum.* (See Figure 9.4.) The same can be reversed for the short side. During this stage of the move, the position may be held as the majority has yet to catch onto the trend. When you see the majority begin to participate, the rate of volume will increase

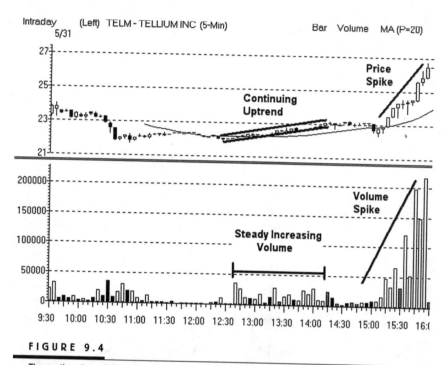

Intraday   (Left) TELM - TELLIUM INC (5-Min)   Bar   Volume   MA (P=20)
5/31

FIGURE 9.4

The continuation of a trend. (*RealTick graphics are used with permission of Townsend Analytics, Ltd.*)

coupled with a steeper angle of the price movement. This is the point at which it is time to observe carefully as price movement can easily accelerate, switching to the euphoria mode. This stage comes naturally after the trend beginning and serves as a preliminary phase before euphoria. If we were to describe the principles in their logical order as subsequent stages of move development, we would put euphoria after trend confirmation. However, we prefer putting euphoria/capitulation first to emphasize its importance as a trend reversal sign. Later we show the logical consequence in typical scenarios and practical examples.

4. Shallow Retracement Trend Continuation.
This principle entails a relatively big volume increase on the price advance with shallow volume on the pullback, indicating a continuing uptrend. (See Figure 9.5.) This shows that there is reasonable support for the stock and no real willingness to sell at the current price by either smart money or the majority. There are often one or two identifiable market participants who show solid support for the stock as they absorb any meaningful wave of selling. In this case, we look for a break of the previous high to provide confirmation that the trend is still intact.

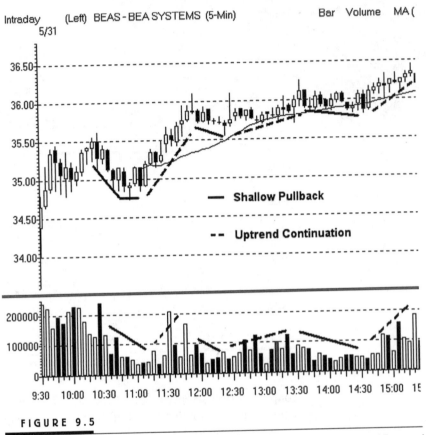

Intraday   (Left) BEAS - BEA SYSTEMS (5-Min)   Bar   Volume   MA (
      5/31

— Shallow Pullback

-- Uptrend Continuation

  9:30 10:00 10:30 11:00 11:30 12:00 12:30 13:00 13:30 14:00 14:30 15:00 15

FIGURE 9.5

Shallow retracement trend continuation. (RealTick graphics are used with permission of Townsend
Analytics, Ltd.)

This situation can be seen in both the trend beginning and trend confirmation stages. It is natural pullback caused either by some profit-taking
or by desire of those who accumulate the shares to limit the movement
until the right time. Other factors can be part of the mix as well, such as a
low level of confidence during the uncertainty of the first phases of the
move or stubborn attempts by the opposite side to resist the move. In any
case, if the pullback is not deep and is accompanied by decreasing volume, it's usually a sign of trend continuation. Throughout the remainder
of the book we provide many setups and examples of how we use volume
changes as indications of what we are going to do.

5. Decreasing Volume Reversal.   *This is a slowing pace of buying with
decreasing volume which indicates that the top of this stage of movement*

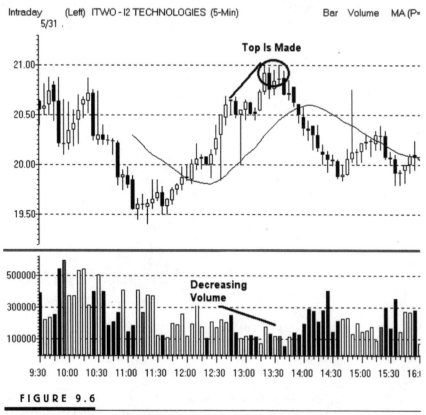

FIGURE 9.6

Decreasing volume reversal. (*RealTick graphics are used with permission of Townsend Analytics, Ltd.*)

is near. (See Figure 9.6.) Most traders refer to this as "Buying is drying up." As the price advances to this area, it fails to attract attention and it slowly slides lower off that high.

Here, again, volume indications help us determine our actions. The idea is simple. As the price rises, buyers do not consider this area attractive; they want to accumulate their shares at lower levels. They evaluate the upside as minimal from here, or they are not confident that buying pressure is going to be strong enough to overcome resistance. At the same time they are not yet motivated enough to start liquidating their positions. This creates a temporary standoff where neither side is aggressive enough to move the price. The volume decreases significantly, and most often this situation leads to a price retreat.

6. Passive Accumulation/Distribution. *Big buying volume without the price changing indicates distribution and means there is a resistance level*

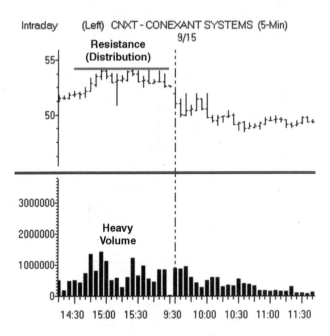

FIGURE 9.7

Passive distribution. (*RealTick graphics are used with permission of Townsend Analytics, Ltd.*)

(passive distribution). (See Figure 9.7.) This is often the case when a stock moves into resistance defined by technical indicators such as a chart or moving average resistance. Early buyers distribute shares they accumulated at lower levels. They feel that the current level is the easiest level in which to unload their intended positions. Many often wonder why they don't raise their offer and fill the rest at a higher price. The answer is simply that, at higher prices, they will have to compete to sell their shares if buying dries up. They basically choose a level that has little competition so that they can distribute their shares to the buyers; thus they are able to complete their intended sales without much effort. This creates a temporary standoff in which both sides are fairly aggressive. Unlike the previous case, volume is big at this level.

This resistance level doesn't necessarily mean that a short should be entered here. As we will see in the following chapters, this kind of situation often leads to consolidation followed by breakout.

Big selling volume without price changing indicates accumulation and suggests a support level (passive accumulation). (See Figure 9.8.) This is the exact opposite of distribution. Buyers are supporting the stock at levels in which the sellers unload their positions. The buyers' intention

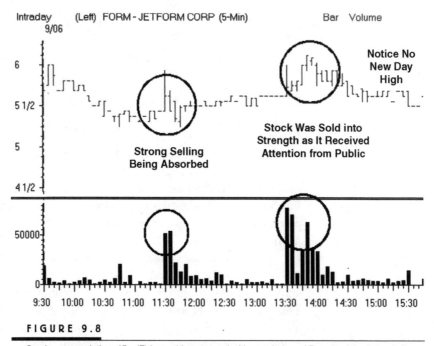

Intraday   (Left) FORM - JETFORM CORP (5-Min)   Bar   Volume
9/06

Notice No New Day High

Stock Was Sold into Strength as It Received Attention from Public

Strong Selling Being Absorbed

9:30   10:00   10:30   11:00   11:30   12:00   12:30   13:00   13:30   14:00   14:30   15:00   15:30

FIGURE 9.8

Passive accumulation. (*RealTick graphics are used with permission of Townsend Analytics, Ltd.*)

is to give strong support to the stock, which eventually leads to the drying up of the selling pressure, thus leaving the sellers frustrated as the solid support holds and leads to a reversal. Should this support level break, all long positions should be closed. Again, as with distribution, this support doesn't necessarily mean that the stock is going to reverse. Consolidation near the low often leads to a breakdown and a further downtrend.

As we can see, this principle describes the situation of a congestion area where one side is betting on the continuation of the trend while the other side places its hope in reversal.

Distribution and accumulation by themselves do not suggest what action we should take. They simply mark certain levels that can be used to form setups. We discuss this in the following chapter as we show how setups are built and played. Notice also that we call this passive accumulation/distribution. It's important to distinguish these two principles from aggressive action. Passive accumulation is bidding, buying only from active sellers. Often it's accompanied by a willingness to drop the bidding price if sellers become too strong. Passive accumulation by itself does not lead to a price advance. Rather, it lays the foundation for a future price increase if and when the sellers get exhausted. Aggressive accumulation is characterized by buying at the offered price, chasing the price, and bidding the stock up. Aggressive accumulation does move the price up as described in principles 2 and 3.

The importance of tape reading is its ability to save us from making market predictions and arbitrary egotistical assumptions about the value of a stock. Your opinion about that stock's price is not important. What is important is where the shift of supply and demand for a particular issue in any time frame moves a stock. The principles described above can be used as a stand-alone system, because they represent what the minority does in order to feed off the majority's reactions to what it thinks should happen. Furthermore, tape-reading principles as we've revived them can be complemented by other studies of trading, including, but not limited to, technical or fundamental analysis.

It's often asked how tape reading relates to technical analysis. They are not mutually exclusive. Tape reading is the root, whereas technical studies and indicators are derivatives. They play the role of interpreters. The market talks to us in its original language of price, volume, and pace. You can read this language on your own, or you can use the help of interpreters to one extent or another. In examples in Part Three we show how we use some simple technical analysis to support and detail the reading of the movement. We don't like to overcomplicate this process. Many traders overwhelm themselves with vast numbers of studies that cloud their perception. This makes their approach too formal and detached from the reality of the market.

With the use of reading the crowd mentality and the footsteps of the minority, we are able to put the probabilities of success on our side. We are not concerned with creating certainties in the market because the market is too random to achieve any kind of certainty. We are concerned with putting the probabilities on our side. An understanding of true market reality increases our chances for success. Remember that there is no Holy Grail of trading. But there is a window of truth into the market, and our tape-reading principles can allow this window to be wide open for your domination of the trading arena.

CHAPTER 10

The Role of Setups

There is a question often asked in many different forums: Does technical analysis (TA) work? The answer depends on what you expect TA to do for you. If you want TA to tell you what the future will bring, then no, it does not. If you want TA to help in your trading, then sure, it does.

To us, TA has no *predicting* value. By this we mean that one or another setup or pattern does not tell us in advance which way the price will go. The value of TA is different. It imposes a structure on what otherwise seems like chaos—price movements.

Following is an illustration: Suppose you see a car on the road, and you try to figure out which way it's headed. *Much like we do when we are looking at stock action and trying to determine which direction it will go from the current price.* There is a crossroads ahead. Until the car actually reaches it, you don't know which way it will go. *This is just like looking at a stock chart for the first time.* When you see the car's right-turn signal flashing, you can assume that the car is going to make a right turn. Is it absolutely certain that it will? No, it isn't. *The stock may head up or down, but is it certain the direction will continue?* The driver of the car can have a change of mind, but the probability of the right turn is high enough. When the car makes the right turn, you can assume with even higher confidence that it will go to the right. Can it stop and back up? Sure, it can. *Just as a stock can go up for only a few ticks and then reverse.* But if you bet on the car going right after making the right turn, you have the odds in your favor. At the same time, you recognize the signals that tell you your initial assumption is wrong—the car reaches a crossroads, turns right after signaling a right turn, but then the car backs up and turns left. *This is the same as seeing the signals that a stock should go higher, watching it go higher for a few ticks, and then seeing it reverse and go much lower.*

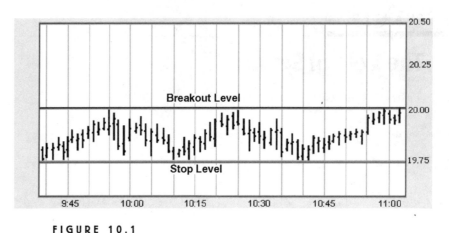

FIGURE 10.1

Trading the range break.

This is how trading setups work. They give you signals. When you have signals, you know what to look for to determine which direction has a higher probability of being taken. For example, a stock is moving in a range between $19.75 and $20. You want to play a break of this range in the direction of the break, assuming that, if the stock breaks to the upside, it's a sign of strength, and vice versa for the break to the downside. (See Figure 10.1.)

Your setup is for a long side trade on the breakout over $20 with support at $19.75. There are two signals. The break of $20 indicates upward movement, and the break of $19.75 indicates downward movement. These signals provide you with your set of if-then scenarios. You also have your safety net. If the price moves through $20 and drops to $19.75 and breaks it, oh well, the driver was drunk.

As you can see, Figure 10.1 doesn't tell you whether or in which direction the breakout is going to happen. It gives you an idea of what you should do if and when it happens. That's what we mean when we say that TA doesn't offer predicting value. TA doesn't tell you which side is going to be broken. But it does provide structure and favorable odds. It provides indications of the most probable direction of the trend. This is one more way in which "Trade what you see, not what you think" works.

Technical analyses work, as long as you read them to your advantage and do not expect them to tell you what to do. They are your tools. Tools do not work by themselves. It's how you master them that determines your success or failure. Traders who expect TA to do their trading are similar to musicians who expect their pianos to play music.

Let's build a set of if-then scenarios, from the simplest one to more complicated ones, and adding new factors that will bring us from pure theory to reality. At this point we will discuss only entry and initial stop placement. Taking profit and stop trailing are discussed next. The example that follows is devoted to a particular setup, "Break out of the narrow range." Later we go over other setups and apply the same methodology of scenario building.

1. *If* the stock price breaks over $20, *then* we buy.
2. *If* the price drops to $19.75 after our buy, *then* we get stopped out.
3. *If* the price breaks below $19.75, *then* we sell short.
4. *If* the price hits $20 after our short sell, *then* we get stopped out.

Now that we have our first signals and our trading idea defined, it's time for more factors to come into play. The first of them is overall market condition. This is a breakout setup, but is the market really favorable for breakouts at this moment? If it is, we can go for a breakout in a broad market direction with confidence and act aggressively. A strongly trending market will act like busy traffic that will not allow our car from the example above to back up and change direction. If we have a narrow ranging market with no follow-through on breakouts, we should choose a conservative approach. Let's analyze what a conservative approach is compared to an aggressive one.

First realize that there is a trade-off on the price you get, the ease of filling your order on the one side, and confidence in the trade outcome on another. You can get the best price by buying the bottom of the range, but there is not the slightest sign of a future breakout. Your confidence is lowest at this point. You can wait for the entire move to be done, and your confidence in it will be 100 percent (what could be more certain than the results of an event that has already happened?). But the price that you get at the top of the move is the worst possible and leaves you no room for profit. Trading is about finding a balance. It's the fine line between where your confidence is at an acceptable level and where the point of entry is affordable.

DIFFERENT METHODS OF ENTRY

Let's look at a case with a long play in a positive market. If you have a really strong trending market moving in the direction of your breakout, you have reason to be aggressive. In this case it would mean entering the stock before the actual breakout. If you see buying pressure building and the price approaching the breakout limit, you can buy at let's say $19.90.

(See Figure 10.2.) It gives you a better price, an easier fill of your order (which might be very hard on an actual breakout, which tends to occur very quickly), and a tighter stop. However, the trade-off is that this inspires less confidence in the breakout itself. The market strength favoring the direction of your trade is what increases your odds for a successful trade and allows you to enter before the actual confirmation of the breakout. Notice that the more aggressively you intend to act, the lower the price of your entry would be. For the purpose of further discussion let's call this the *aggressive method* of entry.

If you are not sure of the follow-through because of the weaker trend, you should wait for the actual breakout to occur, thereby giving you greater confidence in your trade. Again, the trade-off would be the worse price and a wider stop because you buy farther from the support level. This kind of entry would be moderately aggressive. (See Figure 10.3.) Let's call it the *regular method* of entry.

If there is no trend and your confidence in the breakout trade is low, you should adjust your level of aggressiveness accordingly. Before you take this trade, you will want to see as much confirmation as possible. In this case you apply a *conservative* approach, which means that you skip the breakout level itself and wait for the stock to pull back. If it tests new

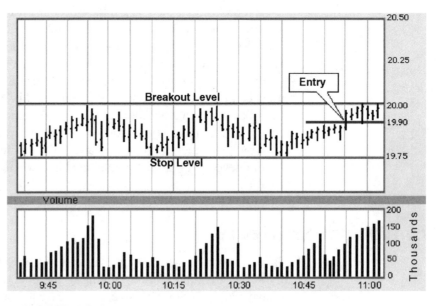

FIGURE 10.2

Method of aggressive entry.

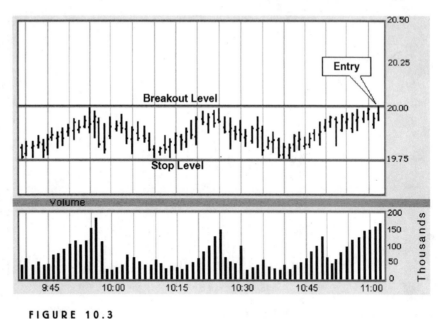

FIGURE 10.3

Method of regular entry.

support (the former resistance level) and keeps above it with confidence, then you've got your confirmation of the strength and you can buy the stock anticipating further movement. (See Figure 10.4.) The trade-off here is going to be the risk of missing the trade altogether if the stock runs on you with no pullback.

Figure 10.4 shows entry just above a new support level. Depending on how much confirmation you want to see, you can wait for a break over the new high of $20.25, thus effectively deepening the trade-off of more confidence for a worse price.

Notice that the breakdown of different ways to trade the same setup can be applied to any setup. When we describe setups in the following chapters and Part Three, we talk mostly about the regular way of entering a trade, which means "Enter at the trigger level." But this distinction as to the method of entry is always possible and is left to the trader's discretion.

There are endless variations on the way you can play the setup, and what you choose becomes part of your edge. Following are a few more setups to give you more ideas to choose from.

You can let the trigger go and wait for the stock to bounce back into your range. At this point you try to enter as close to the stop level as possible. You will need to find the entry at the moment when the stock stalls

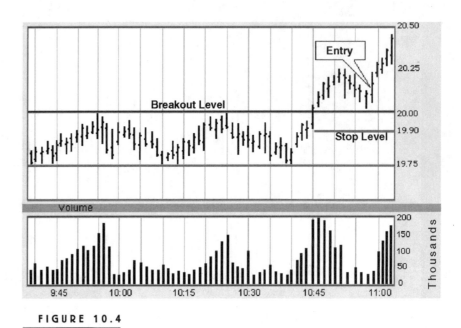

FIGURE 10.4

Method of conservative entry.

and is getting ready to reverse. This way, you can make your stop as tight as possible and your profit potential bigger compared to your entry on the trigger. You also have more confidence as compared to an aggressive entry since your trigger was hit once, thus shaking the confidence of those who believed that the level would hold. Drawbacks are the risk of missing the play altogether if the stock goes in the direction of the setup and never looks back. This play requires perfect timing.

You can enter half of your position at any of the above-mentioned points (at the trigger, near the stop level, before or after the actual trigger) and add another half as the stock hits another indicative point. For instance, if you enter the first half near the stop level, you can add the second half as the stock hits the trigger. Or you can enter the first half at the trigger level, adding the other half if a bounce takes the stock within the range and the action weakens. There are other variations of adding to your position as the stock goes in your favor. Obvious drawbacks are a possible increase in commissions and the possibility of being left with just half of your planned shares if the stock doesn't give you an additional opportunity to enter.

As you can see, setups provide you with structure that you can exploit in any way that matches your risk tolerance, your temperament, and your personal objectives.

There is one more important element to add to your observations: volume. As we know from tape-reading principles, we want volume to increase when the price moves in the direction of our trade. In this case we want volume to rise as price rises and dry up as price pulls back. Figures 10.1, 10.2, and 10.3 include volume to show that we need it to be shaped to increase our confidence in our breakout success.

Now our set of scenarios becomes more complicated. It includes not only the setup structure but also market conditions and our confidence in a successful break. It also includes volume as an element of a general reading of the movement. At the same time there are no more scenarios with the short side since we defined that market as favoring long plays.

The new look of it would be:

1. *If* the market is very strong, *then* we look to buy at the first sign of strength and don't wait for the actual break.
   a. *If* (1) the stock trades over $19.90 and (2) the volume increases on the buying, *then* we enter.
   b. *If* $19.75 is hit, *then* we get stopped.

2. *If* the market is trending but not overly strong, *then* we look to buy the actual breakout.
   a. *If* (1) the stock trades at $20 and (2) the volume increases, *then* we enter.
   b. *If* the price drops to $19.75, *then* we get stopped.

3. *If* the market is uncertain, *then* we look to buy only after the break and a successful retest of new support.
   a. *If* (1) the stock breaks over $20 and (2) we retest it on pullback, and (3) we see volume increase on upward movement and dry up on pullback, *then* we buy it on the first sign of strength over $20.
   b. *If* the stock loses $20, *then* we get stopped at $19.90.

By building scenarios, you can determine your action for any market situation. This is the way in which you discipline yourself and protect yourself from the uncertainty of the market. Instead of trying to guess what the market is going to do next, you determine what you are going to do in response to any development. This is the biggest role that setups play in your trading. They solve the conflict between the necessity of certain action and an uncertain environment.

CHAPTER 11

Stop-Loss Placement and Trailing

We have already discussed the role of stops in trading and the psychological implications of this part of the trader's job. Now we need to see how stops should be placed so that they can do what they are supposed to do, which is to prevent losses from growing on one side and protect us from being taken out of the trade until it's proven no longer valid on the other side.

Let's start with the factors that determine where we put our stop. There are two major factors that influence our decision. The first is market indications of trade failure. We don't want to exit the trade on the first tick that happens not to be in our favor. The market has too much noise, and such an approach would lead to our being shaken out too often. As we discuss in Chapter 10, there are signals that indicate the rising odds of a trade not working. So our stop should be placed under the level that indicates a trade failure if this level is broken. Usually such a level is a level of support for a long side trade (resistance for a short side). The idea is, that if support is broken, we don't want to be long. And, if resistance is broken, we don't want to be short.

Support is often established by the level that a stock has tested several times and bounced off of. It also can be a former resistance that has broken to the upside. After such a break this level acts as support. (This is a commonplace occurrence, so we will refrain from providing explanations of how and why it happens.) Other examples of support are the trend line, the moving average, Fibonacci numbers, and so on. There are different levels of support within different time frames. When supports from several time frames coincide at the same price level, it makes the support more important.

REVISITING RISK MANAGEMENT

The second factor that determines where we put our stop is our risk tolerance. Now and then we face situations in which the price difference between levels indicating trade trigger and trade failure is bigger than what we are willing to tolerate. Should we move our stop closer to the entry price in such cases? No, because it would increase the odds of our being shaken out. This is a mistake we see many newer traders make. Risk management in this kind of situation should determine position size. If our risk is $250 on each given trade, then we go for 1000 shares on the trade with the difference between the trigger and the stop levels being 25 cents. If this difference is 50 cents, we decrease our share size to 500, keeping within our risk parameters and still following market logic.

We need to add two more distinctions here. The first is slippage. If the theoretical price difference between the trigger and the failure level is 25 cents, it doesn't mean that we can get this price automatically in real life. We have to evaluate the risk of slippage, and our major tool for this is Level 2, which allows us to judge the depth of the market for each given stock. As a rule of thumb, signs of a risky stock with the possibility of big slippage are a wide or often-changing spread, a big gap between price levels, small sizes shown by market participants, and few players at each price level. It takes little practice to learn to tell a jumpy, dangerous stock from one that usually trades in an orderly fashion.

The second distinction to risk management is stop padding. This is a more sophisticated technique that factors in attempts by market participants to move the price to the level where most stops are located. This is known as "running the stops." Many traders mistakenly assume that the market makers can see the stops entered in the system. This is not so, but experienced players understand how most traders think, and this understanding allows them to guess where the popular stop levels will be with a high degree of accuracy. Padding means simply moving our stop a little farther, to place it a bit aside from the popular levels so that we won't be easily shaken out. As you can see, the theoretical 25-cent stop can in reality easily turn out to be a 30–35-cent stop. We need to factor this in when we consider our share size.

For simplicity's sake, we discuss long trades. It's easy to apply the same principles to short entries.

Initial Stop Placement

To define the level of an initial stop placement, we need to identify the reason for the trade. Then we can determine the sign of trade failure.

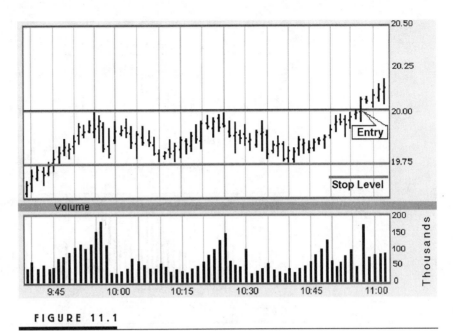

FIGURE 11.1

A breakout trade.

1. Breakout Trade.   A breakout trade is taken on the assumption that, if the stock is trading above a higher limit of the range, then it's going to go higher. The stop should be placed below the support level. Support in this case is defined as the lower limit of the range the stock moved in before breaking out. (See Figure 11.1.)

2. Range Trade.   The reason for entry in a range trade is a bounce from support, assuming that a stock remains within the range. If the lower limit of the range is getting broken, the reason is no longer valid because the assumption hasn't proved correct. The stop should be placed below the lower limit of the range. (See Figure 11.2.)

3. Capitulation Sell-Off.   The entry for a capitulation sell-off is taken on the assumption that panic selling has washed the sellers out and a V-bottom is forming. (See our capitulation setup in Chapter 13.) A V-bottom is a visual representation in which the left side of the V represents sharp selling, the bottom of the V represents the reversal, or pivot, point, and the right side of the V represents sharp buying. The stock is usually trading in uncharted territory for the day, so there are no support levels defined by this day's trading. Considering a higher risk for a larger than expected stop loss due to thin liquidity, this kind of trade's stop loss should be

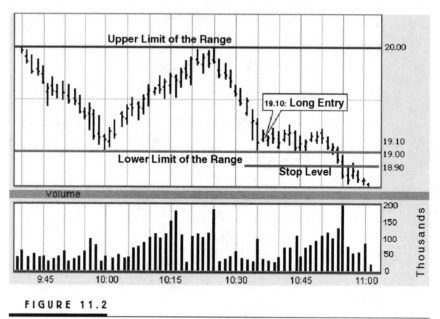

FIGURE 11.2

A range trade.

placed just below the low a stock made on the last decline, within our risk tolerance. In other words, any new low should be considered trade failure. (See Figure 11.3.)

Stop Trailing

As a stock moves in our favor, we want to protect our profits. Usually we combine stop trailing with partialling, or scaling, out, which means the selling of portions of our shares. Most often it's half and half. Sometimes, when the market shows a very strong trend, we can go for half, quarter, and quarter. For example, if we enter with 1000 shares, we can sell 500 and 500 or 500, 250, and 250.

There are some comments that need to be made about this methodology. From the pure statistics point of view, partialling *in* is a better way to trade than is partialling *out*. Do not confuse partialling in with averaging down. Averaging down is adding to your losing position, which we don't do. Adding to your position as it moves in your favor (so-called pyramiding) goes along the lines of "letting your profit run." By partialling out, you limit your profit potential. Also keep in mind that your entry point is usually the point of lowest confidence. As the trade develops, your confidence level rises with new confirmations that your initial

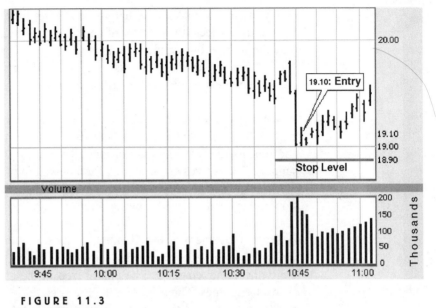

FIGURE 11.3

A capitulation sell-off.

idea is right. It makes perfect sense to enter just part of your position while you have no confirmation and add to it as the market tells you that you are right. If the trade doesn't work, you get stopped with just part of your position. In a real day trader's life, however, other factors come into play. Fast intraday trades do not always allow for multiple entries along with trend, because trends come and go much more quickly than they do for longer time-frame players.

Furthermore, from a purely psychological standpoint it's much easier to keep your position when part of your profit is secured. Of course, psychological comfort is not something that we should let govern our action, as we discuss in Part One. Still, most of us have to maintain mental balance in order not to get burned out from everyday tension. Partialling out serves this purpose well. Is some ways partialling out functions like insurance. In most cases insurance is a waste of money because nothing happens. But in those rare cases when something does happen, insurance saves you from a hard hit. What is it that you insure against when you scale out? It's a trade turning around halfway and hitting your stop. By scaling out, you decrease the size of your win and increase the number of your winners, while still maintaining part of your position in case a stock continues moving in your favor. Insurance also buys you piece of mind, which could be as important as monetary issues. When you trade every day, you need to make sure that you don't get burned out. Again, as with all trading choices it's a matter of personal preference. If you feel you can play the market by scaling in, this is a great accomplishment.

There are several methods to help you determine a new stop placement. They depend on the type of stock movement.

1. Consequent Range Breaks.   Consequent range breaks resemble ladder steps. The stock consolidates under each new resistance level, breaks it, and repeats the cycle. As a resistance level is broken, it becomes a new support. This serves us as an idea for a new stop placement. As usual, we don't want to stay long in a stock that loses support, so we place the new stop under this level, as shown in Figure 11.4.

2. Trend Movement in the Channel.   Trend movement in the channel is presented by a series of breaks and pullbacks without the consolidation stage. Price movement can be chambered in the channel, which consists of two trend lines. The price hits the lower envelope of this channel before bouncing back, and then makes a new high while remaining within the same channel. As it happens, we trail the stop so that it's placed right under the lower envelope on each pullback. In this case, this lower line presents the support, and we want to be out if this line is broken. If the

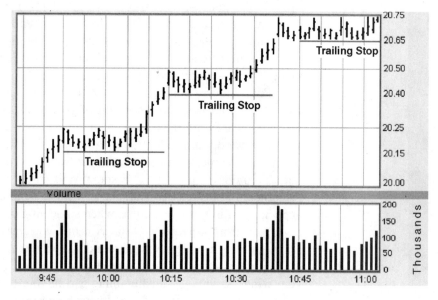

FIGURE 11.4

Consequent range breaks.

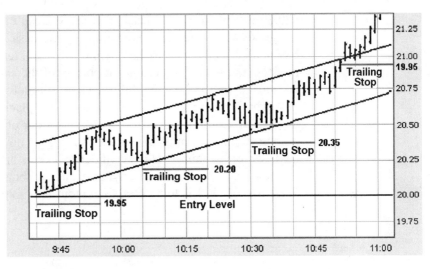

FIGURE 11.5

Trend movement in the channel.

price breaks the upper envelope and moves vertically up, we face the euphoria stage of the movement, and the stop should be moved under the upper line. (See Figure 11.5.)

CONFIDENCE LEVELS

The concept of confidence levels helps us resolve a contradiction that we often have to face. Here is the contradiction: Let's say that your position in a stock goes in your favor to a price level that allows you to trail the stop. Then it retraces from there without hitting your stop. If it's showing strong signs of reversal, what are you to do? You have your discipline demanding that you stick to your plan, while you have a strong feeling that the plan should be altered. This is the eternal conflict between the system and discretionary trading. We feel strongly that any system for intraday trading should allow for a certain amount of discretion. Confidence levels work, in fact, as an indication that it's time to alter the plan. Here is the idea of their placement and use.

Let's say you bought a stock at $20, partialled out at $20.50, and are now trying to let the profit run on the second portion. As the stock breaks the next resistance at $20.75, you trail your stop to $20.45, in accordance with the principles discussed above. Now, $20.75 is getting taken out on the upside, and the stock stalls at $20.95, which gives you a strong feeling that $21 will not be taken out. You don't feel that a trailing stop to

$20.70 is a good idea, because this level doesn't show good support. It cannot serve as a reliable indication of weakness if this level is broken. Essentially, it all comes to the dilemma of, "Do I let the stock hit the trailing stop and give up a significant portion of the current paper profit? Or do I take the profit now and kill the chance for a bigger move?"

That's where we use a confidence level, placing it at $20.75. If this level is broken on the downside, we change our original plan. While our trailing stop is still in place, our exit strategy is now to sell our shares on the first worthy bounce. If the confidence level is broken, we don't expect the stock to go to new highs anymore, and any bounce between the price range $20.90–$21 is to be used to exit our remaining shares.

CHAPTER 12

Trading Setups

In this chapter, we discuss setups that we apply in our everyday trading. They will look familiar to an experienced trader although there is a certain spin on classic setups. For instance, the well-known cup-and-handle formation is tweaked somewhat for intraday trading. Also, such a commonly known setup as the ascending (descending) triangle has a certain twist that we describe.

Most of our setups with the exception of capitulation and euphoria are trend-continuation formations. Capitulation and euphoria are the only trend-reversal setups in our arsenal. But, as you know from the previous discussion, there are many ways to trade the same setup. If a trade fails as a trend continuation, it could be faded for a trend reversal. This approach is in keeping with what we discuss about the role of setups. Although they do not predict the direction itself, they show the signs of direction, and if the signs tell us that upward movement has failed, then a short could be justified. Breaking of the stop level indicates failure. Breaking of the stop level before the setup is triggered invalidates the setup. This way we can define a stop level as a level for fading the setup. This is also known as trading of pattern failure and can be one's trading style.

Also, as you know from early chapters, every setup can be played with a different degree of aggressiveness. So, as you see the description of the setup with a recommendation to buy on the breakout (regular entry), you can apply to this all the possibilities we discuss earlier: buying before confirmation or buying after the breakout and test of new support.

JUMP-BASE–EXPLOSION (JBE) SETUP

The jump-base–explosion setup can be described as consolidation near the high after initial upward movement. The idea of this setup is that an initial upward movement (the J phase) shows the direction of major interest. Then a stock meets resistance and consolidates under this level (the B phase). If the stock is strong enough to stay close to the resistance level without sharp retracement, it means that the path of least resistance is still upward and that the stock is likely to continue in the same direction as soon as it digests the distribution. We prefer the range of the consolidation to be narrow, usually not more than 25 cents. The first stage of the setup (Jump) should be not less than 1.5 times, but preferably 2 times, the size of the range (Base). With a range of 25 cents we get ideally 50 cents or more of the initial movement.

This setup has several variations. They differ by the formation within the consolidation range.

1. Flatline at the High.   Entry should be taken as the flatline makes a new high. The stop is placed under the nearest support, or, if the initial run-up has no pullbacks to indicate where support is, the stop is defined by risk tolerance. (See Figure 12.1.)

2. Consolidation after a Shallow Pullback.   Volume should decrease on the consolidation phase. The buy signal is a break of the upper limit of the range (U). The stop is placed under the lower limit of the range (L). (See Figure 12.2.)

3. Narrow Range Near the High. Volume should dry up on pullbacks and increase on upward pushes. Buy and stop triggers are similar to setup 2. (See Figure 12.3.)

4. Ascending Triangle.   The ascending triangle is similar to setups 2 and 3, with a somewhat stronger indication of successful breakout. This setup is similar to the classic ascending triangle, with the only distinction being that we want this formation to occur within the consolidation range. (See Figure 12.4.)

DROP-BASE–IMPLOSION (DBI) SETUP

The drop-base–implosion setup mirrors the JBE on the downside for a short play. Everything that was valid for the JBE setup is valid for the DBI as well. It has the same formations and the same rules for entry and stop placement. An ascending triangle is going to reverse to a descending one, of course. (See Figure 12.5.)

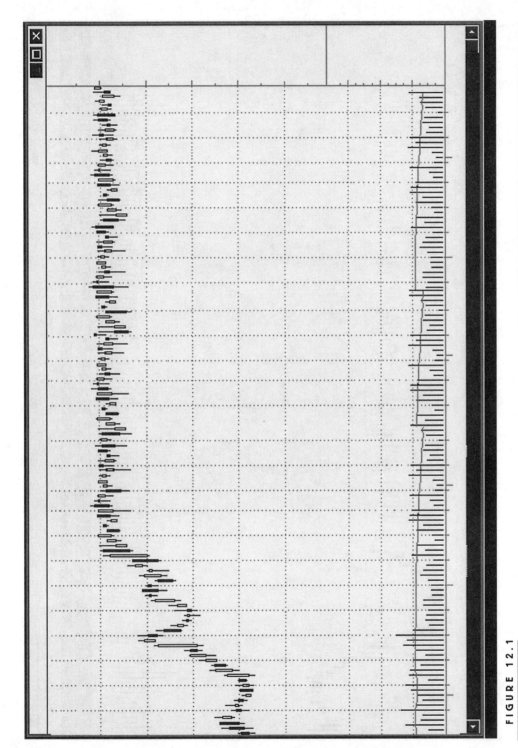

FIGURE 12.1

Flatline at the high.

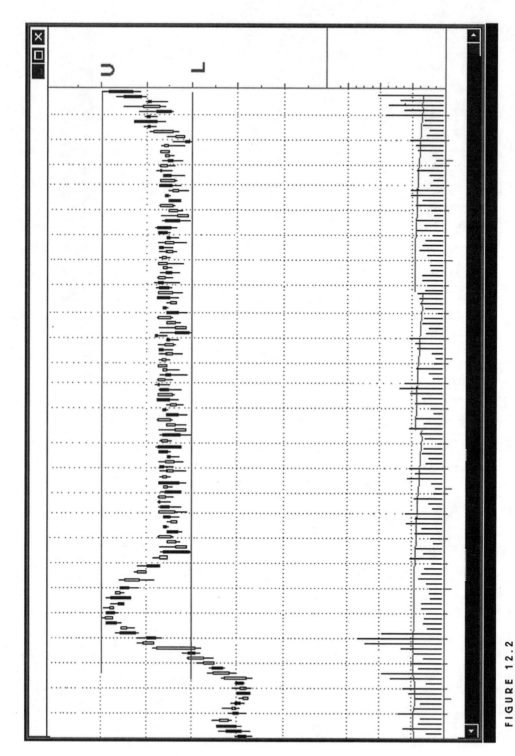

FIGURE 12.2

Consolidation after a shallow pullback.

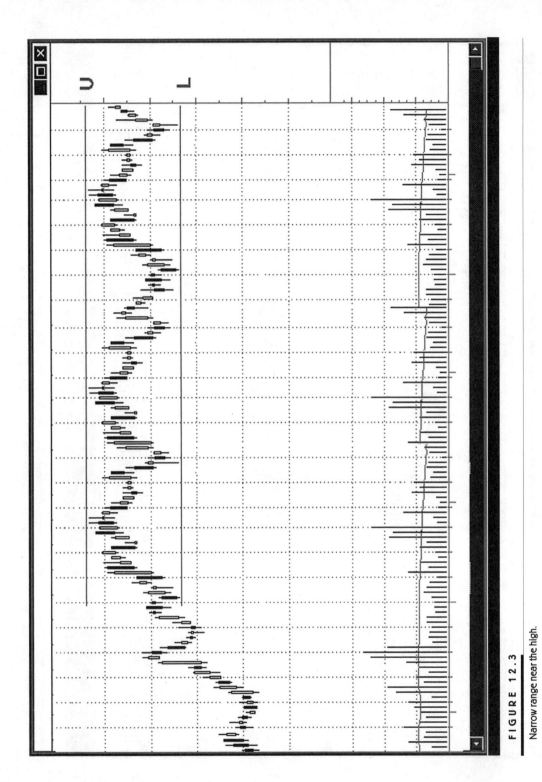

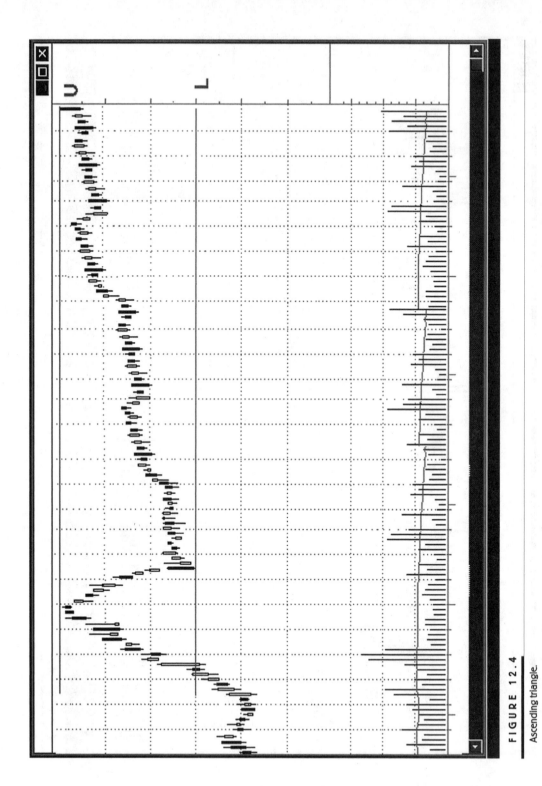

FIGURE 12.4

Ascending triangle.

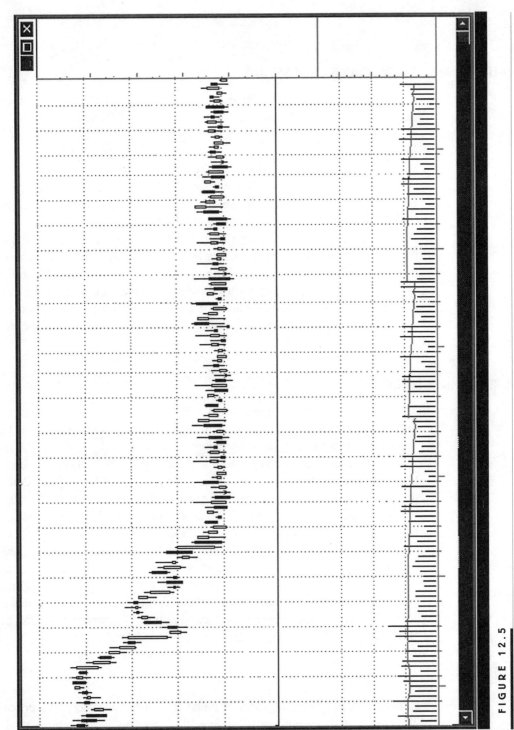

FIGURE 12.5

Drop-base—Implosion setup.

OPEN-HIGH– AND OPEN-LOW–BREAK SETUPS

Open-high– and open-low–break setups are breaks of the range that are played similarly to JBE and DBI setups. The only difference is that these are setups for the beginning of the trading day, so they usually don't have initial movement. The idea is to define the most likely direction of the price movement by the direction of the break of the opening range.

For these setups we want the stock to move within the range, not more than 25 cents. These are setups for the first 15–20 minutes of the trading day.

If the stock breaks the high of the range, we go long with the stop at the low of the range. If the stock breaks the low of the range, we go short with a stop at the high of the range. Since the opening is often quite volatile, this setup is frequently used for scalps unless the market shows a strong trend. Scalpers look for a 1:1 or 2:1 ratio of reward to risk. Holders scale out into a 2:1 reward/risk ratio and look for a trend. (See Figures 12.6 and 12.7.)

CUP-AND-HANDLE SETUP

The cup and handle is also a breakout setup and is very common for longer time frames. It works best on a day's high, although it can be applied in the middle of the daily range as well.

In Figure 12.8, points 1 and 3 are the cup edges at the day's high. Point 2 is the cup bottom. The volume should dry up close to point 2 and pick up close to points 1 and 3. The cup should continue for a minimum of 30 minutes. But more than 30 minutes is desirable. In our experience, the optimal time for a cup forming is 1 hour or more.

Point 4 is the bottom of the handle, and volume should dry up here. The handle should not have retracement deeper than 50 percent of cup depth. The volume should pick up at point 5. The handle should continue no longer than 30 percent of the time of cup formation, 25 percent is desirable. The stop is placed below the handle bottom. The entry point can be taken aggressively or conservatively as described earlier.

CAPITULATION

Capitulation is a reversal setup. It's that fast, sharp decline with vertical movement and volume-pace pickup that are necessary components because they suggest panic.

Capitulation is one of the riskiest setups. It requires fast reactions and well-developed scalping skills because it sometimes provides just a

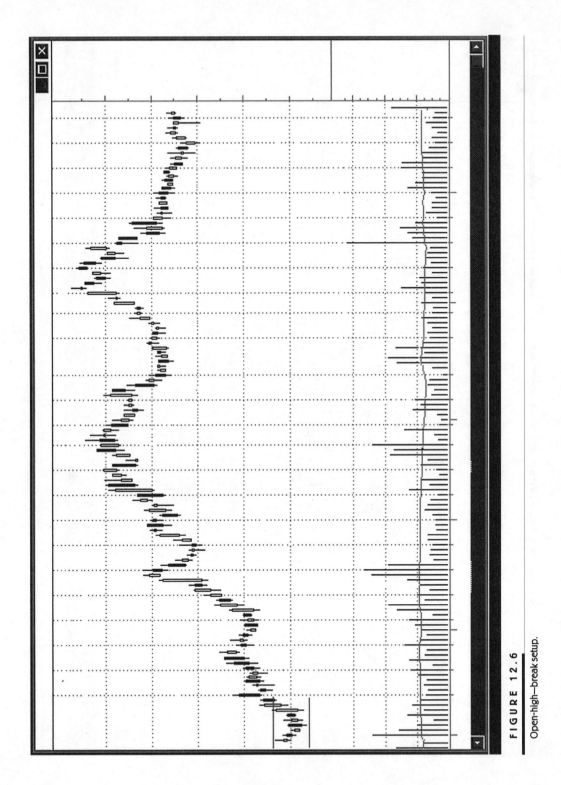

FIGURE 12.6 Open–high–break setup.

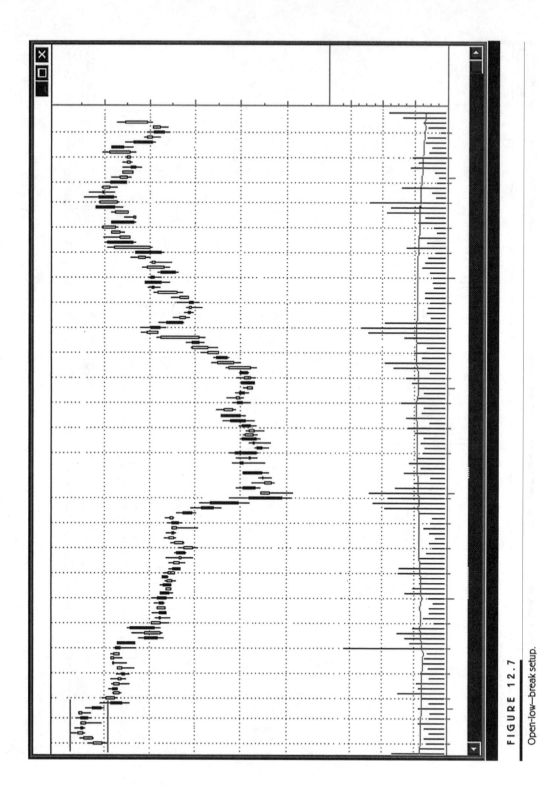

FIGURE 12.7

Open-low—break setup.

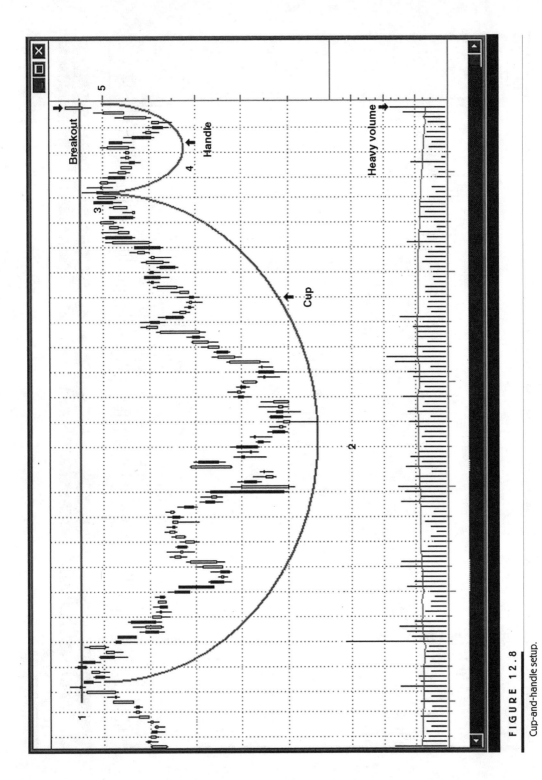

FIGURE 12.8

Cup-and-handle setup.

133

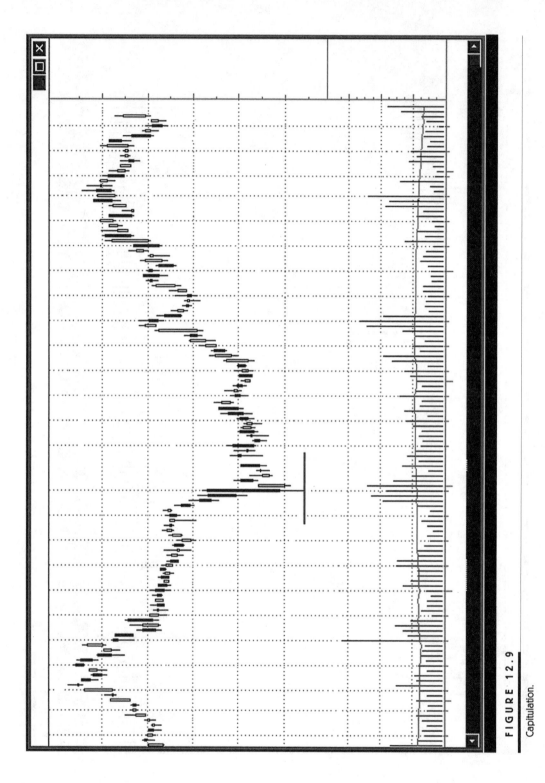

FIGURE 12.9

Capitulation.

small, quick bounce. It could be treated as a scalp or as a hold for the recovery, depending on market conditions. A stop is placed under the level that the stock has bounced from as discussed in previous chapters.

Keep in mind that this setup is more conceptual than others. It doesn't have an exact indication of how big the vertical drop should be to provide the best chances for a profitable entry. In practical examples cited in Part Three, you will see that this setup contains a much bigger "art" element compared to others. (See Figure 12.9.)

We do not describe euphoria as a separate setup here. It's an exact mirror of capitulation. The main reason for not including it in our list of setups is that we avoid shorting strong stocks altogether until we see clear reversal. Shorting strong stocks can be even more dangerous than buying capitulation. In Chapter 13 and in practical examples, we discuss the signs of trend reversal that we use for shorting the upward move exhaustion.

TRADER'S ACTION

Following is an algorithm of the action traders should take when a signal is generated:

1. Define the setup by comparing a stock chart to the charts of setups.
2. Evaluate the risk by volume and the look of Level 2. If you see low volume, a big spread, thin levels, small sizes shown by market participants, and/or a wide gap between levels, you know this is a high-risk stock. Skip the trade altogether or lower your share size. Be prepared to limit your expectations to scalp.
3. Define the trigger point and stop level as the setup suggests.
4. Evaluate the stop from the perspective of your risk tolerance. If the stop exceeds the size of the loss dictated by your risk management, lower your share size or skip the trade altogether.
5. Define the conditions that work in favor of the setup and the conditions that invalidate it.
   - If the stock breaks the stop level before triggering, then the setup is invalidated.
   - If the stock moves in sync with the Nasdaq-100 (NDX), you need the NDX directional support for the setup to achieve a higher probability of working.
   - If the stock moves with no relation to the NDX, you need the NDX to be in favor or neutral to the direction of the setup. Do not take the trade if the NDX moves sharply against your setup direction.

6. Define the conditions of fading the setup. If the stock breaks the stop level before triggering and you get the NDX working against the setup, then fading is a reasonable trade.

7. Define your approach to the trade in terms of aggressiveness depending on market mood. Be aggressive in a trending market and conservative in a choppy market. Pick your method of entry as the setups suggest.

8. As your entry is triggered, initiate the trade without hesitation.

9. Monitor your trade as it develops. Don't let the movements within the range confuse or rattle you. Your trade is stopped out only when the stop is hit. The stop was placed there for a reason. Don't change your mind in the middle of action—most likely it's your emotions talking.

10. As the stock moves in your favor, wait for a clear exit signal to close the trade in full, or partial it out. According to tape-reading principles, slow movement with steady volume indicates a stage where you continue to hold your position. Vertical spikes with sharp volume increases indicate an area and time interval to exit, either fully or partially. Be willing to exit in full in a choppy market by taking the scalp. Ride your position in a trending market, protecting the profit by partialling out and trailing the stop.

CHAPTER 13

Trading Market Ranges and Miscellaneous Points

In this chapter we review some points and cases that "surround" our trading system, so to speak. By this we refer to situations that are not central to our system but that occur too often to be ignored. Also, we discuss those situations that present a particular danger.

As you have seen from the previous discussion, our trading system is trend-oriented. However, the market is not always trending. Despite the fact that trends are relatively easy to find in the small time frames in which we trade, now and then we run into a ranging market. You need recipes for this market condition.

TRADING RANGES

There are three types of ranges we would like to discuss. Those are *regular, narrow,* and *expanding.* Each requires a different approach and presents a different challenge. We have to add that as for trend traders, a ranging market is very tough for us, and we tend to decrease our trading activity when we run into range days.

Regular Range

A regular range is wide enough to allow traders to profit from the movement within the range. Unlike a trending environment, this range requires that traders buy low and sell high. The major challenge is to tell the range from the trend early enough. If traders fail to identify the ranging market, they are destined to lose on false breakout attempts. Usually, if we see the market test the low and high twice and hold, we go into range-trading mode.

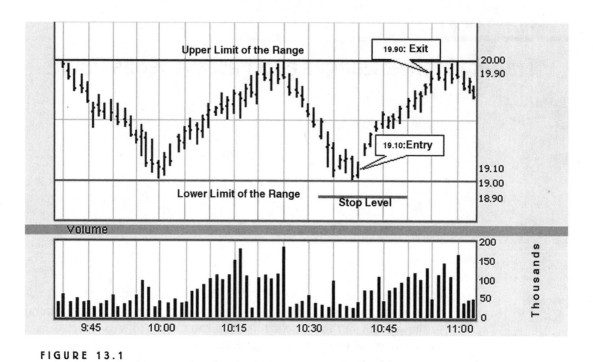

FIGURE 13.1

Regular range.

When you are trading the range, you need to buy at the first sign of strength as the market bounces from the low, or short at the first sign of weakness as the high is holding. Stop placement is self-explanatory, just outside of range bounds (see Figure 13.1). The exit point in this case is just below the upper limit of the range.

If you see the volume rising on upward movement and decreasing in the downward stage, you might want to try to let your profits run. In order to give your profits room if the market breaks the range, you can scale out of your position by selling half your shares at this point. A trailing stop for another half should be placed just below midrange. In Figure 13.2, a stop would be placed at $19.40–$19.45.

The idea behind this is based on the assumption that if a stock is going to break out of the range, it should bounce off $19.50 in most cases. If it's going under the midrange, then most likely the stock will remain range-bound. If a stock is breaking out of the range, then your new stop level should be $19.80–$19.90, just under new support, which forms at $20—former resistance, as discussed in Chapter 12. In this scenario a new set of rules comes into play. Now it would be a trend trade, and the exit should be made as discussed in Chapter 12.

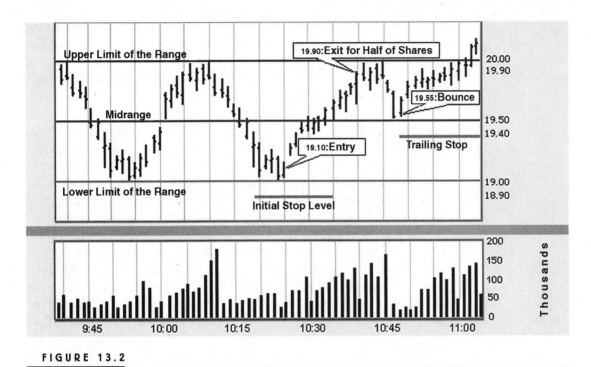

FIGURE 13.2

Trading within the range.

Narrow Range

Trading in a narrow-range market is very difficult. Unless you are just scalping small movements, all you can do is to wait for the breakout of the range. The time in which a market is locked in narrow limits can and should be used for preparing for the break, which means identifying candidates you will consider trading when the break finally occurs.

The problem with a narrow range is that you can't trade within it because as soon as the stock (index) bounces from the low, it's already almost near the high limit of the range, and you have no room for a profitable entry and exit. Attempting to buy at the bottom of the range or short the top is too risky since you have no clear indication that range is not getting broken, and, even if your entry is correct, the reward is too small and doesn't justify the risk.

So, the only thing we are left with is the attempt to play the break out of the range. In order to place odds in our favor, we need to select the stock that will break with high enough probability, or, at least, one that won't go all the way back to the opposite end of the range if the break fails.

We need to play the stock that is stronger than the broad market for a long trade or weaker than the market for a short trade. The idea of this search is quite simple, yet many traders make many losing trades during narrow market conditions because they try to bet on a break without properly selecting the candidates.

For a long trade, the stock needs to hang near the high while the market pulls back to the lower limit of the range. If we get such a stock, then we have a very good chance for it to break its upper limit as the market merely bounces from its lower limit. This situation is shown in Figure 13.3, in which the stock chart is combined with the NDX chart.

As our long candidate breaks the upper limit, we enter it long, making sure that the market is holding the lower limit of the range and bouncing off it. Now, if the market goes to the upper limit of its range, our stock is likely to go with it and often may be even stronger because it's being identified by many traders as a strong one worth trading in an unsure market. If the bounce fails and the market breaks down, our risk on this stock is minimal, because its relative strength won't allow it in most cases to go down as fast as the broader market, and our stop will be as usual. If we

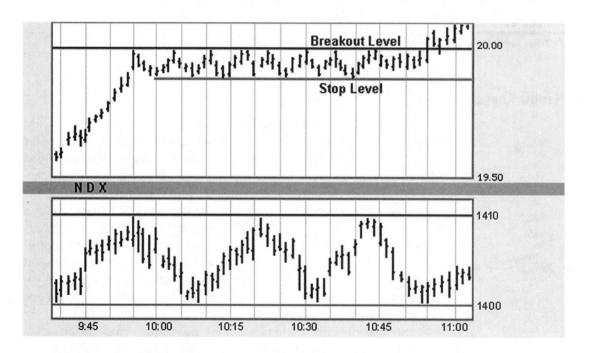

FIGURE 13.3

Trading a breakout from a narrow range.

were to buy the stock that goes up and down in the range with the market, we would practically bet on market direction. In the first case we use the market as an indicator. This is a major difference. The first case is gambling; the second is going with the odds using the relative strength of a particular stock as an indication of its being a likely candidate.

Also keep in mind that this approach is useful as a backup plan in trending markets. As the market is going up, you are playing breakouts and effectively are going with trend. But you need to have a couple of candidates on the back burner for short play in case the market reverses. Instead of guessing which strong stocks will reverse with the broader market, you are shorting those that were weak before and didn't break down because of the overall market strength. As soon as the market weakens, this support disappears and the breakdown comes. A similar approach can be used for finding candidates for a long play during a downtrending market, where you would buy the breakout on market reversal from the lows.

Expanding Range

The expanding range is the worst market we've ever encountered. It is always costing us stop after stop. This is the market that makes new highs, just above the upper limit of the range, then drops all the way back to the low, breaks it, and, instead of continuing to the downside, it bounces all the way back up, repeating the cycle. See Figure 13.4 for an example.

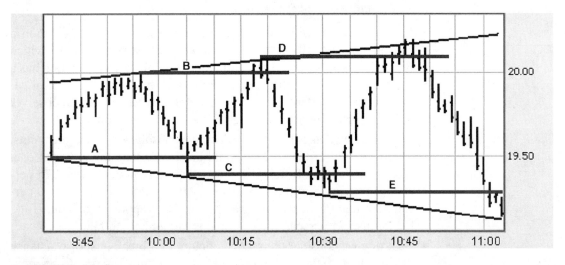

FIGURE 13.4

Expanding range.

A widening range with no continuation on any side makes it very hard to read the movement. Here is what happens when a trader tries to play this kind of market. As level A is getting broken, trend traders go short. Instead of a continuation, the market bounces, stopping them out. At the same time, the breakdown doesn't allow going long for a range trade. As level B is touched, traders don't go short because of the breakout, but attempting to go long won't work either. A spike over the breakout level is too small to allow any room for profit, and the market drops back effectively, stopping the traders out. This vicious cycle repeats at levels C, E, and D. This kind of action is very hard to recognize in time. In theory, you can reverse your position as the market bounces and breaks your stop level. In reality, this is much easier said than done. You can't recognize this kind of action on a first or second failed break, and you don't know which of the failures is going to be the last one.

MISCELLANEOUS POINTS

We would now like to go over some miscellaneous points—those fine distinctions that allow us to correct our action, those factors that should be taken into consideration in a particular situation. These points serve as a means of finessing our system and allow us to adapt. When your system tells you, "If you see A, then do B," these fine distinctions tell you, "Unless you see C." With experience traders can collect plenty of these points that help them hone their systems, and make them more adjustable, more flexible, and more "personal."

- In setups with consolidation, the time factor is important. Too short a consolidation usually leads to a fast, short-lived vertical spike which often signals reversal. At the same time, too long a consolidation has a greater chance to fail. It's hard to define the optimal time of consolidation, since it is different for active and dull markets. A careful observer can develop an intuitive feeling of "too short" and "too long."

- When a stock makes several consecutive consolidations and breakouts, each next step of the ladder should be shorter than the previous one. Ideally the length of each next step is between 50 percent and 75 percent of the length of the previous step. If this ratio is less than 50 percent, the trend is accelerating and is likely to approach its end. If it's bigger than 75 percent, the breakout is more likely to fail.

- As a rule we consider the second attempt of a break (test of resistance or support) to be more likely to fail, and the third attempt to be more likely to succeed.

- In a double-top scenario we look to enter a short position when the price drops below the bottom located between two tops. The stop is placed above the top. We do not short the second top itself.
- In a double-bottom scenario we look to enter a long position when the price rises above the top located between two lows. The stop is placed below the low. We do not buy the second bottom itself.
- When a stock goes through consolidation and you intend to play the break of the consolidation range, avoid entry of the trigger if a stock spikes sharply right into the trigger level. This scenario tends to produce traps rather than valid breakouts. The ideal case is to go slowly approaching the trigger level and orderly break.
- When you select your candidate for a breakout by the narrow-range method discussed earlier in this chapter, make sure it's not a stock that by its nature moves in the opposite direction of the market. Sometimes certain sectors act like this; gold stock in the fall of 2002 is an example. If you fail to take this into consideration, you would most likely buy for such a stock breakout when the market is bouncing, although this is the time for this stock to retreat.
- When you are looking for an uptrend reversal after a strong move, you want to see a stock losing the latest support it has formed on its way up. Avoid shorting euphoria itself since it can easily turn out to be a shallow pullback or new consolidation. Rather you want to see a stock pulling back to the support level, bouncing on the decreasing volume without making a new high, retreating back to the support, and breaking it. This break is a trigger for a short entry.
- A similar approach can be used for the reversal of a downtrend.
- When you are trading a stock that follows NDX movements, superimpose its chart onto that of the NDX to find out how much in sync they are. The best trading candidates are those that move with a slight lag because this allows using the NDX as the leading indicator.
- The process of finding the leading indicator can consist of two steps, including the sector index. It makes the selection of trading candidates and timing of entries and exits more fine-tuned, although somewhat more cumbersome. Some of the most popular are the Semiconductor index (SOX) and the Biotechnology index (BTK).

PART THREE

Practical Examples

In Part Three, we provide a number of practical examples, which are trades taken from the actual experiences of both authors and dissected to illustrate the decision-making process.

In those cases in which the trade was explained to and traded by our students, you will see comments such as "I would" rather than "I did."

The trades that are presented here were made over a number of years, so you will see fractions on some of them and decimals on others. We decided to leave each trade as it was so as not to distort perception. This demonstrates that no matter what changes are being made in technology, the core of the market remains the same, and the principles based on human reactions remain intact. Different time frames are used in the charts, from 1 minute and higher, to show that traders within any time frame can apply the principles.

You will see that many of the trades were based not only on pure tape reading but also in combination with simple technical analysis. We do not intend to go into depth in those studies. There are plenty of great books written on the subject. Rather our task is to show how you can add tape reading to your favorite indicators in order to deepen your understanding.

In the description of the trades, you will see many references to the psychological issues discussed in Part One. Also, there are some repetitions in applying different tape-reading principles. The authors did this deliberately because we want this part to be a way of "putting it all together" for both the technical and the psychological side of trading. We want each trade to be as finished and as self-contained a review as possible, to show the entire process of a trader's thinking as events develop in real time. The repetition of major points that shape up each trade is intended to reinforce the correct approach to any trading situation.

EXAMPLE 1

Accumulation and Distribution

We have already discussed distribution/accumulation principles, which are important because these two principles are often applied by the smart money long before the public catches onto this kind of movement. For example, on this day, Portal Software (PRSF) had news concerning a contract with AOL. (See Figure EX1.) Forgive me for not remembering exactly what the news was. I'm a trader, not an investor, so I'm unaware of exactly what it was. The week prior to this day, PRSF was strong—solid uptrends, no really nasty pullbacks, and so forth. These are normally signs of accumulation from some defined level. Whether this accumulation occurs in anticipation of something or whether it derives from inside knowledge or whatever doesn't really matter. It is how the accumulation behaves that we traders watch for. Buying is slow, stable, not many sharp

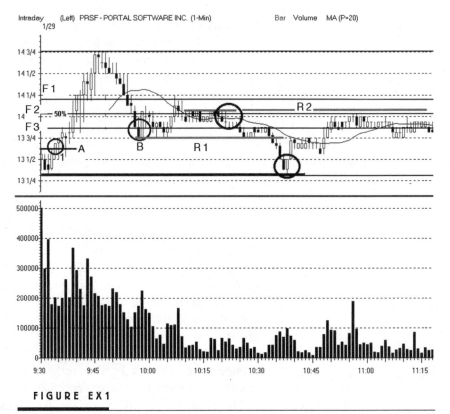

FIGURE EX1

Accumulation and distribution. (*RealTick graphics are used with permission of Townsend Analytics, Ltd.*)

price increases. Pullbacks are shallow and supported. As far as I remember, PRSF didn't have any news catalyst from the Friday before, so it was trading maybe in anticipation of the AOL news that was leaked somewhere. Who knows? It could have easily been a major fund or funds wanting to buy it at current levels. The point is that we had a bit of a run, for whatever reason, into Monday.

The AOL news brought outside attention to the stock, meaning those who weren't watching it from Friday's action now had a reason to watch it. The public was alerted. When stocks are being accumulated, for some type of event, the next phase is distribution. The principle, "The public is always the last to know" or "Buy the rumor, sell the news" usually leads to distribution at some higher level on the day any public attention is drawn to the stock. Therefore, for PRSF on this day, I was looking for a good, defined range and to have a short setup with expectations that this day would have a reasonable distribution at high levels. There were morning impressions of the stock showing the strong gap up on the AOL news. Note that I didn't want to short the gap just because it was up too high or short it. The stock already made its run; it wouldn't hold. This is usually how an amateur thinks and often gets killed because of it.

I wanted to see a reasonable range defined and to trade from the continuation of either direction, with expectations that I would see the sell-off. By defining the ranges, instead of just gambling on some arbitrary figure, I can bring structure to the trade and review my entries and exits, using reality, not thoughts of "I thought it would. . . ." So with my initial impression developed, based on the principles of accumulation/distribution, let's look at the three areas that were tradable.

The first area was a long entry based on the open-break trade. Here is the setup. The stock made an open high of 13^5/_8$ and made small downticks to 13^5/_{16}$ to 13^3/_8$ showing. At this level the support was still strong, and nearly 13^1/_2$ to 13^5/_8$ was showing as some reasonable resistance in the premarket. Had we tested 13^5/_8$ and failed, the short setup we planned to take was a break of 13^3/_8$, with a stop at 13^5/_8$. I then looked for distribution principles to take my stock lower at the open. It didn't break lower because support was strong, the volume was increasing as we approached the open high of 13^5/_8$, and I felt it was a reasonable and fairly safe entry. In Figure EX1, circle 1 represents the buy area on the chart. Line A is the open high-resistance level showing the confirmation of the open-high break. With the risk moderate and the stock still strong, we now needed to define our exit strategies.

Exit strategies are different for everyone. You can be a scalper, a holder, or a swing type of trader. Define who you are and follow our comments as we discuss each setup or trade. Remember, sometimes who you are differs from day to day because the day is trending or the range is bound or maybe something within you feels great or not so great.

If PRSF was to set up on the long side, it would have to break $13⅝ as a confirmation trigger. The stop would be $13⁵/₁₆ support. For a reasonable reward/risk ratio, the stock would have to clear $14. Those who like to scalp the stock would look for a move into $13⅞ to scale out.

Our first exit strategy is for scalpers and those who wish to take quick profits in the early going. Usually, this is where we see areas of volume/price increases with the first resistance for longs/support for shorts. This occurred right under $14. An ISLD offer at $13¹³/₁₆ to $13⅞ would have been for scalpers. Holders continued with the same plan—stop at the low of the day, $13⁵/₁₆ in this case.

For holders, our plan was now to look for the over $14 area in order for our reward/risk ratio to always be at least 1:1. This means that if you have a ¼-point stop, you need at least a ¼-point gain to serve it. As the stock began to climb to $14 and over to nearly $14⅛, we saw another volume increase telling us this was where we wanted at least half our shares to be exited. Remember, volume and/or price spikes are areas where stocks need to be exited with current positions held. It's a function of our tape-reading principles. As we climbed to serve 1:1 reward/risk ratio, we then began to trail stops on the remaining shares to breakeven levels. As we began to show some resistance and volume decrease near the $14½ to $14¾ level, we wanted to lock in profits on another portion at least (assuming we had enough shares to make it worthwhile). At this point we trailed our stop again. This is where we begin to use Fibonacci retracement levels to aid us. The lines F1, F2, and F3 in Figure EX1 going across the chart illustrate this. The first being 38 percent; the second, 50 percent; and the last, 62 percent.

In cases such as this, traders have two options. They can trail the stop tighter to the $14¼ area where the first retracement level is or trail it to the last retracement level, which would be $13⅞. On the fast-pace increase from $14 to $13¾, the scenario is set for the scalp reversal players. Just as fast spikes/volume spikes are areas for covering shorts or exiting longs, we can also use them as reversal pivots for entry, sometimes just for scalping. It depends on the trade. In this case, at $13¾, support was strong, and $13¹³/₁₆ was slowly melting. This made for a reasonable scalp entry for traders with the worst-case stop being $13⅝, which should have been easy to keep, certainly no worse than $13⁹/₁₆ if we really had to get out. On the move back to $14, scalpers exit, and holders of the stock from $13⅝ can take profits on the support bounce from $13¾. From this point, we have no more clear setups, so we let the stock decide what it wants to do.

Our morning impressions were to look for distribution, but not to gamble on it. The breakout of the open-high and pullback scalp trades were valid. Tape-reading principles for entry and exit and chart analysis for trailing stops defined our exit strategy. Now, we had one more play on it. The bounce from $13\frac{3}{4}$ went to $14\frac{1}{8}$ and stalled. I had an inkling that distribution was still an impression, so I wanted to look for a short setup. In this case the range was $13\frac{3}{4}$ to $14\frac{1}{8}$. The play from point B (on Figure EX1) on the scalp reversal leads us to the range defined.

This is shown by lines R1 and R2. Now traders have two options. They can short the high of the range, or they can wait for confirmation of the break of the low and try the short. As we've said before, trading the confirmation is tougher, because the uptick rule doesn't always allow entry into the short. When I find reasonable chart resistance and the high-range resistance is solid, I have no problem taking a short entry at the high of the minirange. In reviewing the trade, I set the stop a bit wider than it had to be: $14\frac{1}{2}$ seemed to be $\frac{1}{4}$ point higher than where I would have liked to have it, but hindsight is 20/20. I used $14\frac{1}{2}$ mainly because it was where the stock began to slow on the tape on the run-up. Fibonacci analysis says that $14\frac{1}{4}$ would be plenty. Either would be fine, depending on which you choose to follow.

As we failed to break $14\frac{1}{8}$ a few times, I began to get an intuitive feeling that it would drop below the support we'd defined, so we went with shorting before the confirmation of the breakdown. This was at $13\frac{13}{16}$ to $13\frac{7}{8}$ depending on where we could get in. I think we saw most at $13\frac{13}{16}$, which was fine. Now that we had entry, we looked for an exit strategy. Once again, we were using support principles as well as tape-reading principles to define the strategy. The break of the $13\frac{3}{4}$ support level and then the $13\frac{5}{8}$ level (as resistance at the open became support on the pullback) confirmed that our downtrend was intact.

Once we got confirmation, we looked for fast selling/volume spike/price spike to cover at least half the shares. When the stock broke $13\frac{5}{8}$, selling began to pick up. When it broke $13\frac{1}{2}$, it became very fast and erratic, offering a great place for scalpers to exit and for holders to exit at least half. I would have liked it to break $13\frac{3}{8}$ for a move to near $13, but when the volume increase on the tape showed us a signal, we took it. From this point, we still had our stop at $14\frac{1}{8}$ on the remaining shares unless we trailed it tighter to breakeven, which was reasonable. For those holding, we still had a tight range, one from which we had no idea what it would do from that point. With half our shares remaining, as long as the risk stayed low, we had no problem holding with the stop plan set and looking for a possible breakdown.

I often find it interesting how our position can dictate what we want to see. Don't let your position dictate what you "want" to see; see what is in front of you. What is in front of us is a stock stuck in a tight range, almost evenly matched. But the short position seems to dictate the short-side bias. In this range, there is nothing more you can determine from the current action other than "it's stuck." Let it do what it wants to do from here and take a stop or more profit. Or, if boredom outweighs greed, then you have the option of exiting with a small loss or gain.

In summary, our initial impressions were based on accumulation/distribution principles. Reality allowed us to go long for a nice play and to scalp for little profits. The short setup offered us entry on a range defined. In each exit, tape-reading principles were defined, shown, and profitable.

EXAMPLE 2

Entry on Pullback

Figure EX2 is a chart of Extreme Networks (EXTR). It shows an example of a pullback into a support area off the move of over $24 on a fairly nice volume climb that moved with the market. When I'm bidding support areas, these are the questions I ask myself:

Risk evaluation—does the stock have tight levels and enough size participation at these levels?

What route would work best in this situation for what I'm seeing on the bid?

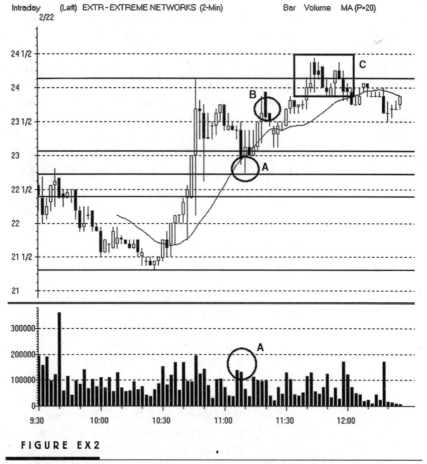

FIGURE EX2

Entry on pullback. (*RealTick graphics are used with permission of Townsend Analytics, Ltd.*)

What is my stop price?

Where is my first resistance area if this pivot works?

Where is my last resistance area if this pivot works?

What is the share size based on risk evaluation?

EXTR was a stock that could get ugly at times, and fast selling often decreased size participation causing at least one-eighth in slippage, if not closer to one-quarter. Therefore I decided that 500 shares was my risk tolerance, not a full 1000 lot by any means. I entered a bid at $22\frac{3}{4}$ with an ISLD order, since I didn't see much ISLD size ahead of me at this level. The reason I chose $22\frac{3}{4}$ was that the market was making a fairly reasonable pullback off its wave of buying and I didn't feel that first Fibonacci level was the best price on relatively slow selling.

I wanted some faster-paced selling to take me to the 50 percent or 62 percent level instead. I used the 50 percent level at $22\frac{3}{4}$ as the area where I saw the increase in selling (see circle A on volume chart) which brought the stock to $22\frac{3}{4}$. The bid was thick at $22\frac{3}{4}$, so I felt safe enough that, if I was wrong, I wouldn't get hammered on my stop with a 500 order. I placed it on ISLD. I was second in line hoping for a panicky seller to hit me. As it turned out, I wasn't filled and didn't have time to reverse and hit the offer when it did hold at $22\frac{3}{4}$ and bounced. I wasn't willing to buy higher than $22\frac{13}{16}$ and the best available was $22\frac{7}{8}$. I got filled with my 500 shares, so then it was time to go with a stop-price strategy. I was using the last Fibonacci level at $22\frac{7}{16}$ for this purpose, figuring that if it lost that price, I would not be confident in the uptrend. So I risked about $\frac{3}{8}$ on the trade.

The first resistance area was $23\frac{1}{4}$, which, if filled, would have given me my 1:1 reward/risk ratio if I had to take it. The last resistance was just over $23\frac{1}{2}$, and you can see how $23\frac{3}{4}$ was showing fairly good resistance (see circle B on Figure EX2). So my downside risk was $22\frac{7}{16}$, and my upside target areas were $23\frac{1}{4}$ to $23\frac{3}{4}$. Using tape-reading principles, buy when other traders are scared (fast selling, capitulation) and sell when they are hungry (fast buying, euphoria), offer out into strength in areas you feel comfortable with, should it provide a profit potential. The break back over $23 to $23\frac{1}{4}$ ran into resistance but held $23 well enough that it had a chance to get closer to the upper target range near $23\frac{1}{2}$. For the scalpers, exiting into strength under $23\frac{1}{4}$ was fine. Holders were looking for a move back to upper resistance and a possible breakout.

Holders had two choices. First, they could exit half their shares into first or last resistance areas and raise the stop on the remaining shares, looking for a break of the high. Second, they could hold the full lot with a tighter trailing stop and failed break of high, and exit into a trailing stop. If the stock broke to a new high, they could offer out into new highs as they feel most comfortable, raising a stop along the way. In this case, we had a break of the first resistance near $23^1/$_4$, with $23 holding, so we exited half into that buying, bringing the stop to just under $23 on the remaining shares. After it failed to break $23^3/$_4$, I chose to bring the stop to $23^1/$_4$ to lock in profits since it wasn't clear whether a new high would be reached. This was a decision I had to make in the moment, although hindsight tells me I should have kept it under $23. This is not important. You trade how you decide, not how you should have decided. For holders with no trailed stop, the break of the high eventually occurred taking the price to near $24^3/$_8$ (area C on Figure EX2) or so before going lower again. The holders had the option to trail their stop again or exit into that break of the high strength. On a day like this, where the market is desperately trying to hold and strength is uncertain at best, I have no problem exiting into an onrush of new buyers. If you like the trade, you can always reenter again into another support area.

To summarize: We found support areas defined by Fibonacci lines, used tape-reading principles of faster selling into a support area to find where to bid. If fast selling didn't occur till the last Fibonacci, fine, bid it there. If selling never picked up, I was less inclined to play congestion bottoms. Then we exited into strength, scalpers near first resistances, holders, at least half anywhere from first to last resistance, hold the remaining shares with a trailing stop and look for break of high. If we were so inclined, we could have held the full lot with a trailed stop tighter to lock in profits. Finally, we could have trailed our stop on what we deemed necessary and what we were willing to risk should the stop get hit. Don't second-guess yourself. It just erodes your confidence and trust in yourself. When you lose these, you lose an important edge. Once the trade is complete, review it for a bit, keep it in your notes, and move on to the next.

EXAMPLE 3

Jump-Base—Explosion (JBE) Setup

The trade illustrated in Figure EX3 was taken during a period when our previous 2 days had shown a nice uptrend, slow and relatively calm, indicating to us that we are seeing a fair market accumulation on many issues. We had two negative events from Cisco Systems (CSCO) the day before the trade and in Yahoo! (YHOO) the day of the trade. Both were absorbed nicely by the broader trend. The day before the trade CSCO interrupted the uptrend at midday, but the market regained its trend after the negative events from CSCO and YHOO were absorbed. On this day, we had a gap down that was met with the same continuation of the uptrend we were seeing. During phases such as these we look for pullbacks and breakouts to enable us to participate in the trend. At such times we frequently buy high and sell higher, which may sometimes be a tough thing for many people to do. In this case, buying pullback to support levels and waiting for new highs is reasonable.

As we noted, the market was showing a nice steady uptrend. Commerce One (CMRC) was one issue that was participating, as you can see in Figure EX3. Therefore, we had to identify areas for entry. The circle A illustrates the beginning of the most recent uptrend and an area that we happened to miss for entry. The steady volume is shown by the bar brackets in the volume section. This suggests that interest continued on the slow uptrend climb. After missing the move from the $20^{1}/_{4}$ area, we saw a nice base in the stock near $21. The two lines R show our range of $21 to $21^{1}/_{4}$. Here we have determined the range for our trading. There were a few prints to $20^{15}/_{16}$ during this time period, but very few sells occurred at these prices. If this trade was not going to work out, we had two choices on the stop. The first choice was selling at $20^{15}/_{16}$ and not waiting for confirmation. The second choice was to wait for all of the $20^{15}/_{16}$ to be eaten and then take a stop loss at $20^{7}/_{8}$.

The first thing traders should do is evaluate the risk. If $20^{15}/_{16}$ goes, would we be able to get out at $20^{7}/_{8}$ safely? If yes, then we have to wait for $20^{15}/_{16}$ to get eaten, possibly hitting a market maker with size or an ECN with size. In the worst case, our exit would be $20^{7}/_{8}$. If no, then we don't wait for too much selling at $20^{15}/_{16}$ to trigger our stop. In this case, if $20^{15}/_{16}$ looks unattainable immediately, find someone at $20^{7}/_{8}$ to hit, an ECN or a market maker with size. So, now we had our stop loss defined. As you progress in your trading, you can figure all this out in a matter of seconds. You bring up a stock, see levels, and know if a stock is risky or not.

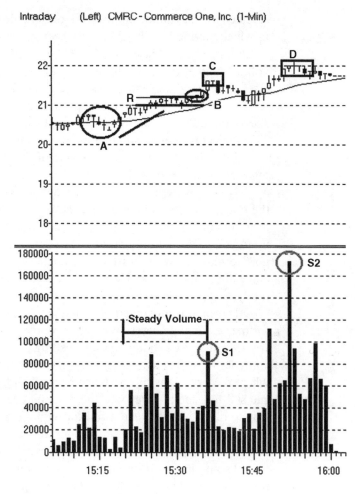

Intraday   (Left) CMRC - Commerce One, Inc. (1-Min)

FIGURE EX3

Jump-base–explosion (JBE) setup. (*RealTick graphics are used with permission of Townsend Analytics, Ltd.*)

Over the years, the most common question we get is how to know whether to buy or wait on volume spikes on breakouts. The answer is that, if a stock shows strong volume into resistance and the volume spikes at the resistance, I'm not inclined to buy this break.

At this point, the buying is usually exhausted and does not have the strength to carry the stock over the break. Or the break is weak, and we are better off trading pullbacks. If the stock shows a nice steady climb or a nice base and we see a volume spike as resistance is being eaten, I'm inclined to buy this break. The difference is that interest on the break rep-

resented by the volume comes from reasonable support, not a strong move
in which buying may have already been exhausted in getting to the resistance level. In this case with CMRC, the latter applies. We had a steady
volume with a reasonable base near $21. The risk was relatively low since
sizes were good and the levels were tight. So a break of the high was a
reasonable trade. The entry as represented by the circle B in Figure EX3
shows the entry. Circle S1 on the volume bar shows the volume spike.
This indicates interest and that breakout was likely to occur.

It is important to remember one of the trading mantras: Tape reading creates higher probabilities, not certainties.

Now that we had our stop loss defined and a plan ready, we entered
the trade. We enter either before the break with conviction for the break
or try to enter at the break price. If you miss the break price or better, it's
up to you to decide how far above the breakout price you would want to
go. Normally, I wouldn't chase a breakout play higher than 3–5 cents,
depending on the risk. However, in some cases, I'm willing, but only
rarely, to go higher—closer to 5–10 cents.

During this movement, I would have liked CMRC to hold above $21
for the remaining shares. We had an entry and we had a stop plan. Next
we needed an exit strategy. Tape-reading principles tell us to watch price
and volume spikes. Scalpers exit full lots into these price/volume spikes,
where the first signs of resistance occur. Holders have two options. They
can sell half their shares into the first spike and, in some cases, raise the
stop to breakeven or keep a full lot with the original plan. In the CMRC
case, we opted to take half our shares above 21^1/_2$, with 21^9/_{16}$ probably
being the best possible exit area. See point C on Figure EX3.

Taking half positions assumes that you have enough shares to make
it worthwhile. For example, trading 200 shares would not be worth the
trouble. Trading 500 shares is more reasonable. And trading 1000 shares
is an excellent move. At this point the scalpers were out of the trade, and
the holders were out possibly half their shares. The next thing we did was
watch for pullback support. Notice that the price move and the volume
spike (as described earlier) usually lead to the end of the oscillation. This
is why we exit into these areas. We also have an exit strategy on the
remaining shares.

Now we wanted to have our remaining shares with a stop at the low
of our minirange which was defined before. This could easily have failed
and cost us a stop on the remaining shares. However, we saw good bid
support at $21 and not much selling to jeopardize the stop. This is a try-
ing period for many. Do you exit or hold? The answer depends on you and
your tolerance for executions. I felt the size of the bid and the lack of sell-

ing as it got to $21 made it reasonable to hold. At that point, we had to look for retest of the high and a break over that for the remaining shares. We were looking for the volume spike once again.

We wanted to sell the remaining shares into the next spike because it was nearing the end of the day (just about 10 minutes left) and I didn't want to hold the stock overnight. The stock made a move near the previous high and broke on reasonable volume with the greatest price spike represented near $22, at which point we'd most certainly be out with the remaining shares (see area D and circle S2 on Figure EX3). This is a good illustration of volume spikes offering us clues to exit. CMRC behaved nicely. During this phase of the break of $21⅝, traders had the choice of exiting the remaining shares into the first volume spike test near $21¾. Or watching for support on the pullback and waiting for another break of $21¾. Action was such at $21¾ that selling continued to be absorbed nicely and eventually broke the $21¾ level, offering us a chance on the volume increase to exit our shares anywhere we wanted between $21¾ and $22. This example demonstrates the application of tape-reading principles to enter and exit on the breakout play.

EXAMPLE 4

Capitulation

Capitulation indicates public participation on the sell side. Traders tend to want to exit at any price they can get, as they sell in panic mode, giving up on their positions. You can see this in any time frame. The two components we want to see are:

Faster selling on a surge of volume and pace

Vertical price drop

Faster selling suggests that the majority is now selling in aggregate, thereby exhausting the selling. Plus, following the assumption that the majority is usually wrong, when members of the majority participate together, it's time to act as a contrarian, in this case, on the long side. The vertical price drop shows that there is no one willing to bid into that selling pressure. Market makers show enough to mark their liability or their need to make a two-sided market, but they don't stick around for long. Eventually, as the selling becomes exhaustive, we see the phase of passive accumulation. You know that this is happening because it is often difficult to establish a large position in a snapback reversal.

In aggressive accumulation, one or more MPIDs (market participation identifications) are looking to support a stock in a slow uptrend, while trying not to alert the public to their intentions. They absorb a lot of selling pressure, and pullbacks can be shallow as these aggressive accumulators are looking to build a bigger position, ready to unload to the public when it hits it on the buy side. So with capitulation, the smart money causes passive accumulation to happen, and we try to participate. As with any setup, these are based on probabilities. We present here two figures that show three separate occasions for capitulation with only two offering the chance for profitability. Don't think that one set of circumstances will always yield a profit. There are always outside events that can skew any setup. In capitulation, maybe there is an aggressive distributor who is not letting a stock rise. All we can do is see the event, adjust for our risk, and see if we get good profit potential.

The first stock is Alpha Industries (AHAA) (See Figure EX4a). You can see a fast-selling phase from $28.25 to just below $25.50. This marks the left side of what we refer to in capitulation as the *V bottom*. The two circles on this chart mark both things we need:

Faster volume selling; you can see the volume spike.

A more vertical price drop from just over $26 to just under $25.50.

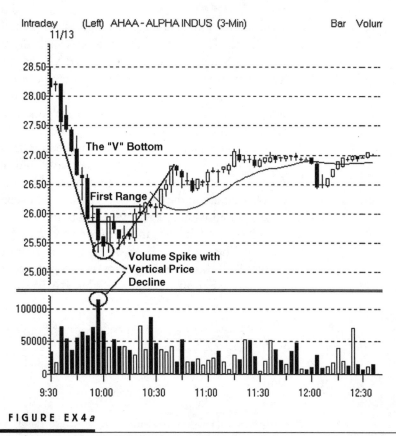

FIGURE EX4*a*

Trading capitulation. (*RealTick graphics are used with permission of Townsend Analytics, Ltd.*)

At this point, it was up to us to find our entry. This is often the most difficult case because this is a conceptual setup. There is no situation in capitulation that says that if you see so many bars at a base, then it's time to go long. The snapback doesn't allow for this. You have to use a little art in this entry, and it's often difficult for many people to buy into such uncertainty. Until you get comfortable with a setup where there is no "set trigger entry," use small share sizes or try to paper-trade it a bit. Get used to the idea of buying into contraction. There's no reason to push it. On AHAA, the entry price and entry size had to be based on risk factors. AHAA tended to have wide levels, and size wasn't always big. I would play no more than 500 shares in order to stay within my risk tolerance. And I'd exit half and half or in full depending on how the stock reacted.

So, how did I find my exit targets? The first area of exit is usually where the more vertical price movement begins. This is somewhat along the same lines as our trend-continuation setups: Suppose a stock makes a base and then falls. Once that support is broken, that usually becomes our resistance. This is the same case in which the vertical price movement becomes evident. You can see on AHAA that we had a small base near $26, so if there was any sharp movement back into $26, we'd exit at least half and quite possibly in full because this kind of stock tends to be erratic, and sure profits are a bad idea. We were patient and held, then we looked back higher and saw another same type of base at just above $26.50. This is where the stock made a stronger top before making a shallow pullback. This is the next area where I would have sold the remaining shares. Of course, it's easy to say what we "should" do. But Figure EX4*a* provides a bit of structure to the trade, so that you aren't seeing a bunch of confusing numbers and wondering why or where to exit.

Now let's look at the Peregrine Systems (PRGN) trade (see Figure EX4*b*). The highest circle on this chart represents the idea discussed above: With faster selling from $17 to just under $16.50, we see a huge volume spike. Entry would be under $16.50, and we needed to look for a

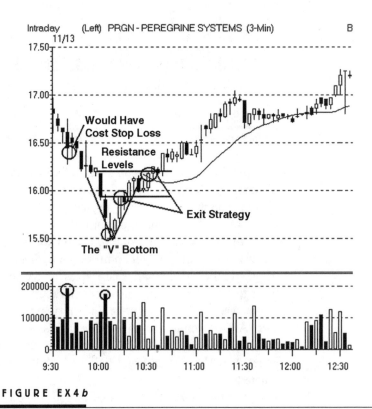

FIGURE EX4*b*

Trading capitulation. (*RealTick graphics are used with permission of Townsend Analytics, Ltd.*)

retest of the high. As you can see on this chart, the setup didn't yield a profit. It might provide a scalp, but most likely it would provide a stop. Once again, we're dealing in probabilities, not certainties. The price went vertical, the volume spiked, and an entry signal was seen. But it failed. So the cycle repeated, but this time it got closer to $15.50. The two lines showing the V indicate more vertical price movement from about $16.25 down to $15.50. So as the stock bounced off $15.50, we had two small resistance areas. One just below $16, where we could partial out, and the other right near $16.25, where we could have taken the remaining profits. The fact that the stock got back to $17 was quite amazing, and I definitely should not have taken full profits on it. I like to scale out into first and second resistances on these kinds of stocks because they offer the better probabilities to get full profits.

The AHAA and PRGN situations don't prove this exit methodology. However, the same ideas apply: With faster selling volume, the price went vertical. This is the time to look for a long-side entry. Determine where the vertical price movement begins and scale out into that. If you have enough patience, use that last resistance as a confidence level. If it breaks it, you can trail your stop or use the next round of buying to exit into. If it continues to break resistance levels, the way PRGN did, you can use that last resistance as a new confidence level. This is really a personal choice: Where do you scale out? However, if you follow technical analysis and tape-reading principles, you can manage to find the optimal points for both entry and exit. Optimal points in this case are those that work most often and are not necessarily the best for each given trade. It's in this that we can be more confident in the probabilities of our trade.

Notice also that we aren't believers in, "Loved it at $28; should really love it at $25; value being created; a certain percentage down." Such statements are opinions about the worth of the stock. Not once have I mentioned the *worth* of a stock in this whole discussion. The worth of a stock in intraday trading is the expression of an opinion; we could care less about it. Our job is to view the relationship between price and volume, and capitulation alerts do a great job of this, showing how the majority panics all at one time, and the smart money looks to profit off that majority participation.

EXAMPLE 5

Capitulation

As noted earlier, capitulation is one of the foundation principles of tape reading. It simply means that selling becomes exhausted as the public struggles to "get out at any price." The public capitulates; it gives up. Keeping with the idea that the public is usually wrong, the minority looks for a long-side reversal. Two things present the entry signal:

Price decline in a sharp, almost vertical manner

Volume increase in a sharp spike, showing that the sell-side volume is approaching or has reached its peak

Let's apply this principle to Netiq Corporation (NTIQ). (See Figure EX5.) The range, labeled A, is about $27.50 to $28. You can see signs of capitulation as the stock drops into this range. We have a spike on the volume chart to the sell side in combination with vertical price movement to the downside.

This would be a reasonable area for entry in the capitulation phase except for one thing. A trader's first consideration must always be risk. Risk evaluation is top priority. Remember our saying that amateurs evaluate profit potential, and pros evaluate risk? On NTIQ, liquidity at this level was really thin, meaning that sizes at each level were small and the depth of the stock had gaps between each level that were too wide. As this stock was falling, it was even thinner than it was at the real bottom. It was one that I wouldn't trade even 500 shares because it was just too thin from a liquidity viewpoint.

However, had I gone in on the capitulation phase at point A, then my trade would have been a stop loss. Chances for a fill were not easy because sizes from the $27.70 area were very small and stock action was erratic at best. Had we gotten filled by bidding into contraction, the most we would have gotten was about $28, certainly not worth the risk. And we'd have held the position looking for a move over $28.25 or so. This didn't happen and we saw new lows.

As the stock continued lower, we wanted to be looking for that faster-selling capitulative phase movement:

Price gets more vertical on the downside.

Volume increase on the sell side is apparent.

We wanted stronger sell-side volume than we saw in the $28 area. As the stock approached this next low on faster selling, we would enter

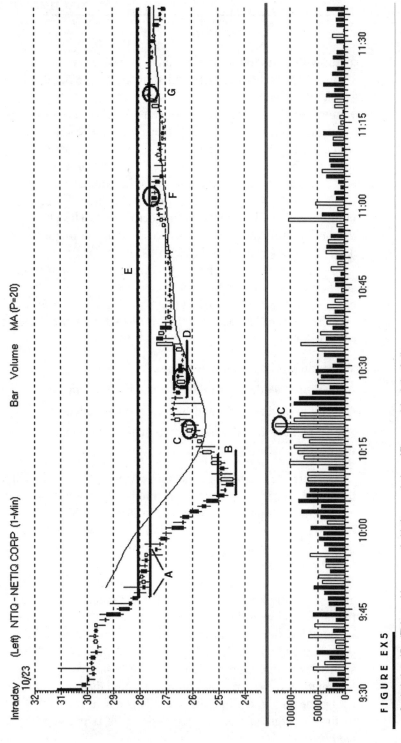

Intraday (Left) NTIQ - NETIQ CORP (1-Min)   Bar   Volume   MA (P=20)

10/23

FIGURE EX5

Capitulation. (RealTick graphics are used with the permission of Townsend Analytics, Ltd.)

again with only 500 shares, because liquidity was still relatively thin. In Figure EX5 the bottom print ended up at about $24.30, so if that broke, I would have been looking to exit with a stop just below that support level. Remember that we always have stops in place because the market isn't about certainties. Faster selling doesn't always lead to a reversal. Nothing in the market works 100 percent of the time, so stop losses are part of the trade for the times that a setup doesn't yield a profit.

You can't know if the bottom is the bottom until 5 minutes later, so don't try to be a psychic—be a trader. If you can learn to live with discomfort, you will do what the majority can't. The phrase that profit and discomfort go hand in hand is not one that the majority knows or uses. This holds especially true in capitulation setups.

At the B range, we had signs of capitulation and reversal. We could see how the first move off this $24.30 area went into about $25 and then came back down. This is often the most difficult time for a trader. Do you take the profit or let it ride? In this situation I usually ask the trader a series of questions:

Where are you right now in trading?

Are you in drawdown, and do you need a few winners?

Are you in a win cluster and feeling good and clear-minded?

Are you a new trader who needs to make some money while in the learning phase?

There are many elements that answer the "Should I sell now?" question. You must understand what mindset you are in and use it to your advantage. Selling at $25 and seeing it later at $28 doesn't matter. You need to exist in *now,* and you need to respond *now.* You can give yourself only as much profit as your inner reality will allow. The market is the best reflection of you.

Now I had entry, and I had a resistance level in the $25 to $25.25 area. At this point I was looking for a resistance level, and volume into that level that would yield a higher reward-to-risk ratio, since the capitulation phase should mark a very good low and lead to filling some of the gaps in areas where the selling begins to get faster. The $25.25 wasn't such an area, but closer to $26.50 was. We saw volume into about $26.30, indicated by the C circle in Figure EX5, and there also was a bit more vertical price movement into this area. This meant that the public was participating in aggregate on the buy side. This is the tape-reading principle *euphoria.*

I wanted to put out my order at this level. As the stock moved into this area, liquidity was not good enough for a fill and the stock then fell faster into the D range, where we saw a base and consolidation. At the D level, I saw support, but also a series of lower highs within this range. This made me want to take the first half of the trade within it. So I offered out 300 shares of my 500. It was taken, and I was ready to trail the stop higher on the remaining shares.

Why didn't I take the full 500? I was willing to risk the remaining 200 to see if a gap filled closer to $28, as seen in the E range. This gave me a target closer to $27.50 to $28, and you can see why from the two long lines forming the E range. This was the same range that had given me a consolidation earlier in the A range. Since this was support and it was broken, I then thought that what had been support would now serve as resistance.

As we got into this $27.50 to $28 area on the first test, we wanted to be scaling out into any kind of increased volume move or at least trailing the stop higher. In this case, I trailed the stop to the low of the D range on the first test of that area. (This first test is indicated by the F circle in Figure EX5). The stop on the D range was $26.30 or so. The pullback into $27 after the first F oval test of resistance held fairly well. As the next test into the resistance (if there would be one) I would watch for signs of volume/price relationships. The point of the G circle showed declining volume, and while the price rose at that high, we had signs of distribution continuing, as well as declining volume. The NDX began to back off at this point, and we were nearing the lunch period when things tend to become less apparent and readable because of the overall lighter volume. Now, it would have been reasonable for us to take the remaining shares as close to $27.50 as possible, rather than waiting for the new confidence level of $27 to fail.

Let's review some of the major points on this trade. First, capitulation reversals require that you adhere to your risk/money management principles. In fact, every trade should, but this is especially so for capitulation alerts because they tend to be less liquid as market participants drop bids fairly easily during their passive accumulation of a new low. Rid yourself of old theories that make sense to the public, but not to those who are using real price action to dictate thin areas of entry and exit. Technical analysis principles let us define ranges and supports and resistance.

Tape-reading principles let us know how volume and price work together to enable us to scale out of positions that go in our favor. These are repeatable and strong guidelines. Understand what mindset you are in as you try to exit the trade. If you are feeling confident but exit the trade just because you have profit, then something is wrong. If you are feeling out of the flow but are trying to let profits run (almost like revenge trading), you are pushing it too hard and need to get your equilibrium back. Throughout my trading career, I've been amazed at how many things we have to think about. Consider this: The chicken asked the millipede, "How, with 1000 legs, do you know which one to move when?" The millipede replied, "If I thought about it, then I wouldn't be able to do it." I don't trade with all these step-by-step issues going through my head at once. They come to me naturally, as part of a progression resulting from years of trading experience. Eventually, as a trader, this is where you need to be.

EXAMPLE 6

Drop-Base—Implosion (DBI) Setup

There are two technical indicators on Figure EX6*a* that I use to help me in my entry/exit strategy. Without going into the mechanics of each, let me say that many people use them, and I find them helpful. They are the 20-period moving average (20MA) line and the Fibonacci levels (lines F). I used these two elements during this trade to give me more self-confidence, while relating them to the ideas of tape reading, which is our foundation for trading. As you can see, the stock was on a clear downtrend from mid \$22s to the \$21 level. Traders have two options on a downtrend. They can either go with the trend and look for short entries, or they can

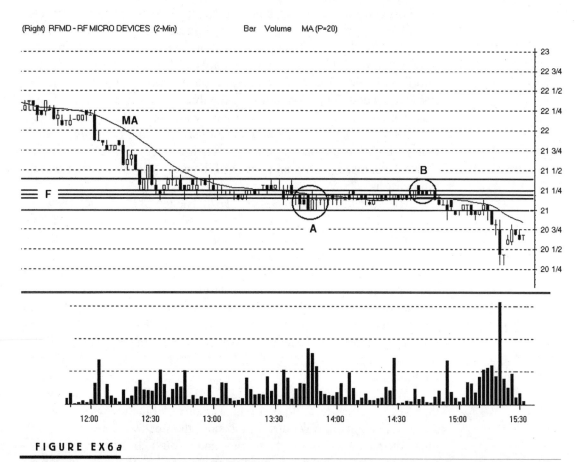

FIGURE EX6*a*

Drop-base—implosion (DBI) setup: entry strategy. (*RealTick graphics are used with permission of Townsend Analytics, Ltd.*)

wait for capitulatory selling and look for a reversal, and then go long off support. I became interested in this stock at point A. I missed the move from the mid $22s to the $21 area while I was watching other stocks. I didn't think that point A was the only area for a setup, but it just happened to be the first one that I saw on this issue for the day.

As RF Micro Devices (RFMD) began to move to the $21 level, we looked for two things: the long black bar in circle A, which indicates strong selling, and the volume increase shown on the volume chart. Normally we look for a reversal in this case and go long. However, my feeling was that we still had a good chance for a downtrend continuation. This wasn't based on any chart or tape. It was more a perception or an intuition that develops from years of trading experience.

In this case, I was correct. If I had been wrong, I have money/risk management in place to keep the loss small. So I created the perception for short entry on this trade, and then I looked for the proper entry setup on it. Downtrend trading has a caveat. You can't short on the downtick. Therefore, we had to let the stock break and try to get filled on the offer or on some small bounce, or we'd identify the top of the range and short into it on buying. The first choice has a lower percentage for a fill than does the second. So in this trade, we did three things. The first, as always, was risk evaluation. If we were wrong, would this stock cost us a huge stop loss? The levels on RFMD were relatively safe, certainly no more than an eighth of a point of slippage. Then we defined the range. In this case, you can see the top and bottom Fibonacci (Fib) lines identified the range for us.

RFMD had a range of $21 to $21\frac{3}{8}$. The top of the range was where we wanted to short into on buying, using a stop no worse than a level higher than top of the range, which would be $21\frac{7}{16}$, and no worse than $21\frac{1}{2}$ if there was really strong buying. At this point it was important to stay calm and let the stock make its move. It was rather torturous; you can see the extremely long base it made within the range. However, this was fine, as the stock remained safe for us. If the spreads had changed or the pace gotten really fast, then it would have been less exciting for me to hold it on a long base. Usually the longer the base, the less likely it is that the stock will make a break of the range which signals a trend continuation.

We wanted buying to take us to $21\frac{1}{4}$ and to use the stop at no worse than $21\frac{1}{2}$, giving us a $\frac{1}{4}$-point risk. The break of the low would offer us 2 to 1 or more in our reward/risk ratio since the stock was safe, levels were thick, the pace was not too dangerous, and so on. I considered this to be a nice setup. Then I saw two things that made me think that I would stop out

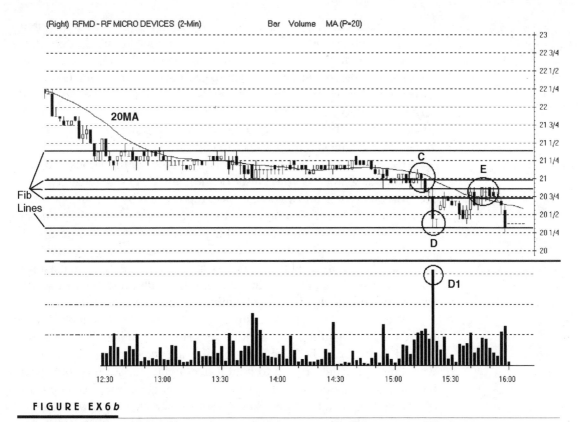

FIGURE EX6b

Drop-base—implosion (DBI) setup: exit strategy. (*RealTick graphics are used with permission of Townsend Analytics, Ltd.*)

of the trade if the stock showed above the 20MA serving as support. Also, the market was making an uptrend into this time period. I felt that if I broke $21^3/_8$, I would need to get the stop executed at no worse than $21^1/_2$ because support was holding and the market was uptrending. This may have followed the buying. As you can see, it never got above $21^5/_{16}$, and our short trade remained open. So we had reasoned our entry, our setup, our range, and our desire for the trade.

Now let's review the exit strategy. Point C in Figure EX6b is where the best confirmation of the downtrend appeared. You can see that in the minutes prior to point C the stock broke below $21, suggesting that the downtrend was still intact. Traders could choose to short the stock here at $21 with a stop no worse than the $21^3/_8$ to $21^1/_2$ area, depending on risk tolerance. I'd have used $21^3/_8$ in this case simply because it couldn't break that price previously when the support on the MA held and the market began an uptrend. So you see, if you wait for trend confirmation, you do have as much cushion in the trade as you would if you had not waited. Some people like confirmation; some prefer to trade before the confirmation. This is up to you. Just understand that, in downtrend trading, waiting for a break of the low makes it harder to get fills. Now that point C showed us confirmation of the downtrend, we looked for an exit strategy. The reward/risk ratio was served at just below $21, so we had room to let this stock breathe a bit. Scalpers could exit at any time. Next, we simply waited for volume and price spikes to exit into.

RFMD behaved beautifully by offering both confirmations to exit at least half our shares. As you can see on the chart, there is a long black candle down at point D and a volume spike represented by D1. This is where we began to bid at least a portion of our shares. Exit into strong buying when long, and cover into strong selling when short (at least a portion, if not all). It's a principle we've discussed many times. Here you could have gotten a fill possibly at $21^{5}/$_{16}$, certainly at $21^{3}/$_{8}$, giving you almost a full point in profit. If we took only half our profits off the table, then we would have to develop a plan for the remaining shares.

We then needed to trail a stop. Looking back on this trade, I have two thoughts regarding the trailing stop. First, I trailed it too tightly. Second, I didn't care because it was getting late and who knew how things would end up. I didn't want to hold it overnight, and scalping profits on the remaining shares was reasonable. Let's talk about the first stop price of $21^{1}/$_{16}$. I chose it because I didn't want former support, now serving as resistance, to be broken. If it was going to be broken, I would take the stop at $21^{1}/$_{16}$. As we can see, $21 wasn't jeopardized in this case. The 50 percent retracement Fib at $20^{7}/$_{8}$ (circle E) was the next line I used, and the 20MA actually cut the Fib at the $20^{3}/$_{4}$ level. Once the $20^{3}/$_{4}$ level was broken, I wanted scalps at the $20^{13}/$_{16}$ level. In hindsight, I should have kept a stop at $21. As it turned out, the stock made another little spike down into the close, offering a chance for another cover near $20^{1}/$_{4}$, but I had no problem taking the scalp near $20^{13}/$_{16}$.

In summary, the stock was in a downtrend, and I wanted a short setup. I defined the range and evaluated the risk. The stock confirmed that the downtrend was still intact on the break of the low. The exit strategy using principles of tape reading for a volume/price spike was used to cover at least half my shares. I used Fibonacci lines and the 20MA to identify a trailing stop.

EXAMPLE 7

Capitulation and Euphoria

Euphoria and capitulation are two of the major elements of tape-reading principles. They represent the most extreme cases of how the minority differs from the majority. Let's first look at capitulation in relation to the minority/majority. Capitulation is the phase of selling that shows a sharp rate of increase in the drop of the price of the stock and an increase in the pace/volume. It indicates that the majority is now trying to sell its stock at any price it can get. In essence, the majority has given up on its long position. Despair, fear overcoming greed—however you want to describe it. In this phase, selling becomes exhausted. When the majority exhausts the selling, the minority passively begins to support the stock at a level it feels is solid for a reversal to the long side. (We discussed this before.)

The minority is passive because it knows that the majority is now alerted to the stock and it can't get the best prices or develop a large position in a stock that has the attention of the world. Stock scanners, filters, chat rooms, news bulletins, and so on all contribute to the attention a stock gets when it makes a "sudden movement" one way or the other. So firms are not aggressive in accumulation when working a position in which the majority is participating.

Let's explore one example of capitulation. (See Figure EX7a.) You can see on this stock the rate of change increase in the price drop. It becomes vertical. At this point, you see the same increase in pace/volume on the volume chart on the sell side eventually hitting the peak. This is where the majority exhausts its selling, and the minority begins to passively accumulate. For our purposes as day traders, this is where we look to bid the contraction. We can, if we wish, wait to see some higher level broken to confirm the reversal, but, if we wait too long, we will be trying to buy with the majority (more difficult as liquidity dries up).

We now have a price drop and a volume spike leading to the setup. The minority looks long with a stop at the low. If we get a solid reversal, we will make higher lows and higher highs much the way Research in Motion (RIMM) does. Where do we look to exit?

I look for the last downward price thrust to find a rebound. In this case, you can see how the last major selling occurs from $36 to $34.50. A rebound to $36 is quite possible. Anything higher than that seems more uncertain. The first rise you see is almost right into that $36 area, just a bit over it. Anything beyond that $36 is for those who scale out looking for a

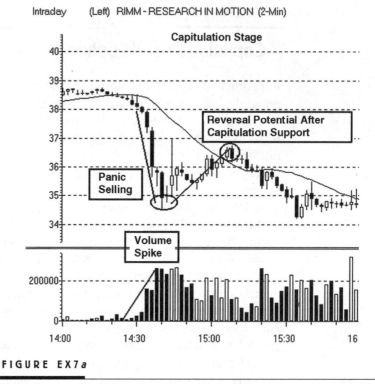

Intraday   (Left) RIMM - RESEARCH IN MOTION (2-Min)

FIGURE EX7a

Capitulation stage. (*RealTick graphics are used with permission of Townsend Analytics, Ltd.*)

stronger move into $38 with a trailing stop because the $38 area is the next major resistance area.

Capitulations are difficult for several reasons:

1. They are usually very fast and often rebound quickly leaving the majority to chase the best price.
2. We don't know if a stock is rebounding or simply pausing slightly.
3. Traders lacking in confidence will rarely go long if liquidity is not on the bid side. However, as we state earlier, most rewards come from the most uncertain situations. Discomfort and profit go hand in hand.

Your major goal in capitulation should be to learn to bid contraction—with confidence. Start with 50 or 100 shares. There is no reason to blow it all learning to bid contraction. But attaining confidence will get you better prices, and your system over time will get back to the same percentage of win/loss clusters as you progress.

The approach opposite to capitulation is euphoria. Euphoria is a different animal. It has some difficult limitations for many, the major one being the uptick rule. In capitulation, you can buy on downticks and upticks. It doesn't matter. In euphoria, you have to fool with the uptick rule. Funny how the market tries to protect us from the downside but not the upside. That and a 25,000 margin rule are some of the greatest ideas I've ever seen.

Euphoria in simplest terms is exhausted buying. It is associated with a rate of increase in price with vertical movement to the upside and the volume/pace spike as well. Figure EX7*b* illustrates this.

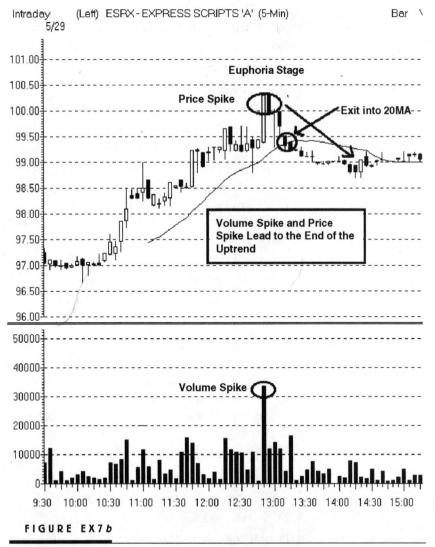

FIGURE EX7*b*

Trading euphoria. (*RealTick graphics are used with permission of Townsend Analytics, Ltd.*)

As you can see, this stock makes a vertical movement into about $100.25, signaling the end of the upside move. Buying becomes exhausted (referred to as panic buying), and the minority now begins the distribution phase. If buying is exhausted, then there are no more buyers to take the stock higher. Therefore, the minority begins to distribute when frantic buying happens, and this frantic buying is seen by the volume and price spikes.

Now that we are able to recognize euphoria, let's discuss some ways to trade it. If you look at the Express Scripts (ESRX) chart, can you see the trend? It's up, and, since we are not "buy bottoms, short tops" traders, when stocks are in a trend, we have three choices when ESRX shows euphoria:

1. Short the stock for fast profit expectations only.
2. Wait for a double-top scenario and see if the trend is indeed broken and shows downside movement.
3. If you are going with the trend, you let the stock spike, make a retracement, and see if that retracement level holds.

If it holds and breaks the previous high, you have a trend-continuation signal, and you go long if the entry price is within your risk tolerance. ESRX shows a great setup for a euphoria short play, but many strongly trending stocks we've seen prove that trying to short euphoria would have resulted in huge losses or only small gains.

The idea is, that when euphoria occurs, if the stock is in an uptrend:

1. Take faster profits from the short side.
2. Wait for a double top if you like it short.
3. If you like it long, watch for retracement support to hold.

However, don't get into the habit of trying to short a strong stock. Sure, there are plenty of times when a strong stock finally breaks down and you have a nice cushion by trying to short the first pop into resistance. However, you must understand that, over time, trying to short tops and buy bottoms simply because they are, in your opinion, due for a bounce or breakdown is not going to serve you well.

There are specific times only that we should employ this strategy:

1. Capitulation—exhausted selling
2. Double bottom—support is holding
3. Euphoria—exhausted buying
4. Double top—resistance is not broken

Early in my trading career I was trying to call tops and bottoms and I continued to fail and fail and fail. I finally changed my tune. Sure you can catch a couple of good plays this way, but, over time, you will usually run into problems unless your reward/risk ratio is high enough to cover your stops.

If you look at it from a mental aspect, which is more difficult to trade:

Stop, stop, stop, profit

Profit, profit, profit, stop

The former is buy low, sell high. The latter is trading with the trend and is more profitable more often and also better from a trading mindset. There are specific areas in which you should buy low, sell high, and we have outlined them based on tape-reading principles—capitulation and euphoria. All others are based on a value judgment or some other reasons that have nothing to do with reality, with price and volume. We as intra-day traders are concerned only with the correlation of price and volume, not an opinion-based methodology. The market doesn't care about your opinion. It has its own way of revealing what is too high or too low. More often than not, a stock can be too high or low longer than you stay solvent.

EXAMPLE 8

Finding Entries in a Strong Trend

Early in my career, I couldn't tell you how many times I got angry at seeing the market rising strongly, while I hadn't made one trade or owned anything on the long side. It was truly frustrating. I see this in many traders whom I talk with. The question always seems to be: When the stock is rising, where should I get in?

Let me go back several years and give you an answer that I was given by a self-proclaimed stock guru. If the stock is rising, just buy it and watch it go higher. You can guess how many times I bought the top. I'd need about the fingers and toes of 10 readers of this book to help me count, maybe even more. This is clearly not the right answer. We need a specific reason for entry. Many times, when stocks are trending all by themselves, against the better movement of a market indicator that is stuck, it's often difficult to have confidence in such plays.

And it's difficult to identify areas for entry because we are not confident when the overall market is narrow. This stems from the idea that we play probabilities, and, over time, our probabilities tell us that trying to play this or that setup, hoping we get the one or two that do actually move, is usually a losing proposition. Let's take two stocks that were moving on the same day, despite NDX inactivity: Inrange Technologies (INRG) and Manugistics Group (MANU). I will go over exactly what it is that prevents us from entry as well as where there are higher probability areas for entry should a trend continue.

As you can see, in Figure EX8a we have an open range, indicated by two lines labeled 1 and 2, that fits well into our risk parameters for open-break plays. However, because of the previous day's fades and a very narrow day, we wanted to back off open plays.

There were 4000 stocks that opened, but how many open-break plays did well? Not many, and with aggression levels relatively low on this particular morning, I wasn't looking for things like INRG or MANU to occur. On INRG, we saw how the circle A signaled the entry for the long setup with a stop at the low end of the range. What we saw next is what I was alluding to earlier, the hardest part of the move. If we missed our entry near $7.65, we would be looking for another entry, but where? Anywhere, and hope the stock continued higher? Obviously not. You can see from the ascending line from about $8 to $8.90 that there is nothing in this whole move to justify an entry. Rather, we needed some type of

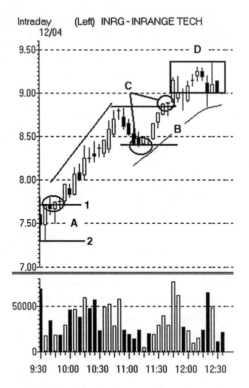

Intraday   (Left) INRG - INRANGE TECH
12/04

FIGURE EX8*a*

Trading trend confirmation. (*RealTick graphics are used with permission of Townsend Analytics, Ltd.*)

move, pause, or base, and then we would push higher. This is what we had in area C. This gave us more confidence for two reasons.

First, if the base is shallow, then the selling pressure is not strong and/or someone is supporting this stock. Second, a break of the high after this base says that there are still enough willing buyers around to indicate that the long side is still the right side, a higher probability. In this case, we had two options. We could buy the low of the base or the break of the high assuming it was within our risk ratio parameters. Did I want to short it? Only if I saw that base broken or if I had seen a possible double-top scenario.

This is why it's not a good idea to short the first spikes on stocks, trying to nail the first top. Trending stocks like INRG or MANU can kill you if you try to fade the move. Rather, on uptrending issues, you need a base broken or a double-top type of movement to confirm that a short-side trade is a better probability. Do stocks come off the first tops? Sure, but the probabilities don't support this over the longer term. You will end up finding yourself doing that "loss, loss, loss, profit" thing by trying to nail the first top each time. In the case of INRG, we had a base to work with. It was a bit wider than we'd like for a full lot, but we now had a reason to buy other than, "Buy it, it's rising." We had a low and a high. If we held the low and broke the high, we had structure built in. Now as we moved into the area marked D, things became "choppy." We saw a spike over $9, a small retracement, a move into a new high, and then selling back under the area where the price spike occurred. No real support or resistance was clear in this box area. It was not a good base, as we had in range B. If we bought the break at $8.90, we'd have scaled out or taken a full lot to protect profits, as shown in box D.

Where INRG went from that point was much less of a probability, so it was better to lock in a profit. The main point on this is that rather than get frustrated because the stock goes without you, you need to understand that all stocks move; all stocks have potential. But not all stocks provide setups that are familiar to you or your system. This is the difference between a pro and an amateur. A pro can let a stock move from $20 to $30 without an entry because nothing is familiar. An amateur will see the move from $20 to $30 and wonder, "Why didn't I buy it?"

The MANU chart shows the same thing (See Fig. EX8b). We had the open-break play, which we didn't play because of the low aggression level. Circle A shows the setup for this and the two lines on the bottom establish the range. As we moved up to $12.30 or so, we finally got a little pullback and a base. This is the range marked B. Traders could buy the low of that range as a cushion and look for a break of the high, or they could buy the breakout of that high base. The next movement from $12.30 to $13.20 offered incredible potential, but not a familiar setup. We had basically a vertical price movement with few characteristics of a base with which to enter. So, while the amateur sees MANU go from $12.30 to $13.20 and feels frustrated, the pro sits patiently, looking for another base to trade from. Being that the stock was still in an uptrend, we looked for a long setup.

We saw a base from $13 to $13.20 and looked for a break of this range in order to be more confident in a long setup continuation. MANU just sat. Was this base building a certainty? No, it was a higher probability. Could we break down from this base? Sure, and those who were short-oriented could look for a break of the low of this base with a stop just over the high. But imagine being the one who tried to short it on the initial spikes discussed in INRG. You'd have stopped out at $12.50. Then again

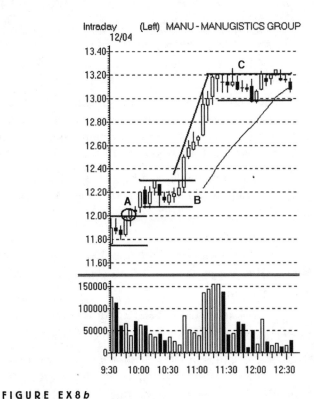

FIGURE EX8*b*

Trading trend confirmation. (*RealTick graphics are used with permission of Townsend Analytics, Ltd.*)

at $12.70. Maybe again at $13. Finally, again, you are short at $13.20, and you see 20 cents in potential.

So you go, stop, stop, maybe stop again, and finally you see potential. Unless you have emotional control here, you will short the stock again, looking at a fourth stop on the same stock, hoping that the potential will outweigh the last three spikes. Meanwhile the stock sits in this range, creating frustration that a potential 20 cents on the short won't cover the stops you've already taken. Moving on a win/loss percentage that, in this case, could very well be 25 percent with your profit not coming near your loss. To me, this isn't the best use of your trading capital and can certainly ruin your trading mindset. This again is the difference between trading at any level for whatever reason versus imposing structure, ranges, and the like into your trading so as to identify similar setups that have higher probabilities to work over time.

EXAMPLE 9

Open-Break Setup

An open-break setup requires much confidence and fast, if not automatic, decision making. I don't normally recommend such plays to inexperienced traders because they require skills that most newer traders don't possess. First, let's go over what exactly this setup is.

1. Risk must be defined by a range of 25 cents or less (at times you can stretch this to 30 cents depending on the action, but this is rare).
2. Watch for the range to be broken either on the high side or on the low side.
3. If the stock breaks high, go long with a stop at bottom of the range.
4. If the stock breaks low, look for a short with a stop at the high end of the range.
5. Look to partial out at a 2:1 or less reward/risk ratio.
6. Scalpers look for 1:1 reward/risk ratio.

Peoplesoft (PSFT) shows a good example of the open-break setup (see Fig. EX9). You can see on this chart the support and resistance levels from the previous day into the close. Many times I use this kind of situation to help me if the stock is staying within this range in the premarket activity for open candidates. PSFT was staying in the $30.40 to $30.60 range and looked stable on the sell side. From the previous day's sell-off, we had a fairly slow and stable uptrend into the close, so I wanted to remain with this trend for the open play. This is why I chose the long-side bias, rather than the short side. As the day opened, our resistance at $30.60 held, and we lost $30.40, hitting $30.35 before the stock made its move. The prints below $30.40 were minimal, and, therefore, to me, selling wasn't really that strong.

In this trade, with a stop right under $30.35, the support level would be the entry. This kept me in the long-side bias, which is where I wanted to be, and it provided me with a reward/risk ratio of under 25 cents. If the action broke, I'd be looking to scale out somewhere in a 2:1 or lower reward area. In this case, I got a break, which was confirmation that an uptrend move at the open was higher. Those who wait for confirmation tend to get more confidence but worse prices. That's the trade-off. Position yourself on the side of the break with higher probability before confirmation, and you get better prices and less confidence. Position your-

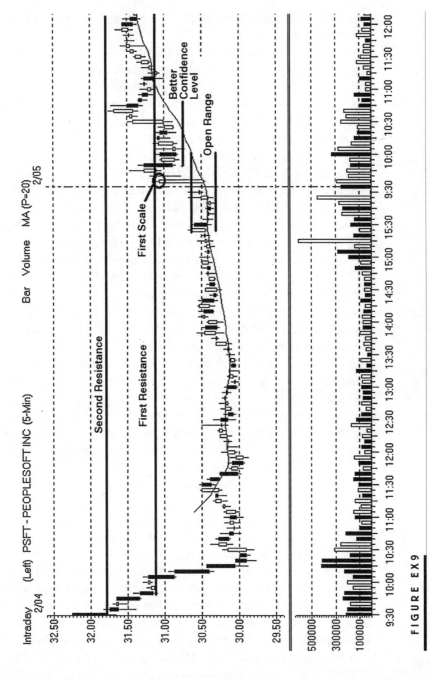

FIGURE EX 9

Open-break setup. (*RealTick graphics are used with permission of Townsend Analytics, Ltd.*)

181

self with the bigger crowd after the break, and you get more confidence, but worse prices.

This is why, when I feel confident about a trade, I frequently try to get ahead of the setup rather than waiting for confirmation. My win/loss ratio usually doesn't improve by doing so (unless I'm in a win cluster), but my profit per trade improves for the trades that are successful. This is one side of the trade-off. When I have entry and receive confirmation, I look for an exit strategy. For this, I use my 2-day charts.

As you can see from the previous day's action, there was on PSFT strong selling from $31.25, marking eventual capitulation into under $30. Therefore, on the principle that what was support would now be resistance, this $31.25 would serve as resistance. Traders stuck with these higher prices in the sell-off would be looking to exit near $31.25, trying to recoup some paper losses. This added to the distribution pressure.

You can see on the chart the vertical price movement into just over $31, showing some resistance, as expected. A target was $31.25, but remember that it's price action that determines how near the target we want to take profits. If it's slow into $31.25, it should be easier to get nearer $31.25 for an exit. If we see faster buying which indicates majority participation, then we would want to sell into that buying under $31.25, where we can find liquidity. Offering this out is usually the best policy because price improvement can happen when buying is erratic on the strong side.

My confidence level was wrong for a proper scaling out. I placed it too tight at $31.10 on the pullback from $31.45. A better confidence level would have been where the line is marked accordingly. There is a base here, and it's above our entry trigger of $30.60. You can see a base formed, then a break of that base leading to our second resistance level at $31.70. Even though I didn't participate in this move, we see the same action. It shows faster buying into resistance indicated by vertical price movement. This is again where we would want to scale or take in full shares (assuming we held shares).

So, in review, my entry was fine and based on a solid setup. My first exit was solid, based on tape-reading principles combined with technical analysis. My second exit was not stellar because my confidence level was brought in too tight and missed 50 cents or so in potential. Let's focus on the lesson learned. Don't trail confidence levels too tightly just because you are eager to book profit (I'm often guilty of this). Rather, let stock action dictate where you begin to issue confidence levels and trailing stops. You can always find fault with yourself. You can't ever find fault with the stock action. It's the ultimate truth in intraday trading.

EXAMPLE 10

Open-Break Setup

First let's talk about premarket information. In the morning from 8 a.m. to 9 a.m. I'm fairly quiet, just gathering active stocks, which are dictated either from an up or down gap or from news that might bring some interest to a stock. At around 9 a.m. I focus on premarket support and resistance levels. At 9:20 a.m. or so, risk evaluations become easier, and I make my final list the last 10 minutes before the market opens. This is fairly basic preparation. I don't make predictions about where the market will go. My job as an intraday trader isn't to predict. Rather it's to define ranges and trade from them.

When I watched Finisar Corporation (FNSR), I saw a premarket high of about $17.10 and support at $16.85. (See Figure EX10.) For open plays, I like the ranges to be narrow, within 25 cents, before I go one way or the other. FNSR opened at under $17, and I saw market strength and wanted to look for open-high–break plays. With FNSR under $17, resistance at $17.10, and support at $16.85, I felt this was safe enough. An entry at $17 or better with a stop at $16.85 was a 15-cent risk. If the price slipped by 5 cents, I'd still be within my 25-cent risk tolerance ratio.

The bottom line represents our open low of $16.95, and entry was given at $17 or better. In this case, the line labeled "confirmation" was the area that, if broken, had the best chance to see a trend continue based on premarket resistance. As you can see, the stock spiked right over it, but not yet benefiting me much for my risk. I wanted to see it closer to $17.40 to $17.45 for scalpers. Holders should take half their position off the table. The next spike took the price into $17.40, and, at this point, the risk became higher.

Spreads were widening, sizes at bids were smaller, and levels were not thick. More often than not, when this happens, I want to take half, even if the target is not met. In this case, I'm reducing risk. When bids disappear and prices fall too fast against me, I don't want to have to get rid of a full lot. Fortunately, the stock resumed in my favor after my first half. (See the second circle (A) in the chart.) The volume increased and the rate of price change was nearly vertical, so I applied the tape-reading principle that suggests in this situation to exit another portion or all my remaining shares. The stocks moved to just over $17.80; see the spike in price followed by a decrease in volume. This is where I wanted to take another quarter of the position if not the full lot. In this case, $17.65 was a high target, leaving me to miss out on about 15 cents more in potential. But,

184

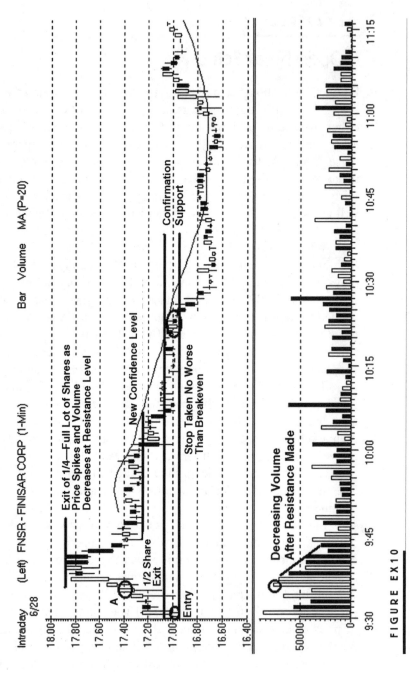

Intraday   (Left)   FNSR - FINISAR CORP (1-Min)   Bar   Volume   MA (P=20)
6/28

Exit of 1/4—Full Lot of Shares as
Price Spikes and Volume
Decreases at Resistance Level

New Confidence Level

Confirmation

Support

Stop Taken No Worse
Than Breakeven

1/2 Share
Exit

Entry

A

Decreasing Volume
After Resistance Made

FIGURE EX10

Open-break setup. (*RealTick graphics are used with permission of Townsend Analytics, Ltd.*)

when volume picks up like that, it's best to offer out into the strength at a reasonable level and not try to get the highest tick. The most expensive decisions are usually made within the last 10 to 20 cents of stock movement. Don't get caught being greedy and trying to get the highest tick.

I am occasionally close to the top ticks, but certainly not every time—not enough of the time to be greedy. For those who hold a quarter of their original position, they must use a stop-loss strategy. In this case, I identify "confidence levels," which are areas to which the stock pulls back after making a new continuation signal in the trend's direction. If the stock breaks the confidence level, I feel the ability of the stock to continue in the desired direction has a much lower probability. For example, after the stock broke $17.40, my first exit, I wanted to use any move back to under $17.50, and closer to 35 cents as a confidence level. This is illustrated by the line "New Confidence Level" on the chart. If a stock breaks this line, you have two options. You can use the next buying wave to exit the remaining shares over that confidence level. Otherwise, keep the original stop and look for the trend to reverse. If the stock goes below the confidence level, look for the next wave of buying to exit into. I wanted $17.50 or higher to justify the risk of taking 30 cents more in losses by keeping a stop at the $17 breakeven level.

Unfortunately, there was a big seller holding it at $17.40, and so I never had the opportunity. The remaining quarter of my shares was stopped out at no worse than $16.95 to $17 (see the circle on the support line). This is another good illustration of applying technical analysis principles of support and resistance to complement tape-reading principles for exit strategies. Notice that I didn't use arbitrary amounts like 25, 50, and 75 cents and whole numbers to dictate decisions. I allowed the stock action, through the form of support and resistance levels, as it dictated, to create my confidence levels. This way I brought structure to what might seem like chaotic movement.

EXAMPLE 11

Open-Low—Break Setup

On open-break plays, as you know, we try to identify a tight range of 25 cents or less, with moderate risk. We also like to watch the premarket action that occurs 10 minutes before the open to assess support or resistance as we move to the open within a range.

PMC-Sierra (PMCS) was a stock in a situation that fit these parameters. (See Figure EX11.) I was short biased that morning, and I watched mostly for open breakdown plays as the strength into the close from the previous day hadn't followed through much in the morning. So I looked for open-low–break plays (short setups) rather than open-high–break plays (long setups).

PMCS in the premarket was having trouble breaking $17.50 and was stuck in a tight 10-cent range of $17.40 to $17.50. This satisfied my range parameters. Liquidity was deep enough for me to get a solid fill if the stock set up. This satisfied my risk parameters, because, if PMCS failed, slippage would be minimal.

The next thing I looked for was the signal: The break of $17.40 was the setup trigger. Traders have two options:

1. Wait for the break to occur, hope to get an uptick closest to the setup price, and then let the uptick buying take you out.
2. Enter prior to the signal, which is more aggressive and takes a considerable amount of experience and a feel for the stock.

The caveat for the first option is that you might not get an uptick close enough to the setup price, which would adhere to your money management principles. The upside is that the stock tipped its hand, and, by breaking support, had a higher probability of a continuing downtrend, so you know that the short is the way to go.

The caveat for the second option is that there is a greater chance that the stock will never break support and you will have to stop out because the signal for the continuation of the downtrend isn't given. The upside is that you get better prices if the signal indeed does present itself after your entry. In this case, you enter while things are calm and quiet, making it easier to get your shares. Compare this to the first option in which you enter when everyone else is also trying to enter. So your trade-off is confirmation and fight for shares or no confirmation and easy-to-get shares.

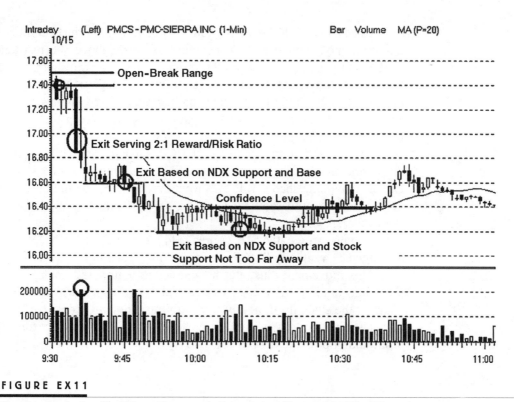

FIGURE EX11

Open-low—break setup. (*RealTick graphics are used with permission of Townsend Analytics, Ltd.*)

Two lines on the chart show the open-break range. The circle shows the entry area. Our entry after a $17.40 break with a stop at a break of $17.50 gives us about 15 to 20 cents in risk, depending on the exact fill.

To get a 2:1 reward/risk ratio, we had to be near 40 cents, at least on the first partial. To add tape-reading principles to this, we looked for faster selling and a volume increase (spike). This allowed us to cover all that we wanted because we could buy into that strong selling, effectively covering our short at least in partial. You can see this happen on the drop under $17.20 into $16.80, leaving an exit at $16.80 to $17 as the area for the first partial for holders and for a full lot for scalpers.

We now had half of our shares remaining. After a small base at $16.60, the price spiked up as shown by the white candle and dropped back into support. The stock looked somewhat nervous, so I wanted to exit another quarter of my shares. I had pretty good cushion now, so I wanted to try to ride this trend a bit more.

I had more than a quarter of my shares left and a fairly solid cushion, combined with the NDX not able to break above the resistance; PMCS had support at 16 from the previous day, so, from here, I established a confidence level. In this case, it was the high of the range from the first $16.20 bottom. The line marked accordingly shows it at just above $16.40. A confidence level says: If a stock goes over this, then I'm less convinced that the stock will see new lows.

As the NDX continued higher, PMCS began to base a bit higher near this confidence level. I wanted to use the next selling back into $16.20 to exit the remaining shares. If PMCS went over $16.45, I would be less convinced that I would see new lows, so I would liquidate my remaining shares there.

As you can see, the $16.20 area held pretty well as the NDX continued higher. Eventually PMCS reversed slowly back to the upside.

This movement illustrates how structure is imposed upon what can seem like random numbers. We see real support and resistance levels made by the stock itself, not by some arbitrary thought process of "where things should bottom or top" because of nonquantifiable reasons like profit-taking pressure or walls of worry.

EXAMPLE 12

Trading within the Range

Take note of lines H and L on Figure EX12. They outline the daily highs and lows; the high was $22^{11}/_{16}$, and the low was $21^{3}/_{8}$. Also we have Fibonacci lines (Fib), which outline a minirange within the larger range. This is based on action throughout the morning session. All pivots before circle 1 were missed as entries because we were watching other stocks we were playing during the morning session, not because they were invalid setups. Let's go to our first setup shown at point 1. This circle represents the area of a short setup.

I defined the low and the high of the range using the low of the retracement from $22^{1}/_{2}$ and the 62 percent Fib retracement level from that. Also, notice the thin line (20MA) moving across $22^{1}/_{2}$. This added confidence that the short setup would be profitable. So we had a setup, but we still needed to do a few things first. We needed to evaluate risk. Remember that when you are trading within the range, you need to beware of bid and offer levels/sizes. If the levels are wide, meaning more than 10 to 20 cents between the offer and next level, you need to back off because they are too wide. If the levels are tight but the sizes at the offer/bid are too small, you need to evaluate your share size. If the levels are small, then trading smaller share sizes than your normal full lot is better. I watched Corvis Corporation (CORV) during this setup, and I evaluated the $21^{7}/_{8}$ bid. There was plenty of size that, if we identified CORV as support here, I had no problem buying the low of the range.

The same applied on the short area on this play. The offer at $22^{3}/_{16}$ was okay, but the offers at $22^{1}/_{4}$ and $22^{5}/_{16}$ had plenty of participation, so that if the play failed, we had no problem taking a close stop. Risk was moderate at worst. Now we had entry setup and risk evaluation. Next we defined an exit strategy. We had two options. The first was to trade within the range (for scalpers) or hold for break of the support level, in this case $21^{7}/_{8}$ or $21^{3}/_{4}$. (I notice this chart has a bar to $21^{3}/_{4}$ prior to the defined support level at circle 2, but it is a mistake on the part of the data feed.) As the stock broke support (circle 2), the pace never picked up, meaning that we weren't as confident that the downtrend was going to be strong and we were possibly in just a range trade. Therefore, we could scalp here for a range trade at $21^{7}/_{8}$ or lower. Or we could hold half the position, and exit half the position with the break at the $21^{7}/_{8}$ level, thus confirming that a downtrend was a better possibility for the remaining shares.

The technical analysis portion of this confirms that the downtrend is

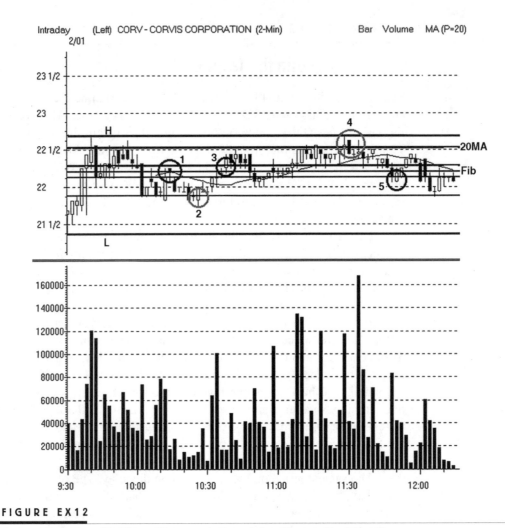

FIGURE EX12

Trading within the range. (*RealTick graphics are used with permission of Townsend Analytics, Ltd.*)

intact. The tape-reading portion made me less confident in the break of $21^7/_8$, which offered a strong downtrend on that break. Volume wasn't strong in this case. For holders of the stock, we had options to trail the stop or keep it at no worse than breakeven levels since we provided ourselves with the cushion of shorting the top of the range. Circle 3 represents the area in which we exited the remaining shares flat at no worse than $^1/_{16}$ because levels were safe enough that exit at $22^5/_{16}$ was fairly easy. So we had our short within the range finished, with scalpers taking about $^3/_8$, holders taking $^3/_8$ on one portion, and flat to $-^1/_{16}$ on the remaining shares.

The next play was the breakout. I liked it long on the breakout (which costs a stop loss in the end). We had a continued retest and failure of that \$22$\frac{1}{2}$ level. The trend began to go slowly higher, futures began to look a bit stronger, and I felt a break of \$22$\frac{1}{2}$, with a tight stop, was a reasonable play. In hindsight, the chart shows us that range trading was still more profitable. This is the "buy low, sell high, short high, sell low" strategy, using defined ranges. So we took the setup on the breakout trade with an increase in volume at the high and the test and retest failing and finally breaking. We identified the market maker FBCO as our seller at \$22$\frac{1}{2}$. A couple of blocks went off as the market maker lifted, and the market improved a bit. There were plenty of buyers, support was stable near \$22$\frac{1}{4}$, and the majority of the signs for a safe breakout play were there. Plus, I had a good feeling at the time that we'd see a move over \$23 on the break. As we had a \$22$\frac{1}{2}$ break, the setup was confirmed, and entry was taken on the confirmation or before for those more confident of the trade than I was. The risk evaluation remained moderate as levels were still tight and sizes were good enough that $\frac{1}{16}$, no more than $\frac{1}{8}$, would have to be given up on the stop if you were a bit slower than most.

Next I defined my exit strategy. Since this stock didn't provide me with at least a 1:1 reward/risk ratio, I was forced to plan my stop loss. I used \$22$\frac{3}{16}$, the last Fib level on the retracement from the \$22$\frac{1}{2}$ level. I had less conviction that the stock would continue up if it got below that level. Circle 4 represents breakout confirmation. Circle 5 represents stop confirmation. During stop loss, traders often wonder, "Do I hold it and wait for stop-loss confirmation? Or do I exit before it goes through that level? If I wait for confirmation, what if I can't get out at $\frac{1}{16}$ to $\frac{1}{8}$ below the stop price?" Fear of a greater loss begins to take their focus away from what the stock is doing. They become so focused on how much money they are going to lose that they lose sight of the stock action.

All this adds to the noise in your head about whether or not you exit before the stop is hit. Two options are available in this case. Mechanically speaking, the stop price is simply a price that says if the stock starts selling (assuming long) at this price, the trade has less of a chance to continue in the direction that would make your position profitable. A break of this price confirms that you need to be out of the trade. That's mechanical. The price you exit at is personal; it's mental and needs to be decided calmly and without hesitation or regret. This is a function of your execution abilities. If you are just learning executions, you don't have experience in how to get out of stocks that are below stop prices or in certain types of faster or erratic selling. This adds to the fear of greater loss and greater noise in your head because you don't know whether or not you exit at x price. The way to get over this is to trade smaller shares so that an extra $1/4$ point doesn't kill you, and it allows you to exit the trade, relieve a bit of stress, and then watch the stock's action. Then, in the next trade, you panic less, and you have less fear that the stock will move 1 point against you. Eventually, you lose this fear as you accept that you will not always get the best exit or always stop at the best stop price. Sometimes, slippage occurs. It's part of the nature of trading.

To review trading within the range, as shown by CORV example, there are a few steps to remember. First, define the range you want. Either use the smaller range or the daily high or low. The range is dependent upon your time frames. Second, do your risk evaluation. Make sure the bid (long trade) or ask (short trade) is safe enough that a break won't kill you on executions. Third, try to use the low or high of the range for entry. If you can't, feel free to hit a price a few cents away. Fourth, once in, define your exit strategy. Fifth, define a profit strategy if applicable. Scalp within range, a half lot at confirmation, hold a half, and so on. Sixth, if your trade is to be a stop loss, do not panic or feel that you blew a stop if you have to give up an extra few cents on confirmation. Do not let the stop loss (the "How do I get out?" fear) distort your reading of the trade. One trade should never make or break you. Over the course of a month or year, it's the average gain or loss that matters. A few cents here or there on a trade exit will not matter. Just don't take huge hits that force you into bankruptcy. Once you make the decision to exit, exit at a price that is easiest to get, even if you give up a little to do so. Use the stop-loss price as a guide. Last, learn to trust your thoughts on when to enter and exit. If you can't trust yourself in trading, you fail to understand yourself and provide yourself the opportunity to succeed.

EXAMPLE 13

Drop-Base—Implosion (DBI) Setup

The first thing we see in Figure EX13 is a nice downtrend from $63\frac{3}{4}$ to $62. I was not watching this stock to play either the downtrend or the reversal from $62. But it provides a good lesson on capitulatory selling that leads to a reversal. You can see the corresponding volume bars rising at the point of reversal.

From this we see a reversal point at the $62\frac{7}{8}$ area. So we had a minirange defined at $62 to $62\frac{7}{8}$ (R1 and R2). The second test of the low held. If we were looking to trade within the range, we could enter the trade at $62\frac{1}{8}$ with the stop under the $62 low. As you can see in this graph, the volume was a bit erratic. We earlier described a situation in which a lower volume on a price rise creates a scenario in which the downtrend is still intact. Volume in this case did not pick up tremendously at the $62\frac{1}{4}$ area, and there was a little shelf of three bars at $62\frac{1}{2}$ that was serving as resistance off the second test of $62. At this point (area 1), I entered the short $62\frac{1}{4}$ with a stop at $62\frac{1}{2}$, assuming a risk of $\frac{1}{4}$ point—$\frac{5}{16}$ point at worst. As you can see, this trade stopped me out (circle 2) because the retest and break of $62, which would have kept the trade valid, did not occur.

I was forced to take a $\frac{5}{16}$ loss on the trade as the $62\frac{1}{2}$ price level was eaten too quickly for a fill. As the stock moved higher to the minirange high again, I had a reasonable and fair play to short the second retest of the high. However, in this case, one of the two things needed wasn't present for the short: Buying was slowing, and this supported a decision to short the minirange high. However, the offer was thin, and, if any pickup in pace occurred, the stock would be a higher execution risk, much like it was at the $62\frac{1}{2}$ level.

This is the difference in trading just off a Level 1 or a chart only and seeing depth off a Level 2. In this case, I did not see depth, so maybe I would enter and look good. However, all too often, not being able to see depth is a detriment to short-term trading. And the few stocks that jump on you will outweigh the converse side of the issue.

Next we started to see the slide off the $62\frac{7}{8}$ area picking up pace again. Any retest of the low would be the third test, and, with pace increasing, I felt it was reasonable to look for another short entry. We saw a test of $62 and a small bounce that allowed me an entry. At this point, the same setup occurred, an entry near $62\frac{1}{4}$ with a stop at $62\frac{1}{2}$ (area 3).

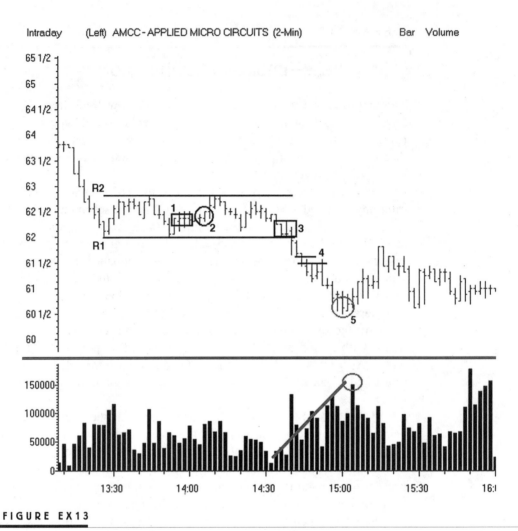

FIGURE EX13

Drop-base—implosion (DBI) setup. (*RealTick graphics are used with permission of Townsend Analytics, Ltd.*)

This time, the price broke on increasing volume. If it didn't break, I would have taken a stop at 62\frac{1}{2}$ or 62\frac{9}{16}$.

The break of $62 confirmed that the downtrend was still intact, so I started to plan my exit strategy for the position. Scalpers normally want to exit short positions at the first signs of strength, which, in this case, were defined in the area where the horizontal line 4 is. The 61\frac{5}{8}$ to 61\frac{11}{16}$ area was fine for scalpers taking $\frac{1}{2}$ point or so depending on the execution level. I chose to bid half my shares near the 61\frac{1}{2}$ level, since the stock was showing a bit of a support level in the 61\frac{1}{2}$ to 61\frac{3}{8}$ area. Taking $\frac{1}{2}$

to $^3/_4$ point on half of the position was reasonable for the risk assumed, which was $^1/_4$ to $^5/_{16}$ point.

After I took a profit on half my position, I lowered my stop to the breakeven level on the remaining shares. With any buying at \$62 to \$62$^1/_4$, I would exit the rest of the position with a small profit or a flat trade. As the trade continued moving in my favor, I looked for capitulation selling to close my position. From about 2:50 to 3:10 (14:50 to 15:10) EST, I saw increasing volume with the stock dropping faster. This is where I had the choice to take full shares on the trade or to lower the stop to about \$61$^1/_4$. Notice that the \$61$^1/_4$ area is the area that broke, sending the stock to under \$61 (circle 5). I elected to take the rest of my profits near \$60$^3/_4$.

EXAMPLE 14

Stop Loss

Let's now look at the Yahoo! (YHOO) trade on which I took a stop loss. (See Figure EX14.) This is an interesting trade because it ended up doing what I needed it to do after I took my exit. The interesting thing here is that it did this on action that didn't support the same setup and reasoning that I had on my previous entry. In other words, it gave a valid entry for a set of reasons. I was stopped out. Then it reversed to profitability, but those reasons weren't there this time.

We opened the day with specific NDX targets for support and resistance. We had 1500 as support from the previous day and then small upside resistance at 1515 and 1555 as more major resistance in the short term.

FIGURE EX14

Stop loss. (*RealTick graphics are used with permission of Townsend Analytics, Ltd.*)

As we approached NDX 1500, we backed off short ideas and playing within a range. So instead of breakdowns, I was looking for reversals. You can see some stronger selling on YHOO into $18.05 and a bit of a volume spike indicated by the circle in the volume section of the chart. This tape-reading principle, tied to the bias of the reversal in the NDX, made me go with a long-side position and look for a reversal signal. I entered long at $18.10.

As the stock moved back into that $18.30 resistance represented by the resistance-level line, it failed, as noted by the circle. This started me thinking that the trade would not work because, also at this point, the NDX was trying to stage an uptrend reversal.

Next we saw faster selling to new lows, just under $18, while the NDX uptrend was still intact. This gave me no confidence in YHOO to reverse at this point. If it can't reverse with the rest of the market, to me, it's on its own merits—trading without regard for the general market direction—and I have no confidence in trying to play it in the direction of the broader market.

So this cost me a stop loss because it didn't act the way I needed it to. You can see in this chart at the bottom near $18 that the stock finally did what I needed it to. You can see a series of higher highs and higher lows as represented by the numbers 1 to 5.

Why didn't I buy it at $18? Because, if it couldn't rise over $18.30 when the NDX was moving higher, why would I expect it to rebound to uptrend reversal signals now? At this point in the trade, $18 or $17.90 or whatever gave me no confidence to reverse, because it couldn't reverse earlier. So I missed it.

What happened from $18 to $18.60 was what I wanted to have happened from the $18.10 entry. It just didn't happen, so I took my stop loss but held my approach intact. I can't second-guess my reasoning. I can improve it. But I can't second-guess it. This is a great lesson that shows that sound reasoning does not always lead to profit. It also shows that the same reasoning in one situation can often make us miss out on opportunities in others.

It's a game of probabilities that over time will make it possible not to care about one YHOO trade. Stick to your discipline, your system that you know works for you. View the trades that don't work out as simple losses, nothing else. They don't make you a bad trader, a bad reader, or a loser. They simply are losses inherent to the system—to any system.

EXAMPLE 15

Drop-Base—Implosion (DBI) Setup

The trade illustrated in Figure EX15 was a short setup at $38.75. Scalpers were looking around $38.30 to exit in full and holders to partial. For holders, the next target for profit would beat $37.70 for the remaining part of the position.

As you can see, a series of lower highs formed which led to a break of support, as shown by the two lines forming the descending triangle. Once the support broke, by going with the trend, we looked for a short entry marked by the circle with a stop, in this case no worse than $39.05, which was the last range high before the support broke.

This range was a bit wider than I liked for our normal trading and the stock was a bit too volatile, so I elected to use a half lot to stay within my money management principles. We see that the trigger setup was given, entry was taken with a half lot, and we started looking for an exit strategy. In this case, I looked for supports/resistance areas from the previous day because the intraday chart doesn't allow me to see anything below the current intraday range support. This is similar to individuals who use large time frames for the overall trend and then small time frames to look for entry, like in a swing or position type of trade. Since I look for faster profits in my trades, I find a 2-day time frame to be fine.

In this chart, we see that some support from the previous day was near $38.30 and then again near $37.70. These are labeled by two lines from the previous day. When we got near these areas, I looked for simple volume indications. If we had slow selling into it, I had a greater probability of seeing it continue lower because not all sellers are washed out. If we saw faster selling into it, we had a higher probability for a base to be made, and quite possibly a reversal.

The long vertical price bar (circle A) on the chart suggests that it was time to exit for scalpers, and for holders to take half. I did the latter. From this point on, instead of keeping the stop at $39.05, we could institute a trailing stop or a confidence level.

I normally establish trading stops and confidence levels by using the last range high before the next low is reached. In this case, we had $38.80 as the new confidence level. In essence this says that if the stock goes over this level, I have less confidence that I will see new lows and so I will use the next selling activity to exit into. The confidence level on the chart is in the $38.80 area. There was a tick over, which told me to exit.

The stock didn't make new lows from that point, suggesting that cre-

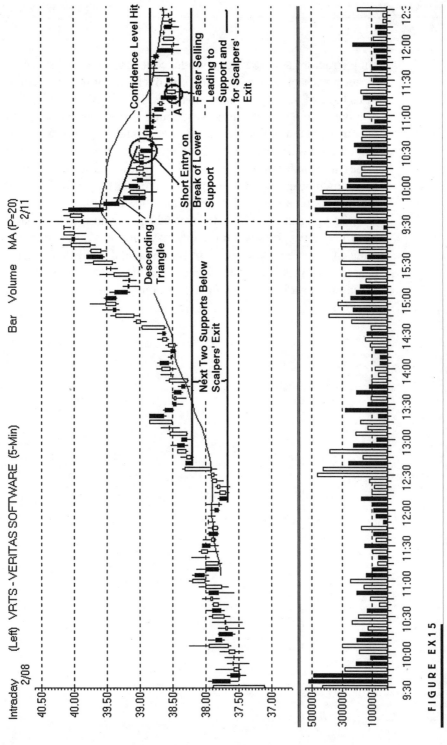

FIGURE EX15

Drop-base—Implosion (DBI) setup. (*RealTick graphics are used with permission of Townsend Analytics, Ltd.*)

199

ating structure among stop, confidence level, and current price allows us to not give back any profits, thereby overcoming the problem that many of us have of turning a profit into a loss. I don't mind seeing profit or part of a profit go flat. But I mind very much seeing a profit become a loss. If we break the confidence level, we should exit no worse than flat. Hopefully we will get a little countermove to enable us to exit at a better price, just as Veritas Software (VRTS) shows us we can because it sold back down near $38.50, which is much better than $38.80 and much better than taking a stop at $39.05 on the remaining shares.

So you can see why entry was taken, how to use the 2-day 5-minute chart to see supports when the intraday support is broken, how to determine an exit strategy using these supports, and finally volume indications near those levels. Confidence levels add more structure to the trade, alleviating the problem of turning a profit into a loss.

EXAMPLE 16

Jump-Base—Explosion (JBE) Setup

The first thing we see on the chart in Figure EX16 is the move from the open to $21 on relatively stable volume. The fourth volume bar shows a slight increase in volume as the pace increased off the $21 level (line 1). Traders could have tried an entry when they saw bid strength and interest coming into the stock, with a stop no worse than selling at $21.

I was able to enter at $21³/₈. To me, taking the trade ³/₈ off the bottom was somewhat too far for a reasonable entry price. I considered this

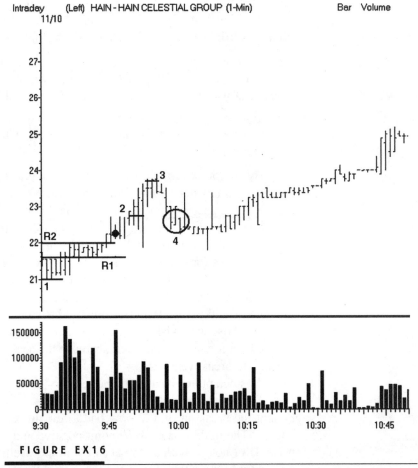

FIGURE EX16

Jump-base—explosion (JBE) setup. (*RealTick graphics are used with permission of Townsend Analytics, Ltd.*)

to be chasing, as my risk tolerance was $250. But I felt strongly about this trade and decided to stretch my risk tolerance a little. The optimal entry for me would have been $21¼ or better in order not to consider it chasing, but entry at that price was nearly impossible.

The next few volume bars show a volume spike while at the same time the stock move to $22. According to tape-reading principles, acceleration in the price advancing, an almost vertical movement, is usually not sustained and indicates the end of this stage of the move (euphoria stage). A rise in price in conjunction with a volume spike is where the majority of traders who entered off the $21 level would be exiting. I liquidated my shares into this buying at $21⅞.

Further, this $22 level, as you can see on the chart, serves as new resistance for the next 10 minutes or so. The pullback from the $22 area came to a level of $21⅝. This pullback from $22 to $21⅝ serves as our minirange (lines R1 and R2). There are two options when this happens:

1. Buy the low of the pullback of the minirange, in this case, no higher than $21¹¹⁄₁₆ with a stop at $21½. Then you have the choice of either scalping within the range of $21⅝ to $22 or holding for a breakout of the high.

2. Watch for the test of the high and the look of the break, and buy the breakout at $22.

By the "look of the break" I am referring to the strength in the bid; the ask gets smaller as the pace increases. You can see on the volume chart that the pace was increasing into the break.

Since the stock showed all the signs of breakout, I reentered at $22. We see that the next volume bar at 9:47 a.m. is another volume spike. On breakout plays for scalpers, those who take faster profits on larger shares, volume spikes should be considered a good reason to exit. The solid black circle on this chart at $22⅜ represents the price strength combined with the volume spike. I sold my position on this spike.

For those who wished to hold for a continued uptrend, this would be a good area for selling half their shares at the scalpers' target and trailing the stop to breakeven.

As stock pulled back from the scalpers' exit area, it held the $22 support. This situation is a tough spot for traders. For example, traders who bought the breakout of $22 now had a few things running through their heads. "The trade was ⅜ to ½ point positive and is now testing my buy price. Do I hold it with a stop at $21⅝ or exit, selling at $22? If I exit at $22 and it holds, I'll be frustrated for not holding. If I exit at $21⅝ by not trailing my stop, I'll be frustrated for turning a $^3/_8$- to $^1/_2$-point gain into a $^3/_8$-point loss."

Traders must rid themselves of such thoughts. Instead, as the stock is climbing they should be planning their exit strategy, "Okay, the stock is positive. I'm either going to keep the stop at 21^5/_8$ or trail it to breakeven. I don't want to take a $^3/_8$ loss on a failed breakout. I'd rather take the flat trade. Maybe I'll use 21^{15}/_{16}$ so that, if $22 fails, I take a small loss but my break of the $22 stop is confirmed."

The idea is that traders have to have the exit strategy. This lets them focus on the stock activity as the stock moves. Cluttering their minds with thoughts of profit and loss does not allow for clear thinking and the application of tape-reading principles. The less they are focused on the action itself, the more their emotions control the trade. Successful traders must maintain self-control at all times. They must define their strategy and execute it when the time comes.

Fortunately, in this case, the $22 held. At this point, the former resistance of $22 now has changed to support. For me, if there were any signs of selling at $22, and I would have exited the trade. With $22 as our stop, we wanted a move to over 22^1/_2$ to occur.

In the chart, we again see a volume increase as well as the break of 22^1/_2$. At that moment, holders of the stock began to consider exiting at least half their shares above the 22^1/_2$ level into strength. 22^3/_4$ is a good level to sell into strength on the price and volume increases (line 2).

Holders would trail the stop to 22^1/_2$ as we broke over $23. The next few volume bars from the point at which we took half our shares began to fade. The slowing pace of buying with decreasing volume indicated that the top of this stage of movement was near. We now wanted to look for a price to exit our remaining shares. As the stock moved over the 23^1/_2$ level, buying dried up considerably (line 3). We saw a drop in the bid to 23^1/_2$ and then 23^3/_8$ within minutes. If you waited and didn't exit into strength, you would have to go as low as 23^3/_8$ (circle 4).

The lesson here is that exiting after confirmation of the top is more difficult. Those who wished to hold the trade longer were stopped out later at 22^1/_2$ on the trailed stop represented by the circle.

EXAMPLE 17

Jump-Base—Explosion (JBE) Setup

In Figure EX17, let's first look at the time period just before 10:30 where
the stock moved from $29^{1}/_{2}$ to $30 on a relatively good volume spike.
Unfortunately, I missed the pickup in pace at the $29^{1}/_{2}$ level. What we
saw next was a tight range. The shallow pullback and the absorption of
selling suggested a possible continuation of the uptrend. I allowed the
stock to define its range from $30 to $29^{3}/_{4}$.

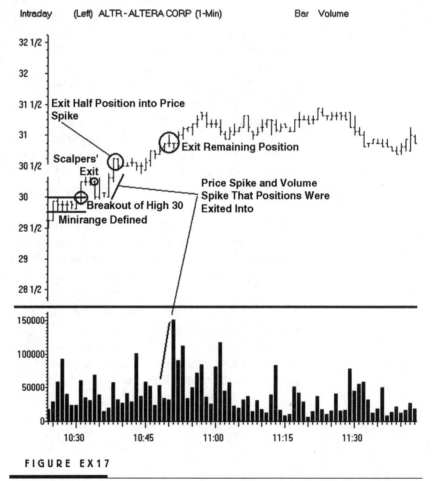

FIGURE EX17

Jump-base—explosion (JBE) setup. (*RealTick graphics are used with permission of Townsend Analytics, Ltd.*)

I wanted to play it for breakout, so I made a choice to buy the bottom of the minirange at $29^{13}/$_{16}$ with a stop at $29^{11}/$_{16}$. The range was too narrow to scalp in, so I planned to hold the stock for the breakout of the high.

Bidding the low of a minirange assumes bid strengthening. If the bid appears to be weak and a break of the low is imminent, then we need to understand the strong possibility that the stock will not hold the low of the minirange, and we need to pull our bid. In this case support was pretty strong as the stock neared the low of the range. As you can see on the chart, the price spiked to the $30^{1}/$_{4}$ to $30^{5}/$_{16}$ area and then got stuck there. At this point in the trade, when it looked as if the breakout was going to fail, I started to feel nervous about continuing. At the same time I had a fairly good cushion thanks to my entry at the low limit of the range, so I held it with my original stop in place. The pullback after topping in the $30^{1}/$_{4}$ area came to $29^{7}/$_{8}$, and I put my finger on the mouse and got ready to exit. Support held and the stock upticked off this level. As the stock went over $30^{1}/$_{4}$, I decided to raise my stop to $30, not allowing my profit to disappear.

The ascending line in the bar chart shows a moderate price spike. The circle shows the area $30^{1}/$_{2}$ to $30^{5}/$_{8}$ where I exited half my shares.

The stock had another shallow pullback after my exit. Selling was again being absorbed. I tested the $30^{5}/$_{8}$ level again and broke it. Notice the ascending line in the volume chart indicating a large spike. I wanted to look to exit the remaining shares on this larger volume. I chose the area of $30^{3}/$_{4}$ to $31 as a reasonable exit area. On the break of $30^{3}/$_{4}$, the stock hit a high of $31 but there were plenty of sellers on the ask at $31. I exited at $30^{7}/$_{8}$, taking fairly good profit on the second half of my shares.

We can see on the chart that during the next 15 minutes or so the stock climbed to $31^{1}/$_{2}$. So by exiting into the volume spike, I left about a ^{1}/$_{2}$ point on the table. However, on breakout trades, we never know how far they will go. By trading within these ranges, trailing stops, and following tape-reading principles, we can bring order into our trading and let the rest of the profits go to those who see things differently.

EXAMPLE 18

Drop-Base—Implosion (DBI) Setup

ADC Telecommunications (ADCT) (see Figure EX18) closed right below $19 on the previous day. It opened with a slight gap up. Approximately 20 minutes after the open it hit $19 again. That was a short signal for ADCT.

At that moment someone asked me if it was a good time to buy ADCT. Apparently, "buy low, sell high" was deeply ingrained in his trading. I told him that I had just sold it short, and I explained that the "buy low, sell high" principle was in direct contradiction with another: "Trend is your friend."

If you go with the trend, why would you want to buy low or short the high? If a stock is trending down, wouldn't buying the low be fighting the trend? Every new low confirms the continuation of the trend and should be shorted, not bought. The same goes for shorting of strong stocks. I am sure that you have seen plenty of examples of traders getting killed trying to pick the bottoms or tops. Trading is not about picking tops and bottoms; trading is about determining the trend. Actual buying and selling points within the trend need careful consideration as you try to either pick up the shares at the bottom of a pullback or at breakout level or go with some kind of hybrid, buying half of your position on the bottom and adding to it on breakout.

Is there a situation in which you buy low and sell high? Yes, there is. You can do this when you have determined that the stock is trading within the range, not trending. But, as soon as the range is broken, you have to switch to another kind of trading: Buy high and sell higher or sell short low and buy back lower.

This is why traders who go with "buy low, sell high" do poorly in a trending market. I have seen (and I am sure you have, too) plenty of them getting killed during the huge market run-up of 1999 through early 2000 as they tried to short the tops. The same happened to those who tried to buy bottoms during the market decline in 2000–2001.

Let's return to the ADCT chart. I shorted ADCT when it broke $19 to the downside (trade 1 on the chart). I placed a stop at $19¼ because the stock unsuccessfully tried to penetrate this level during a weak attempt to bounce, so $19¼ became the natural resistance.

ADCT broke down pretty quickly. At around $18 it showed some support, and I had covered the short in full. I watched it going down more, and, later on, ADCT found more support at $17½. It made several weak

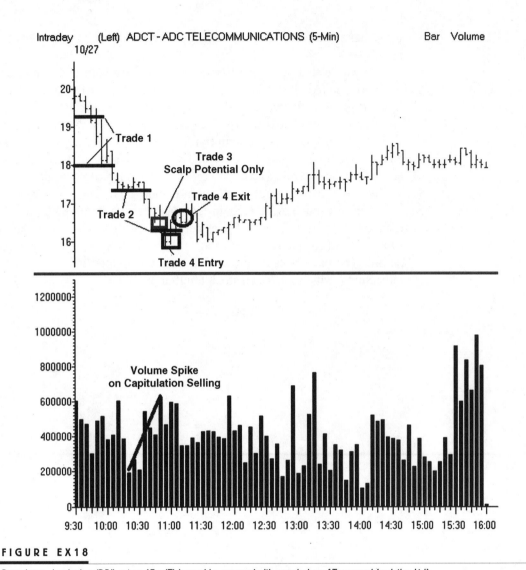

FIGURE EX18

Drop-base—Implosion (DBI) setup. (*RealTick graphics are used with permission of Townsend Analytics, Ltd.*)

attempts to bounce from this level, and then the volume dried up. Unsuccessful attempts to bounce led me to the conclusion that the downtrend was still intact, and another short signal was generated (trade 2). It took traders of ADCT about 20 minutes to realize that the stock was destined to go down. I covered it just below $16\frac{1}{2}$.

Note the volume spike as ADCT went down to $16. That was capitulation: fast selling on sharply increased volume which usually indicates the end of selling and offers a reasonable expectation of a reverse. This is what makes me reverse from "sell low, buy back lower to buy low, sell high."

It was at that point that I started to look for a bottom buy because it really looked like the trend was about to reverse. I made two attempts: The first led me to a flat trade at $16^1/_2$ (trade 3). The stock sold down once again on exhausted selling, which I believed was the last gasp of selling.

I took my next buy attempt at $16^1/_8$ with a stop at $15^7/_8$ (trade 4 entry). Placing a stop in this case was easy—any new low, and we had to admit that the downtrend was still there. The closing of the trade was easy as well. As a scalper I got my $^3/_8$ point (Trade 4 exit).

I didn't touch ADCT again that day, despite its nice climb after a double bottom was formed. It was certainly worth another long play, but I lost my feel for its movement and could not read it as clearly as I could before. The pace became pretty flat; volume stopped giving any useful indications, which made the stock tough to read.

EXAMPLE 19

Trend Continuation

In Figure EX19 the circle marked 1 is a long entry after capitulation selling. This is illustrated by the declining line in the price section and the circle in the volume section. A steep price decline on sharply increased volume indicated capitulation and led to a long entry called at $75^3/_8$. The stock spiked at over $76, where I made my exit.

Let's take a look at what has happened. The price stalled at around $76, and the volume dried up. You can see the two lines marked as bear flags, one in the price section and the other in the volume section. A relatively big volume increase on the price advance with shallow volume on the reaction indicates a continuing uptrend. Here we have reversal of this principle for a downtrend: volume drying up on a short-lived rally indicates a continuing downtrend.

I interpreted this as an indication of potential further decline and prepared to short JDS Uniphase Corporation (JDSU) at a new low, as it would penetrate $75 to the downside. We didn't want to short it at around $76. Although this is a valid play, in this particular case we refrained from doing it because the stock was moving extremely fast, which can be dangerous, and we needed more confirmation of direction. It was easy to short it at around $76 only to see it making a double bottom $^1/_2$ point lower and then jumping higher. That's why I made the short entry at under $75 as the stock made a new low. My actual entry was $74^3/_4$, which was all that was possible considering the speed of JDSU.

The next stage of the movement was accelerated selling, which is marked as capitulation on the chart. When selling became furious at under $74, it was the time to cover and/or go long. As you can see, the cover and reverse would have happened at around $73^1/_2$ to $73^5/_8$.

The next event is quite remarkable. It's an exact repetition of what happened on the first rally. The stock spiked to $75, and again, as in the first case, the price stalled and the volume has dried up. The same principle was applied, and this is indicated by the bear flag, which suggests that the downtrend is likely to continue. The price broke down fast once again and reached the previous low. The line marked "previous low broken" shows the level of that low. And, once again, the entire cycle repeated itself. The new short entry was $73, just below the previous low, and the new capitulation took the stock to new lows on increasing volume. You can see a sharp volume spike drop to under $71. This spike alerted me to the bottom being close, and the stock rocketed from here. The next stage

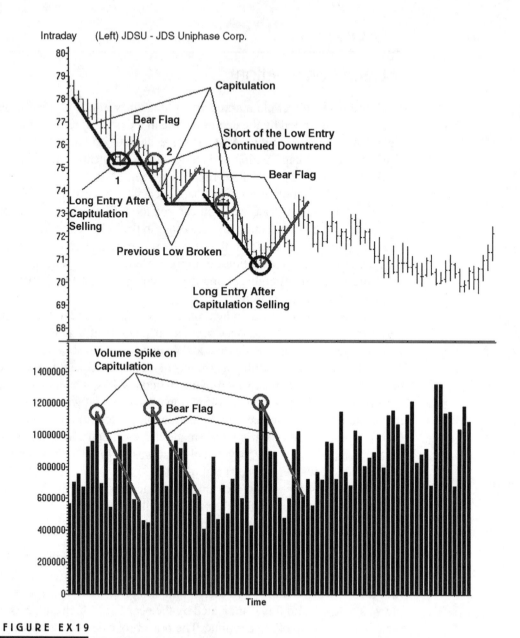

Intraday   (Left) JDSU - JDS Uniphase Corp.

Trend continuation. (*RealTick graphics are used with permission of Townsend Analytics, Ltd.*)

was again the bear flag, and the stock met resistance at the level where it bounced the previous time—at around $73.

Former support became new resistance. After the stock had dropped from this level, it became much less readable mainly because the price movement and pace became plainer, which usually makes readability low.

EXAMPLE 20

Open-Low Break and Reversal

Network Appliance (NTAP) (see Figure EX20) was lower right from the opening, and it had a nice open-break trade possibility. Its early range was $25.20 to $25.40. When it broke $25.20, I took this to be a signal to take it on the short side, with a stop just over the high of the narrow range. I wasn't aggressive on my open plays that morning, so I missed it because of my lack of aggression.

The downside movement is shown in the area with two lines and the circle A. This movement was resistance from the previous day. I looked here for some possible support in order to form a range that would lead me to trend continuation or reversal. During this period of movement, I stayed with the trend and went with a short bias, looking for a breakdown of support.

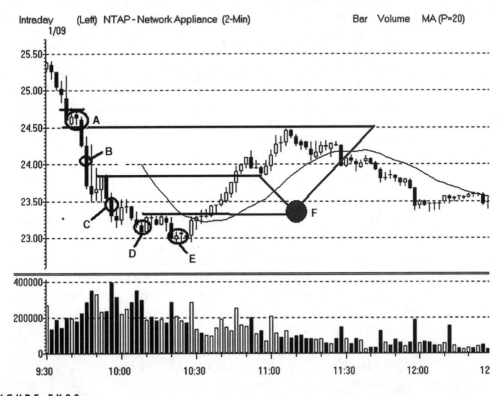

FIGURE EX20

Open-low break and reversal. (*RealTick graphics are used with permission of Townsend Analytics, Ltd.*)

Entry was taken just before confirmation, but liquidity at this point was thin, giving me only half my shares of the original order, before moving lower. When I get less than my original order, around 500 to 600 shares, I look to scale out half and half, rather than half, quarter, quarter. In this case, as entry was taken on the breakdown of this range near $24.50, I looked for an exit strategy that would yield a near 2:1 reward/risk ratio. Selling was faster into the $24 area, and I looked to scale out into that faster selling. In this case, the faster selling took the stock lower to about $23.60, leaving me with around 35 cents in missed potential because I scaled out nearer $24, but what could I do? I saw what I needed, I had no idea how far the stock would drop, and I could scale only as I saw fit.

I then had half my shares left, so I used the next rebound as a confidence level, in this case just under $24, near $23.80. If I were to go back over $23.80 from here, I'd be less convinced that I'd see new lows on the movement. Fortunately, it didn't happen, and the stock moved lower for trend continuation.

At this point, there was another fast selling phase with vertical price drop movement into about $23.20. I took my exit just under $23.50 as the faster selling hit again on the remaining shares. This is shown by circle C. This gave me about 2:1 in my reward/risk ratio for the first lot. I scaled out of the second lot and achieved a 4:1 reward/risk ratio.

We saw capitulation movement a few times on this stock. But instead of trying to trade the reversal at $24 and $23.50, I looked at something nearer $23 because the 2-day chart showed the previous day's support there. When I got a few signals working together, my confidence in the trade became a bit stronger.

We now had:

1. Faster selling (capitulation showing exhaustion and leading to a high probability of reversal)
2. Support from the previous day that I thought would hold on the day of the trade

Faster selling into a support is a good reason to bid the issue, because you have selling exhaustion and clear support. If they hold, it should be a nice reversal. If they fail, you have a clear stop exit strategy.

I took entry at $23.27, and looked for a movement back into resistance levels to scale out or exit in full depending on the action. I took my stop as the stock broke back below the low, which did not get me to a reasonable reward/risk ratio (circle D). This stop loss was defined by the lack of buying into a resistance level, and then the failure of the former low to hold. I didn't reenter the stock because I lost confidence in its ability to recover. Further action proved me to be wrong.

Let's see how a trader should have acted if this entry was taken. Circle E represents the real low. Let's assume that we caught it. Many traders often have a tough time distinguishing where to exit reversals. In these cases, I try to establish two things:

1. Areas where the downside movement begins to become more vertical. This is along the lines of "what was support, should now be resistance." The level where support breaks, and the point at which the price becomes vertical, should now be an area of resistance.

2. In areas where there are ranges, use the high of a range to establish a resistance level that the stock needs to eat through if the upside reversal is to continue.

This situation is represented by the three lines tied into the black circle labeled F.

Let's assume we took entry near $23. We kept an eye on that $23.40 area. You can see the resistance it made between circles D and C. If we broke that, we could have used $23.80 as a next one. But if we broke $23.40, we would have some cushion to work with so that I wouldn't care as much about closer resistance. I could have scaled into this area if I had wanted to.

The next movement resistance was back again at the $23.80 area—the former confidence level. The price moved to this level at 9:50 a.m. and then dropped sharply to $23.30—an area of resistance again. If the buying had been any faster, I'd have looked to exit another portion of my shares. By doing so, I would have given up a little more movement to just over $24.10. Remember, we are defining areas in which things are *likely* to happen, not creating certainties where things will happen. So let's assume that I still held a half or a quarter of my position. The most likely resistance would be where my original entry was made. You can see on the chart how the price moved right back to $24.50 and failed to continue, as this former support, once broken, then served as the ultimate resistance.

If we broke $24.50 with stability, I have trailed the stop, moved the confidence level up to just under $24 (you can see support there on the shallow pullback), looked for final resistance at $25.20 or so, and exited in full to close the daily trade. Rarely do we get that lucky. But the lesson is:

1. Don't guess on where to exit (or enter for that matter).

2. Find the areas of support and resistance.

3. Use the correlations of price and volume to find areas for entry and exit.

4. Use areas in items 2 and 3 as guides for stock movement on retracements.

5. Scale out as the stock moves in your direction.

6. Keep your stop if items 1 through 5 fail to be profitable.

EXAMPLE 21

Drop-Base—Implosion (DBI) Setup

In Figure EX21 we see a fairly sharp sell-off at the open—an almost vertical downside price movement associated with a volume spike. As the stock bounced from $16.25 to $16.60, we got stuck in the range. This range trade didn't allow much for conviction on direction bias until we saw some clues. Examples of such clues are:

1. Are highs and lows higher or lower than those made on a previous move within this range?
2. Is the volume increasing or decreasing on advances and retreats?

In this case, the high of $16.60 gave us a retest of the $16.25 low and then a lower high at $16.50. This is where I went with a short-side bias rather than looking for reversal. As we finally broke $16.25 support, I entered short. Short setups are inherently more difficult than others. The uptick rule negates ease of entry if the stock drops too fast. Fortunately, Comverse Technology (CMVT) fell and then came back to $16.25 for the entry.

In this kind of situation a common question is: If stock falls before entry, how far do you let it go before you refuse to chase? Usually, if the trade doesn't serve at least a 1:1 reward/risk ratio on the first break and then come back to that best short price, I'll go with it. If I see it serving 1:1 right away, I'm less confident in it and am less likely to enter if it comes back to that price.

The support line on the chart shows the support. When the support broke, we went with the trend and found the short entry. The initial stop (shown on the chart) was placed at the previous high made within risk tolerance after the setup formed, in this case, just above $16.50.

With risk of about 25 cents, scalpers would exit near $16 for 1:1 reward/risk ratio. I wanted to hold for a better exit because the bounce looked weak.

From the $15.95 support level, we had a move back to about $16.15. This was now our new confidence level after we retested the lows. This meant that if CMVT were to go higher, back over $16.15, I would be less confident that we would see new lows. If CMVT were to go over $16.15, my option would be to set the breakeven stop on the remaining shares or use the next round of selling back into support to cover.

As you can see, the stock did not get near this level again. Rather it moved into "congestion." Two horizontal lines denote the congestion in

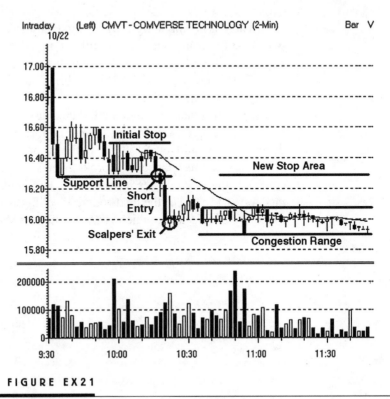

Intraday   (Left) CMVT - COMVERSE TECHNOLOGY (2-Min)   Bar V
10/22

FIGURE EX21

Drop-base—implosion (DBI) setup. (*RealTick graphics are used with permission of Townsend Analytics, Ltd.*)

this area, one just above $16 and one just below.

Congestion occurs when the number of buyers is equal to the number of sellers in a narrow range. In this case, it was very difficult to discern direction. I had two choices:

1. I could hold a full position until the low of the range broke, keeping my stop-loss level intact.

2. I could hold a partial position. I could cover half the position into support, and thereby lock my profits.

If the stock broke the high of the congestion, I could use the same strategy I used with the confidence level, letting it hit a stop at no worse than breakeven, or I could use the next round of selling into support to exit my remainder. If the stock broke the low after I had covered the first half, I could then add the half back again, because the continuation signal was given. Or I could not add that half back and just let the remaining half that I had ride as the continuation signal was given.

There is no single right way to trade it; these are just options. Choose what best fits your style. I went with the first option, held my full position and waited for $15.95 to break down. It did, and I covered my short into $15.75. This level served a 2:1 reward/risk ratio, and there was faster selling with increasing volume.

If traders had covered half their shares at this level, they would lower their stop to $16.15, our former confidence level. Their new confidence level would be $15.95, on the principle that what was support should now be resistance. If it broke over $15.95, I would have been less confident that I would see it under $15.60, so either it would hit the trailing stop at $16.15, or the next round of selling would take it back into the $15.60 to $15.75 area, which is where the exit should be taken.

EXAMPLE 22

Trailing Stops and Confidence Levels

Two days previous to the trade shown in Figure EX22, we had very good action and were aggressive. On October 28, however things became dull, and it seemed that the resistance levels were getting sold into, rather than being broken out of. Trading became rather narrow and lifeless, leading us to October 29. The open-break plays were not worth much on the long side, and we had backed off, looking for short setups as the NDX moved lower throughout the opening. Siebel Systems (SEBL) was my focus from the short side as the NDX was failing to overcome resistance. Resistance at $18.55 looked like the top, as NDX lost its low.

The two diagonal lines are descending and show lower highs and lower lows, which creates the look of a downtrend. With the NDX failing lows and SEBL already in a downtrend that started near 3 p.m. on the previous day, I wanted to go with a short setup bias.

The range from $18.05 to $18.55 was too wide for me to enter with a DBI setup, meaning to short the low. This setup is used to short into resistance on a downtrending issue. I had the trend with me in the stock as well as the NDX cooperating, since it broke the lows. This simply added to the probabilities that I would get what I needed when I took the entry.

The two lines, one at open resistance of $18.55 and the other being low support at $18.05, gave me my range (labeled A). The entry was shorting into that resistance, with a stop just above it at $18.65–$18.70. Circle B illustrates this setup.

As the stock pulled into the range of C, we had congestion—a stock making a smaller range, then buying equals selling. This happened at about $18.20. At this point, the NDX began to sit in a narrower range. There simply was no way to know what would happen during the congestion phase. Guessing which side would win wasn't our goal in this situation. Our goal was to let the buyers or sellers tip their hands and go with that side of the trade.

Since we were already short and downtrend-biased, we positioned ourselves for a downtrend movement scenario. Scalpers would take a full lot off the table at a 1:1 reward/risk ratio. There wasn't any reason to risk a scalp in congestion. Holders needed a better reward for their risk, but, in congestion, on a narrow day, they needed to think of capital preservation, rather than aggressive scaling. Since we couldn't break the support near $18.20, I took half my shares off the table.

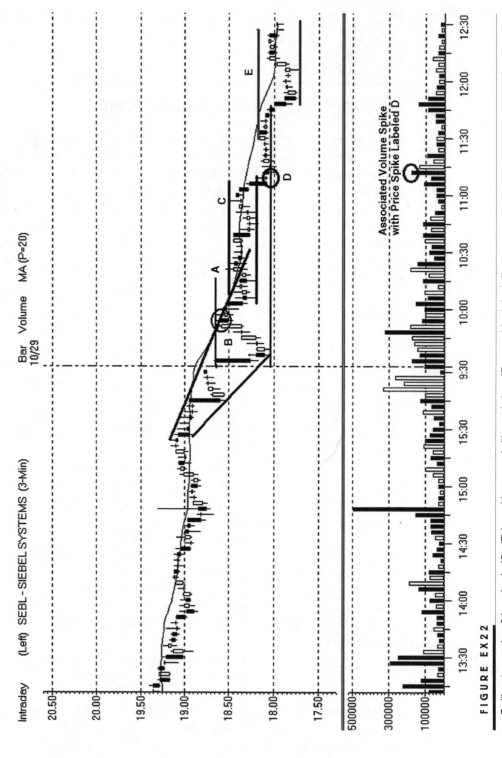

FIGURE EX22

Trailing stops and confidence levels. (*RealTick graphics are used with permission of Townsend Analytics, Ltd.*)

Then I moved my stop to a breakeven level and waited for a breakdown of the congestion range. I had already locked in profits on the first half of my shares. As you can see, we got the breakdown and the trend-continuation signal. We got faster selling into $18 on this phase, and, when you get faster selling into a level, you want to partial out again. So on this round of selling, marked by circle D, I covered a quarter more of my shares.

An important tape-reading principle states that faster selling shows exhaustion and that the trend becomes less certain from that point. Starting at 18, another range started building, from $18.15 to $18. When it broke again, I still owned a quarter of my shares, and I had a choice: take the remaining quarter of my shares or trail the stop. You can see how the volume spiked again at 11:45 a.m. on a more vertical price drop to $17.70. This would be the signal to exit your remaining shares if you wish to, and it's perfectly valid to do so. That was what I did.

Another possibility would be to see how much of a downtrend we could ride with the remaining shares. In this case, I used confidence levels and trailing stops. Confidence levels simply say to me: If the stock breaks this level, I'm less confident that the trend will continue. The trailing stop says: If the stock hits this, I'll take the remaining shares off the table no matter what.

As we moved into breaking support of $18, we needed to establish the confidence level. This is marked by the line E. It is simply the last range high before the stock finally fails support. So if SEBL broke $18.15, I would be less confident that we would see new lows.

The above situation would warrant our trading in the following manner. The stock breaks $18.15, so we will either let it hit our stop price or use the next round of selling to cover the remaining shares. Your risk is that you lose the profit if it hits the stop. Your gain is that you will get better price cover if you use the next selling round to go back under the confidence level. If you aren't comfortable with the confidence level, meaning you don't want to let it hit the stop, then trail the stop tighter to this $18.15 area. It's simply a matter of where your aggression lies. If you want to see if you can ride a trend, then your confidence level is fine. If you would rather take the full profits, then trail the stop tighter and lock in the gains.

What is your mindset? Are you in a win cluster? Do you ride gains while you read the market correctly? Are you in a drawdown or slow-bleeding phase? Don't try as hard to ride gains because it will get you closer to revenge trading, trying to make it all back in a short period of time. Maybe you should trail stops tighter in this period so that you get the sense that you are seeing things well and profiting from them—creating that winning attitude. There are more reasons to trail the stop or to use confidence levels than just, "It's going in my direction." The market is a reflection of you, and you are willing to give yourself only what you think you are worth at a particular moment. If you are feeling well, maybe scaling out is better for you because the stock is moving in your direction and you want to stay with your confidence. If you are feeling confused or in a down period, taking full profits to get used to the feeling of profits is better. Eventually you can go back to scaling out if the market allows you to do so.

This trade helps to identify three important things we use every day, even if we don't naturally or consciously understand why:

1. Technical analysis helps to define the structure.
2. Tape-reading principles help to define the entry and exit points (price/volume relationships).
3. Exit strategies help to pull us through flat or negative periods and move better during positive periods.

EXAMPLE 23

Jump-Base—Explosion (JBE) Setup

The first thing we see on the chart in Figure EX23 is a move from the $73 to the $74 area on relatively stable volume. There was a small price spike right at $74 where traders in from lower levels would be exiting. As the stock began to pull back, we noticed a shallow pullback to $73⅝. So, we established the range from $73⅝ to $74. The broader trend continued to show strength during this time period, and QUALCOMM (QCOM) is a stock that may follow a broader trend a bit better than others.

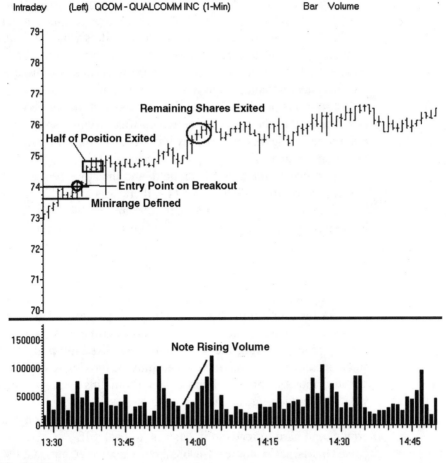

FIGURE EX23

Jump-base—explosion (JBE) setup. (*RealTick graphics are used with permission of Townsend Analytics, Ltd.*)

Traders have two options in this case. The first is to buy the low minirange, in this case, at $73⁵/₈. The other is take the offer at $73¹¹/₁₆ if you feel that $73⁵/₈ isn't attainable. In either case, with selling at $73⁵/₈, you need to get ready for the stop exit. If traders wished to bid QCOM, they could scalp within the range or wait for the break. Here, the stock made a break of the high, offering the setup for a long trade. Buying for a breakout required a stop at $73⁵/₈.

We saw the initial break as being weak; the stock price came back down to $73¹¹/₁₆ and held. At this point, if I saw any selling at $73¹¹/₁₆, I would be ready to hit the bid fast for an exit. Many times, a failed breakout makes a great short. We wouldn't want to get caught in stronger selling.

With the hold of the low minirange and a move back to new highs, we looked for a reasonable exit strategy. The price spike that put us to near $74³/₄ was the area for this. We can see a price spike associated with a volume spike in this area. This is where traders would exit at least half of their positions and raise a stop to near breakeven if not absolute breakeven on the rest. I used $73⁷/₈ as a stop because I wanted to use $74, the previous resistance, to now serve as support.

From this point we saw basing for about 20 minutes. We wanted to raise the stop to the $74¹/₂ level, which was serving as the bottom of the minirange during this period. Any break of that and we would take the rest of our shares at $74³/₈.

Fortunately the $75¹/₂ level held, and the stock broke the $75 level. Notice that on the pullback to $74¹/₂ there was an inclining volume rise leading to a volume spike at about 2:05 p.m., or 14:05 on the chart. This is the next point at which traders looked to exit their remaining shares. The $74¹/₂ level wasn't jeopardized, so anyone holding for the break of the $75 level would be looking to exit into this spike.

Taking profits within the $74¹/₂ to $75 range was reasonable. For those who held, this is the action that they would be looking for to exit.

As the stock moved to the $76 area, we noticed that the volume dropped considerably and that the market participants were jumping on and off levels, making the trade hard to read. At the point at which the stock became hard to read, we'd certainly be looking to exit, if we hadn't already, into the price/volume spike. From this exit, you can see the volatility on the issue as the day wore on.

There were a few other possibilities, but the action was jumpy, erratic, and hard to read, so it was best to back off.

This is an example of a breakout trade from an established minirange, using price/volume spikes to define the exit strategy as we approach it from a tape-reading point of view.

EXAMPLE 24

Cup-and-Handle Breakout

The day the trade took place (See Figure EX24) there was a nice uptrend, with the majority of the potential taken from breakout trades and pullbacks. Stocks such as TUTS, CRDS, ATHM, and NEON were making new highs, and those issues that had been beaten up over the previous year were showing signs of reversals from their lows.

Adtran Inc. (ADTN), however, was a stock that was down on that day after guiding estimates lower for the quarter. So we had a negative

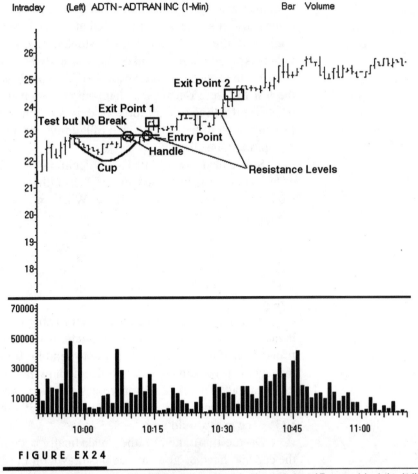

FIGURE EX24

Cup-and-handle breakout. (*RealTick graphics are used with permission of Townsend Analytics, Ltd.*)

gap on negative news in a market that was showing pretty good strength overall. Whether or not the broader trend mood gave some excitement to the ADTN uptrend from its lows is uncertain, but the idea of playing breakout trades was reasonable.

Tape-reading principles are usually the same in any market, for any kind of stocks, with or without news surrounding them. The stock tells us what to do at any given moment. In this sense, the setup occurs, and the tape tells us whether to enter or not. We move from there to the exit strategy.

We can see on the ADTN chart a move from the $21 area. One of the principles of tape reading is illustrated on this move. We had steady volume with an increase in price. This is so-called good buying. The end of the move is shown as a top near $23 with the volume spike. This is normally when "everyone wants in on the stock," and the smart money begins to sell shares it accumulated at lower levels. If you go over chart after chart after chart on any given stock during the day, you can pick out volume spikes and price spikes that normally lead to the end of a move. It is a simple accumulation/distribution principle based on the public being the last to figure out what is happening. When it does figure it out and wants in, it's time to look for your exit. Volume spikes are indications of fast buying or of the public's fear of holding a losing position, which leads to capitulation selling.

So we next saw a pullback on declining volume. Again the principle of tape reading is that you can see that pullback on declining volume, so we look for an uptrend to continue. What we saw next was a situation in which the stock tried to break out again and failed.

The circle (Test but No Break) on the horizontal resistance line demonstrates this failure. At this point, the range defined from the touched and the failed break was $23–$22³/₄. If traders entered below $23 before the confirmation, they would have had to use the low of the minirange as a stop level.

As always, there is a choice when trading breakouts: Buy before the breakout occurs and trade your convictions or wait for the breakout confirmation and have your order ready to send in. By using money and risk-management principles, you will decide how far you are willing to chase the breakout. This depends on your stop price and your entry price. The setup in this case was a ¹/₄-point stop. But if you couldn't enter until $23¹/₈, the stop would now be $23³/₈.

On the third attempt, the break finally occurs. The chart illustrates the cup and handle. You can see this drawn on the chart with the first horizontal line, the cup, and the two diagonal lines, which show the area where the handle will formed. Notice how the volume repeated this formation, confirming the validity of the cup-and-handle setup. Normally the breakout occurs on the third attempt of the high. In this case, the cup had an unusually short time to form, but the setup still worked well.

Now, our stop was set at $22\frac{3}{4}$. Therefore, our risk was assumed (gamblers create risk; traders assume risk) and it was no worse than the $22\frac{11}{16}$ to $22\frac{3}{4}$ level. We now needed to follow the principles of tape reading for our exit. When the stock broke $23, scalpers exited into a price spike, which you can see in the first upside price bar, and you can see the movement leveling off after the price spike. Volume increased, offering a reasonable chance to exit into strength. For those who were willing to hold the trade, we needed a break of the resistance area near $23\frac{1}{2}$ to $23\frac{5}{8}$. So the first square used (exit point 1) offered a chance to sell at least half of our shares and for scalpers to exit this full lot.

Next we had a familiar principle again: shallow pullback on decreasing volume. This suggests that it is still reasonable to expect a continuation of the uptrend. In this situation, traders raised their stop to breakeven after selling a portion of their shares.

Resistance broke, and we looked for a price spike/volume spike to exit into. We were able to hold the trade near the $24\frac{1}{2}$ level, where the second square on the chart (exit point 2) shows the area of exit.

Notice what happened at the $24\frac{1}{2}$ level again. It had a shallow pullback, and volume decreased a bit. Then the stock price formed a little shelf and then broke higher once again. By exiting, I missed out on another $1\frac{1}{2}$ points, but the trade was traded based on principles that tell me when to exit. Those who are better holders of a stock than I am could follow the same principles and exit on the next spike between $25\frac{1}{2}$ to $26. Eventually the trade got too long for my time. My intuition does not last long for each trade, and it's tough for me personally to hold a stock all day when the stock action and the principles of tape reading are telling me to exit.

EXAMPLE 25

Capitulation

Figure EX25 is a 2-day, 5-minute chart. Capitulatory selling is represented by the first two vertical price bars at the open on February 14. Why didn't I try to go long near $32.75? After all, there was fast selling, some support in that area, and so on. In fact, this was just one of those intuitive responses. I didn't believe that this was the area that would give a solid reversal for quick profits. And I was proved correct. I looked for something closer to $32. You can see some congestion and support from the previous day in this area. If we got faster selling into this level, then I would be far more confident of the stock's probability to reverse. As you can see, the reversal occurred right at $32 and gave an entry signal on buying into contraction.

As the stock broke $32.20 (the small range high from $31.95), I felt it had a better chance to get some profit potential. So the entry was either:

1. Wait for contraction of fast selling into support (normally only aggressive traders do this).

2. Wait for $32.20 to break and go long (get confirmation, but fight for shares).

I chose the second option. Now that I had entry, I needed an exit strategy. You can see again from the previous day that there was resistance at just above $33, and this should provide resistance on the day of the trade. Also, on that first round of faster selling into $32.75, we got some support and then failure. On the principle that what was support should become resistance, we wanted to exit from this area with at least partial profits.

You can see that when the stock broke above $32.50, some vertical price movement began into $32.75, where it was smart to exit at least a portion. I did just that. Scalpers might be out in full.

As we pulled back from that resistance just under $33, we held $32.45 pretty well. We then wanted to trail our stop to at least breakeven and use a confidence level on the remaining shares. As we moved back into $33 and failed one more time, this was where I wanted to exit another quarter of my shares.

Exiting in full is reasonable as well because your profit is locked in and you have no worries from there. In this case resistance at $33 proved to be too strong, and my trailed stop at $32.35 was hit and taken.

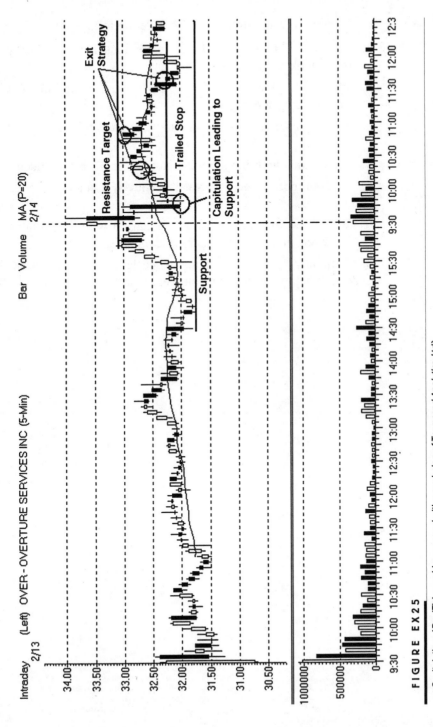

FIGURE EX25

Capitulation. (*RealTick graphics are used with permission of Townsend Analytics, Ltd.*)

Lessons from this example include the following:

1. Faster selling into support from the previous day and intraday is a good area to look for a reversal.

2. Look at resistance levels from the previous day and intraday to determine some upside targets.

3. Look for price/volume action into these areas to begin to exit in full or scale out.

4. If you scale out, bring a trailing stop to establish a confidence level.

5. Scale out more at the next resistance level, if you have enough remaining shares.

6. Let the rest ride and see where it can go with a stop no worse than breakeven, and hopefully somewhere higher.

7. Eventually you will hit a resistance level, at which point the NDX doesn't help your position confidence, so you can exit in full there.

EXAMPLE 26

Open-Low—Break Setup

For the situation illustrated in Figure EX26, we had a range of $43.15 or so to $43, and liquidity was good. The break of $43 gave confirmation of a downtrend signal. The stop was placed above the open high at $43.25. If there was to be a higher-probability downtrend trade, then the stock shouldn't go over.

There were two possibilities for entry:

Before the breakdown, ensuring an easy fill, but with no confirmation.

After the breakdown, with confirmation, but with a more difficult fill.

I chose the first simply on aggression in the downtrending market. The NDX 1500 area was holding as support, but there was no major selling. Our tape-reading principles suggest that slower selling into support give us less chance of a rebound; rather we would hit congestion and see new lows. The quick premarket gap higher faded into the open, meaning that sellers put pressure on the buying and moved the market lower. So I was on a more short focus for open-break trades.

Broadcom Corporation (BRCM) had a good open range shown by two lines on the chart. I went in aggressively with a short at above $43 before the trigger, which was based on all the above. Had it hit $43.25, I'd have taken my stop with no regret because my aggression would have been justified and my reasoning was sound.

Let's now move to the exit strategy.

You can see the three circles on the chart of where I partialled out. I used tape-reading principles of faster selling to cover, which made it easier to get a favorable fill. This action doesn't necessarily get you the best prices, but you can be assured of an easier fill. In this case, as we moved into $42.60 on the longer black bar, I took half my shares off to lock in profits.

I'm not usually looking for more than a 2:1 reward/risk ratio on open trades, so this trade offered a bit more than my normal profit targets. Also, with half my shares locked in on profit, I wanted something nearer the $42 area. This was not based on "guessing," but rather from the previous day's support. I saw faster selling into this area, so I partialled out another quarter of my position, keeping a fair cushion from my entry to see if I could ride the other quarter a bit longer.

This was a purely aggressive judgment call. Taking all the remain-

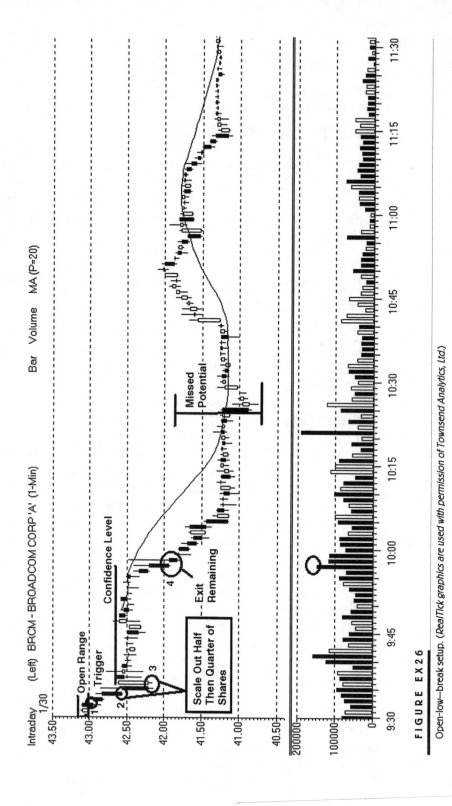

FIGURE EX26

Open-low—low—break setup. (*RealTick graphics are used with permission of Townsend Analytics, Ltd.*)

ing shares into that round of selling was perfectly valid, too. I felt that I had the overall trend with me, that I had BRCM action with me, and that it was worth holding on another quarter of my shares for movement under $42.

I then had a quarter of my shares left. It was now time to make a confidence level. This is different from a *trailing stop,* which means that if you hit the stop-loss level that the trade is exited at, take the stop. A *confidence level* means that if you hit the confidence level, you're less confident in seeing better prices in the prevailing trend.

I judged the confidence level based on retracements. You can see how BRCM held at above $42 and went to $42.60 before backing off again. If we were to go over $42.60, we would show a higher high, and I'd be less convinced that we would see a lower low. So instead of taking a stop here, I used the next round of selling under $42.60, and my stop was at breakeven. Then I tried to get a better fill somewhere under $42.40 for the remaining shares.

The risk is that you get a breakeven stop. The reward is that you get a better price under the confidence level for more profit. This is your decision.

You can see how this level held well enough to give us a move at under $42, which is what I wanted for the remaining quarter of my position.

The tape-reading principle of faster selling is shown on the chart at the circle—the one with the vertical price bar that is labeled 3. On the volume chart, you can see the volume spike to the sell side. These two things combine to say to "cover it all."

My target profits were met. I had confirmation according to tape-reading principles, so I took my profits and moved on. And, by doing so, I missed out on nearly 1 point more in potential.

Do I care? I don't. I played the trade as well as I could within my system. So I'm happy with my assessment, my aggressiveness, my scaling out to lock in profits, and my final exit on my remaining shares. Everything was in sync for this trade, so I have no reason to regret missed profits.

EXAMPLE 27

Fading Breakout

This example on Adobe Sytems (ADBE) describes how to fade the break-out setup. Again, to *fade* a setup is to initiate a position contrary to what the setup should bring in profitability. You will see how volume indications on this setup offer a higher probability for a short setup than a long setup on the break of resistance from the open. Thus *fading* the long setup means initiating a short position after the failed breakout of the resistance. (See Figure EX27.)

In the chart, the resistance is clearly marked from the open high at the $37.50 level, which leads to a move into support near $36.70. From this support, a reversal forms and moves the stock back up to the $37.50 level. Quite often, 30-minute highs will form a significant level that traders key in on for watching for some kind of reaction from the market.

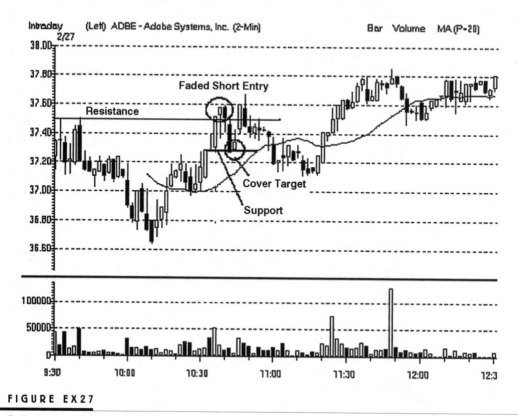

FIGURE EX27

Fading breakout. (*RealTick graphics are used with permission of Townsend Analytics, Ltd.*)

In this case, the stock trapped the buy-side players and rewarded the short-side players.

As the stock moved higher into the $37.50 level, you can see volume indications that showed a steady buy-side slant. Near the 10:30 a.m. period, however, volume began to increase, and eventually the volume spike corresponded with a price spike. Tape-reading principles suggest that minority action is slow and stable and that majority action is erratic and unstable. Given the increase on the buy side in relation to the volume as well as the price increase being more vertical *into* resistance, there is higher probability for the breakout to fail on that retest. Traders want slow and steady buy-side volume into resistance because it shows good support. A volume increase and a price spike into resistance show that the probability is higher for the buying to have been exhausted and that there won't be enough buying on the break of resistance to keep the stock moving higher for profitability.

This leads traders to fade the breakout in the hope of seeing the break of resistance trap more buyers with unsustainable upside movement resulting from exhaustion buying. Traders initiate a short position on the break of the resistance and look for the trade to move back below the resistance point for better confidence. Traders then look for a break of the most recent support to confirm that the downtrend is intact from that faded break. This support level in the ADBE example would be around $37.30.

This is regarded as support from the level that paused briefly before reaching back over the 30-minute highs. Scalpers who wish to initiate a 1:1 reward/risk ratio for this trade would look for a cover into this support with a stop at the high of the level from which the trade would be faded or shorted into. Those traders who wish to scale out of the position would then exit a portion of their position into this support level and trail the stop to breakeven levels. If the position were to break this $37.30 level, traders could then begin to pick out their next support target based on the previous price action and to look for an exit on the remaining position. In this case, we would see support at the $37 level. Unfortunately, the stock never got that low and moved back into resistance, where the remaining portion of the trade would be exited at breakeven levels.

EXAMPLE 28

Short of the Range Resistance

This example of Brocade Communications (BRCD) illustrates trading within a range. Tape-reading principles within the range show why taking a short position into the resistance level at the early range was a higher-probability setup rather than initiating a long position looking for a breakout.

On the day of the trade (See Figure EX28) the stock was in an afternoon downtrend on good volume consistency, showing that the near-term price action was suggesting more downside ahead. Given that the stock gapped up the next morning into the previous day's resistance level combined with the previous day's afternoon price action, we would be looking for a short setup from the open. Having missed the early entry on the open-break play at $26, we were forced to wait for a range to form in

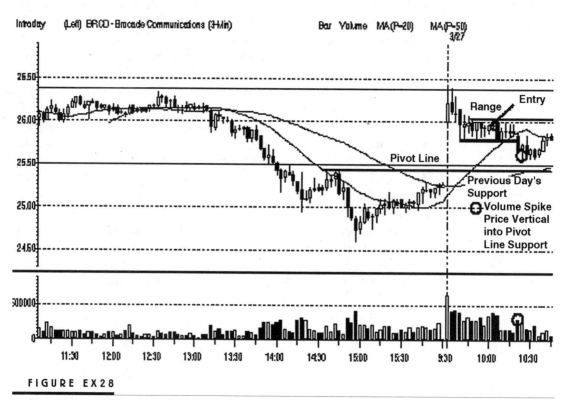

FIGURE EX28

Short of the range resistance. (*RealTick graphics are used with permission of Townsend Analytics, Ltd.*)

order to assess the action within the base to determine if shorting the trade was still a good possibility.

As we watched the range forming from $25.75 to $26, we saw that any move back into resistance would be associated with higher volume. The tape-reading principle of large buy-side volume associated with no increase in price suggests distribution and a resistance level. In this case, traders want to initiate a short position within the range at or near the resistance level with a stop right over that range or at the most recent high, depending on their risk tolerance. Regardless of the risk tolerance, any break over resistance from this point would make it less likely for us to expect a break of the low. Therefore, our exit strategy for a stop loss must be more focused.

Once entry was taken on the short side at the nearest point to $26, our exit strategy for profitability became important. We had our stop-loss strategy in place, so our profit exit strategy was our focus. In order to gain an idea of where we could exit in full or scale out, we needed to look at the most recent support levels. The first idea that we had for exit was derived from the principle that gaps tend to be filled. If this was the case, then being able to scale out along the way down to the previous day's closing price at $25.30 would be our target. If we were looking to be more conservative in our profit objectives, then the previous day's most recent support area near the $25.45 level would be our target. This was again based on the principle that what was resistance would now serve as support. The previous day showed a move into the $25.45 level at about 2:45 p.m., or 14:45 on the chart. This level should get support on the open retracement.

Now that we had our targets selected, it was important to use our tape-reading principles to aid us in determining just exactly when it was time to exit. Again, as the stock moved, as long as it was stable and steady in volume indications associated with a gradual descent in price movement, we were confident that we could hold for better profits. As soon as the trade became more erratic, where the price dropped fast or the volume rose precipitously, then it was time to exit in full or scale out of the position. In this case, our profit objective wasn't met because the faster selling phase of the breakdown occurred almost immediately into $25.60. However, by utilizing an entry into resistance near $26, we provided ourselves with a profit cushion that we wouldn't have had if we had waited and entered on the setup trigger. This goes back to an entry strategy that is based on your own aggressiveness and risk tolerance. By entering into resistance, we assured ourselves of a good entry with a full position, but we gave up the downtrend confirmation, thereby making us less confident about the trade. If we had waited for actual confirmation, we would have given up our profit cushion, but we would have been sure that the downtrend signal was valid.

As it turned out, the trade never got to the desired level, and those who were looking for a 1:1 reward/risk ratio type of profit were happy enough to exit into the $25.60 level. Those who were looking to scale out had to take at least a breakeven exit on any remaining shares. However, the example does a good job of illustrating volume indications during the range-formation process to dictate an entry and then to show us the exit point based on the faster selling associated with the price drop the $25.60 level.

EXAMPLE 29

Open-Low—Break Setup

This example (See Figure EX29) illustrates an open-low–break setup in which we initiated a short-side entry on the break of both the open lows and the previous day's support area. The reasoning behind the short-sided entry was based on the previous day's action into the close as well as the NDX indicator moving into a larger resistance area overall. We saw a series of lower lows into the close after a nice uptrend throughout the day. A possible pullback was in the cards, which, while profitable, wasn't a huge reward/risk type of trade and would be one for traders who make larger-sized trades and look for smaller profits. Those looking to scale out of this type of trade would most likely be stopped out at breakeven on the remaining profit.

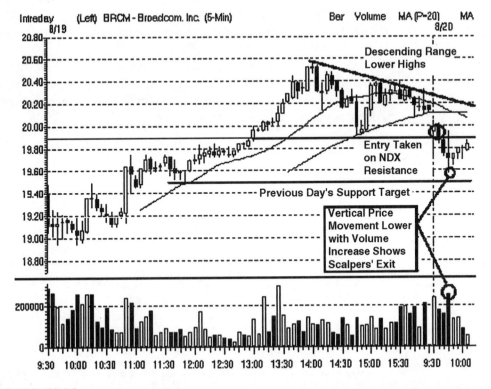

FIGURE EX29

Open-low—break setup. (*RealTick graphics are used with permission of Townsend Analytics, Ltd.*)

The entry was taken on this trade after an open range consisted of the support from the previous day at $19.90 and the day of the trade's high of $20. Once we were unable to break over $20 on the open and then broke the previous day's support as well as open support, the short side should have been taken for a position with a stop at the break of the open high. Once the entry on the short side was filled, we needed to look for a profit strategy based on the previous day's support levels. In this case, we had a support level near $19.50. If the trade had begun to move into this area, we wanted to be looking to exit in full for smaller profits on a larger share size.

In this example, we wanted to be aware of the majority action behavior. In this case, we saw faster selling into $19.60. This was illustrated by the more vertical price movement to the downside associated with the volume increase on the sell side. Given that we were seeing exhaustion on the sell side, it was time to cover into that faster round of selling for a quick 2:1 reward/risk ratio or less. In this example, the $19.50 support level gave us an area in which to look for erratic behavior, indicating majority behavior. Once we saw this type of action moving the stock into the $19.60 area, it was time to enter the cover order and look for a fill to exit the position in full.

We see on this chart that after the open faster selling, the stock recovered and moved back to the entry level, showing that any remaining shares had a lower probability for profitability and would have been exited at no worse than the breakeven level.

EXAMPLE 30

Open-Low—Break Setup

This is an example of an open-low–break short setup on F5 Networks, Inc. (FFIV). It leads to a good reward/risk ratio, but it also shows a degree of missed potential because of traders taking faster profits at higher levels. (See Figure EX30.) The open range was from $20.30 to $20.55 (shown by two lines). Once the stock began to lose the $20.30 level, a short position was initiated with a stop at the high of the range, $20.55.

Given that we had our stop-loss strategy in place, we needed to be looking for areas of exit based on our risk tolerance. If we wanted to take faster profits for a 2:1 reward/risk ratio or lower, we would have looked

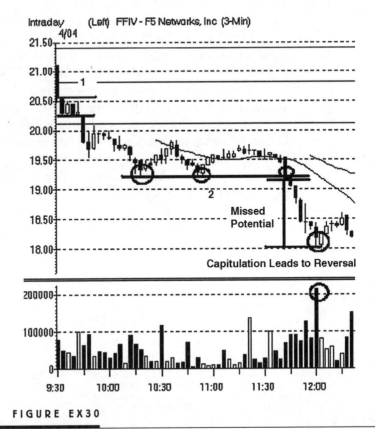

FIGURE EX30

Open-low–break setup. (*RealTick graphics are used with permission of Townsend Analytics, Ltd.*)

for faster selling into the $19.75 level. The stock shows erratic behavior on the sell side, and thus a good area to exit the trade. At 9:45 a.m. we saw an increase in sell-side volume and a more vertical movement to the $19.60 level, offering the opportunity for covering into that level with near the 2:1 reward/risk ratio.

Traders who were looking for something more substantial out of the trade would be looking for faster selling under that $19.60 support. Should this $19.60 level have been broken to the downside, we would have brought our stop to breakeven levels once we began to scale out of the trade. In this case, we had some faster selling into the $19.30 area; this was associated with the little volume spike just before 10:15 a.m. As we held this level, what we should have done and what we did were two different things.

By rights, traders should have brought their confidence level to the retracement highs at $19.75 and looked for a break of the support near $19.30 for a downtrend continuation signal. Instead, at the second test of the $19.30 level that held, the exit in full was taken.

What happened next was that the trade made a lower high, broke the support level near $19.30, and then hit a capitulatory movement, taking it to the $18 level, which made the exit near $19.30 seem somewhat foolish.

Hindsight can be quite a killer sometimes. However, don't let it deter you from trading on your discipline. I firmly believe that for every missed profit like this one, there are 10 other trades where you are happy enough to have taken the profit when you did and actually increased your account over time rather than waiting for trades with bigger profits. Essentially, take the home runs when you can, but don't beat yourself up about missing a few. One trade should never make or break your account. Trading is a sequence of events that slowly builds your account up over time. Missing big profits here and there won't or shouldn't affect you much.

EXAMPLE 31

Drop-Base—Implosion (DBI) Setup

This example illustrates a solid downtrending stock on Medimmune (MEDI) after the 30-minute lows were broken. (See Figure EX31.) This situation is described as the DBI setup in earlier chapters and examples. Because we have discussed this setup many times, we left all the levels and points of reference on the chart unmarked. So it is up to the reader to identify them.

   We essentially had a tight base near the $26.30 support level, which, when broken, offered the short setup trigger. The base formed was the support at $26.30, and resistance was just above $26.40. In this case, with barely a 10-cent stop-loss range and the stock being liquid enough, traders could utilize a larger position size because the stop level was smaller compared to other trade setups that normally show a 25- to 30-cent range.

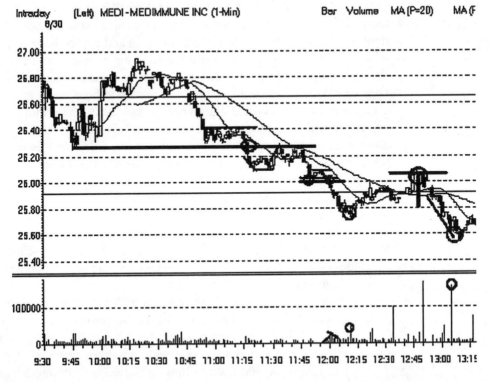

FIGURE EX31

Drop-base—implosion (DBI) setup. (*RealTick graphics are used with permission of Townsend Analytics, Ltd.*)

Once the trade setup was triggered on the break of support, with a stop loss in place, we needed to look for a profitable exit strategy. In this case, with a 10- to 15-cent stop-loss risk level, a simple move into $26.10 to $26.15 would yield a scalper's exit with a 1:1 reward/risk ratio. According to tape-reading principles, majority action tends to be more erratic than minority action, so we looked for faster selling into this level. You can see on this chart that we got faster selling to $26.10 and then a reverse back into resistance.

The important aspect of this behavior is that, on the retracement back into the highs, volume stayed relatively light and the trade was unable to break back over the $26.30 level with any conviction. The principle that what was support should now act as resistance held true, as the $26.30 support level was behaving as a resistance level, and the downtrend was still intact. Those traders who were unable to get a profitable exit on the first move into $26.10 now had a second chance as we saw the trade move lower to $26.

Movement to $26 showed a sharper price drop, which offered plenty of opportunity to exit for those looking for smaller profits on a full exit of the position and who were unable to exit earlier. Next we saw another tight base at the $26 level that tried to retrace and moved back to $26.10, which was former support that was then serving as resistance. This again showed that the downtrend was still intact and those traders who were holding for higher reward/risk ratios were safe to hold while looking for a move under $26 to scale out. What we saw next was a more vertical price drop with a volume increase to $25.75. This was where traders were able to scale out at least half their original position. Once this profit was taken, it was important to begin a trailing-stop and confidence-level strategy. In this case, we had a $26.10 resistance, which was the level that served as a distribution point off the $26 support. This would be our trailing stop. Then we had our $26 support area that was broken and which offered a move to $25.75 where traders could begin scaling out. If the trade were to retrace back over $26, then we would be less confident that the trade could continue lower. So we would use the next round of selling under $26 to exit the remaining shares.

The next part of this trade shows how a plan well made is often not well executed. It happens to the best of us. In this case, we saw a little break of $26.10, in effect, taking our trailing stop. After the trailing stop on the rest of the position was taken, we could see that the support at $25.75 was taken out, and faster selling to $25.60 was offered for greater profitability. However, as our trailing-stop discipline took us out of the trade, we were unable to grab that extra profit.

One important point on this is that you shouldn't let the outcome of one trade alter your trading discipline. One trade does not make a system, and, while this trailing stop didn't allow for greater profits, over time, sticking to your discipline will save you from disasters. It's the aggregate results that matter, not one trade.

Cup-and-Handle Setup

The situation shown in Figure EX32 is another good example of a cup-and-handle setup, this one on KLA-Tencor (KLAC). We saw the stock basing nicely through the lunch period. Then at around 2 p.m. it began to form the start of the cup. During the retracement of the cup, we saw the volume begin to pick up a little. Normally, we would want the activity to die down when it forms the bottom of the cup. But this is art, not pure science. Learn to look at imperfect setups as opportunities.

Once we got our cup formation, we moved right back into the resistance at just above $43. From this resistance, we saw a small, narrow base formed at above $43. This was the handle that eventually led to the long-side trigger entry. In this case, the entry was taken at no higher than $43.25 with a stop at $43, the bottom of the handle range. Again, volume indications suggested that our uptrend was intact as it increased as the stock increased. When we began to see euphoria as defined in our tape-reading principles, we had to begin to partial out. In this case, we saw a little spike just before 3 p.m., the 15:00 time period, into $44. This was when we needed to take at least half our position in profit.

Then we saw the volume spike at about 3:10 p.m. coincide with resistance at $45. This was when we needed to decide whether to take a quarter of our position or exit in full. The decision to exit in full was, in hindsight, not the best exit. However, deciding while things are happening and reviewing a chart are two different things. The trade still gave a good $1.75 per share on that last half of the position.

Those who held the quarter of the shares left, needed to trail their confidence and stop levels. In this case, with the pullback from $45 into $44, we would then place a stop at breakeven and a confidence level at $44. If the stock broke $44 again, then we would have to use the next round of buying to exit the remaining shares. If we couldn't get this buying, then we would exit somewhere between $43.25 and $44, depending on the action. In this case, we made a base at the close, so that we could exit under $46 or decide to hold the remaining portion overnight to see if there would be a gap up the next day to sell into at a price higher than $46. These are each valid decisions that need to be made as we see these volume/price correlations throughout the trade.

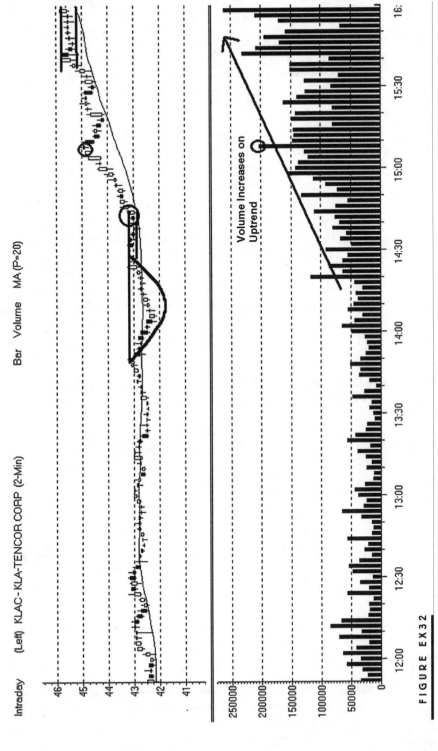

Intraday   (Left) KLAC – KLA-TENCOR CORP (2-Min)   Bar   Volume   MA (P=20)

Volume Increases on Uptrend

FIGURE EX32

Cup-and-handle setup. (*RealTick graphics are used with permission of Townsend Analytics, Ltd.*)

EXAMPLE 33

Cup-and-Handle Setup

This example of Intersil (ISIL) is a cup-and-handle setup. (See Figure EX33.) As we watched this trade from the opening, we saw stable selling to about $17, and then what we call a rinse effect happened on the break at $17. A *rinse effect* is when a stock barely moves out of the risk parameters, which takes traders out of their positions, and then the stock resumes the desired movement, after the traders take their stop loss. We saw sharp movement, which could be characterized as a minicapitulation. After this occurred, the stock regained its foundation and then moved nicely back to the $17.45 resistance area. The action from $17.45 to $16.80 and back to $17.45 formed the cup of this trade. The handle, represented by the two diagonal lines, showed a base forming near the $17.45 resistance.

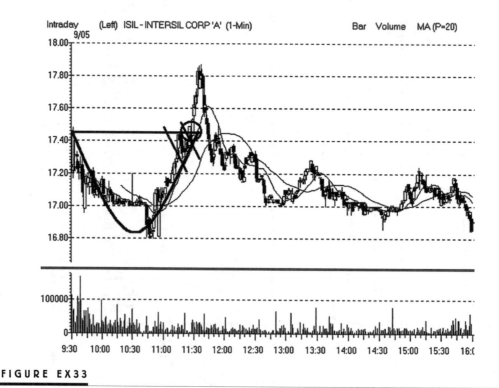

FIGURE EX33

Cup-and-handle setup. (*RealTick graphics are used with permission of Townsend Analytics, Ltd.*)

What was happening was a blow-off event followed by a well-supported reversal. Aggressive accumulation was happening in this case, as there were hardly any pullbacks on the way back into resistance. Once we reached resistance, the bullish resolve was about to be tested. We knew this because a base from about $17.35 to $17.45 was formed. The bulls were still in charge. A break of $17.45 would confirm the handle part of this formation as a good breakout trigger. We saw the breakout at $17.45, and this moved the stock to $17.85 or so. Upon seeing this breakout, traders would have entered prior to the trade setup trigger with a stop at $17.30 or on the break of $17.45 and hoped to get filled on their full share size.

As the trade began to get euphoric, meaning that there was a panic on the buy side as shown in the vertical price movement associated with the volume increase, we would look to exit into this at least partially. In this case, an exit above $17.75 would be the most likely on at least half the position. A confidence level would then be placed at just under $17.45 on the principle that what was resistance should now be support. If this failed to hold, then the rest of the trade would be exited at no worse than a breakeven level if we saw enough buying back at over $17.45. If the trade fell deeper, then it would be exited at $17.35 on the remaining shares, cutting into the profits we made on the first half of the position. You can see that the latter case occurred, and we were forced to exit the remaining shares below $17.45 as the stock hit our stop price of $17.35 at 11:45 a.m.

You can also see that it was wise to take the stop as this stock continued lower into the close and would have wiped out all our gains had we not stuck to our stop-loss management.

ARCA (Archipelago) Very popular so-called active ECN. It not only posts trader bids and offers but also actively works orders by trying to match them with those of other ECNs and market makers.

Black Box A nondiscretionary system that allows an individual to trade entry and exit signals without understanding why those signals are given.

BTK Biotechnology index.

Decimalization Switch of the increments of price from fractions to decimals. It limited volatility to a certain degree. It had a big impact on scalping strategies. Before decimalization, stocks were trading in $^{1}/_{16}$–$^{1}/_{8}$ increments, which equaled 6 and 12 cents, approximately.

ECN (Electronic Communication Network) ECNs allow traders to post their own bids and offers to a central order book to provide liquidity. Instinet was the first of them. During the market boom of the late 1990s, many new ECNs appeared.

ISLD (Island) One of the biggest and most popular day trader ECNs. It provides great liquidity and lightning speed.

Level 2 Presentation of Nasdaq data in the form of a box containing color-coded bids and offers posted by market makers and ECNs. For a while, Level 2 was described as a tool offering retail traders opportunities equal to those of market makers. It became less significant with the introduction of decimalization in the spring of 2001.

NDX Nasdaq-100 index.

SelectNet Order-routing system which allows traders to negotiate their orders with market makers electronically. With the introduction of SuperSOES in 2001, it has lost its role with retail traders.

SOES (Small Order Execution System) For a while this system was a major weapon of day traders, allowing them to execute their orders against market makers with lightning speed. After some rule changes it lost its significance. It was replaced by SuperSOES in the summer of 2001.

SOX Semiconductors index.

Times & Sales (T&S) Presentation of Nasdaq data in the form of scrolling; trades are usually color-coded. Shows size, price, and time of each trade.

INDEX

ABOUT THE AUTHORS

Vadym Graifer emigrated from the former USSR during the transition to a capitalist economy when increased, unwanted Mafia involvement in business affairs made day-to-day living more difficult. After fleeing the former USSR, he settled in Canada and chose stock market trading as a profession in his new society. He lost 75 percent of his trading capital before discovering the principles of tape reading, which allowed him to become a successful trader, providing a better life for his family in a much safer environment.

Graifer has expanded his professional career and has become a full-time professsional trader, mentor, and author of the online book *Job-Daytrader*. He is also the founder of RealityTrader.com, a private mentoring service that includes online education and communication of the tape-reading principles, methods, and techniques that he uses every day.

Christopher Schumacher is the CEO of GST Capital Group, LLC. He is a professional trader, and as a private trading mentor for RealityTrader.com, he trains traders from all over the world. He writes a daily column for TheStreet.com's RealMoney financial Web site and is a featured trading expo seminar speaker. He is a published author and has given guest lectures at The Ohio State University's Fisher College of Business as well as offered his knowledge and market views in other financial media, such as Yahoo! FinanceVision, E*Trade financial program "The Edge," AOL MarketTalk, Multex, TraderInterviews, *Chartpoint* magazine, and Innerworth.

Schumacher resides in Columbus, Ohio, and in addition to his professional career, he enjoys volunteering his time teaching soccer to 4- to 6-year-olds, running in charity events, and being involved in the lives of his two step-daughters, Maggie and Katie.